Virginia Woolf: The Novels

Kristine D. Miner

ANALYSING TEXTS

General Editor: Nicholas Marsh

Chaucer: The Canterbury Tales   *Gail Ashton*
Shakespeare: The Tragedies   *Nicholas Marsh*
Virginia Woolf: The Novels   *Nicholas Marsh*
Jane Austen: The Novels   *Nicholas Marsh*
Thomas Hardy: The Novels   *Norman Page*

Further titles are in preparation

Virginia Woolf: The Novels

NICHOLAS MARSH

St. Martin's Press
New York

VIRGINIA WOOLF

Copyright © 1998 by Nicholas Marsh

St. Martin's Press, Scholarly and Reference Division, 175 Fifth Avenue, New York, N.Y. 10010

First published in the United States of America in 1998

This book is printed on paper suitable for recycling and made from fully managed and sustained forest sources.

Printed in Great Britain

ISBN 0–312–21374–3 clothbound
ISBN 0–312–21375–1 paperback

Library of Congress Cataloging-in-Publication Data
Marsh, Nicholas.
Virginia Woolf, the novels / Nicholas Marsh.
p.   cm. — (Analysing texts)
Includes bibliographical references and index.
ISBN 0–312–21374–3 (cloth). — ISBN 0–312–21375–1 (paper)
1. Woolf, Virginia, 1882–1941—Criticism and interpretation.
2. Women and literature—England—History—20th century.   3. Woolf, Virginia, 1882–1941—Outlines, syllabi, etc.   I. Title.
II. Series.
PR6045.O72Z81525 1998
823'.912—dc21   97–50472
                                                              CIP

For Georgie

Contents

General Editor's Preface

This series is dedicated to one clear belief: that we can all enjoy, understand and analyse literature for ourselves, provided we know how to do it. How can we build on close understanding of a short passage, and develop our insight into the whole work? What features do we expect to find in a text? Why do we study style in so much detail? In demystifying the study of literature, these are only some of the questions the *Analysing Texts* series addresses and answers.

The books in this series will not do all the work for you, but will provide you with the tools, and show you how to use them. Here, you will find samples of close, detailed analysis, with an explanation of the analytical techniques utilised. At the end of each chapter there are useful suggestions for further work you can do to practise, develop and hone the skills demonstrated and build confidence in you own analytical ability.

An author's individuality shows in the way they write: every work they produce bears the hallmark of that writer's personal 'style'. In the main part of each book we concentrate therefore on analysing the particular flavour and concerns of one author's work, and explain the features of their writing in connection with major themes. In Part 2 there are chapters about the author's life and work, assessing their contribution to developments in literature; and a sample of critics' views are summarised and discussed in comparison with each other. Some suggestions for further reading provide a bridge towards further critical research.

Analysing Texts is designed to stimulate and encourage your critical and analytic faculty, to develop your personal insight into the author's work and individual style, and to provide you with the skills and techniques to enjoy at first hand the excitement of discovering the richness of the text.

NICHOLAS MARSH

A Note on Editions

References to the three novels studied in this book, *Mrs Dalloway*, *To the Lighthouse* and *The Waves*, are page references to the Vintage editions of 1992, published by Vintage Books (Random House), and based on the Hogarth Press editions of 1990.

PART 1

ANALYSING VIRGINIA WOOLF'S NOVELS

1

Virginia Woolf's Style

Virginia Woolf's works are strongly idiosyncratic, strange, a surprise to the new reader. Teachers sometimes ascribe this impression of strangeness to Virginia Woolf's *style* and treat the books as 'difficult' texts. This atmosphere of mystical difficulty surrounding the books is misleading. In fact, the strong impression created by Virginia Woolf's writings is a whole impression: the *structure, characterisation, themes,* and other elements of the whole text contribute to our surprise as we read. The *style* is not 'difficult' in itself.

We will therefore approach Woolf's writing with confidence. As with all literature, we expect that the features we notice in language and style will help us to realise the novelist's main concerns and her perception of life-experience. We will dip into the novels taking samples of the way Virginia Woolf writes, but we will not pre-select passages because we think they are important. We begin with an open mind: we may find constant characteristics in her writing, or differences between the novels, or both. Our approach is like that of a scientist who wants to discover what makes the natural world work. We hope to discover what makes these books work, and we can call our method an *empirical* approach. Research is always done in this way, and literature is not a different, mysterious kind of study.

* * *

In this chapter we sample extracts from three novels, carrying out a preliminary analysis of each. Here is an extract from *Mrs Dalloway*, found by opening the book at random and selecting a scene that makes some sense on its own. Clarissa Dalloway, wife of Richard Dalloway, MP, is at home repairing a dress she will wear to her party the same evening. Peter Walsh, a man she nearly married more than twenty years before, visits her unexpectedly, having just returned after five years in India.

'Who can – what can –' asked Mrs Dalloway (thinking it was outrageous to be interrupted at eleven o'clock on the morning of the day she was giving a party), hearing a step on the stairs. She heard a hand upon the door. She made to hide her dress, like a virgin protecting chastity, respecting privacy. Now the brass knob slipped. Now the door opened, and in came – for a single second she could not remember what he was called! so surprised she was to see him, so glad, so shy, so utterly taken aback to have Peter Walsh come to her unexpectedly in the morning! (She had not read his letter.)

'And how are you?' said Peter Walsh, positively trembling; taking both her hands; kissing both her hands. She's grown older, he thought, sitting down. I shan't tell her anything about it, he thought, for she's grown older. She's looking at me, he thought, a sudden embarrassment coming over him, though he had kissed her hands. Putting his hand into his pocket, he took out a large pocket-knife and half opened the blade.

Exactly the same, thought Clarissa; the same queer look; the same check suit; a little out of the straight his face is, a little thinner, dryer, perhaps, but he looks awfully well, and just the same.

'How heavenly it is to see you again!' she exclaimed. He had his knife out. That's so like him, she thought.

He had only reached town last night, he said; would have to go down into the country at once; and how was everything, how was everybody – Richard? Elizabeth?

'And what's all this?' he said, tilting his pen-knife towards her green dress.

He's very well dressed, thought Clarissa; yet he always criticises me.

Here she is mending her dress; mending her dress as usual, he thought; here she's been sitting all the time I've been in India; mending her dress; playing about; going to parties; running to the House and back and all that, he thought, growing more and more irritated, more and more agitated, for there's nothing in the world so bad for some women as marriage, he thought; and politics; and having a Conservative husband, like the admirable Richard. So it is, so it is, he thought, shutting his knife with a snap.

'Richard's very well. Richard's at a Committee,' said Clarissa.

And she opened her scissors, and said, did he mind her just finishing what she was doing to her dress, for they had a party that night?

(*Mrs Dalloway*, pp. 34–5)

Look at this passage closely. It is not written in an unconventional way. We have no difficulty at all in following the story: the author clearly states who speaks and who thinks ('Exactly the same, *thought Clarissa*', and 'mending her dress as usual, *he thought*'). The author uses direct and reported speech clearly ('"And what's all this?" he said', or 'He had only reached town last night, he said'); and gives us ample narrative detail of movements and actions ('taking both her hands; kissing both her hands' and 'And she opened her scissors', for example). The author writes in the third person. Here we have a conventional narrative telling us the actions, thoughts, conversation, and some of the feelings of two characters. The elements of this narrative do not differ essentially from those found in Dickens, Jane Austen, or George Eliot. Our first look at the passage, then, has laid one myth to rest. This is not a strange new narrative technique, but a classical technique. If Virginia Woolf's novels have a peculiar flavour, it is not because her narrative consists of odd or original elements.

Now look again, thinking about the kinds of sentences there are in the passage. First, they vary between the very short, terse single sentence (two of them in this passage are only five words long); and unusually long and loosely constructed multiple sentences such as the one beginning 'Here she is mending her dress', which is seventy-eight words long. Of the two longest sentences in the passage, one gives Mrs Dalloway's thoughts and reactions when Peter Walsh appears; and the other gives Peter Walsh's thoughts and reactions on seeing her. The shorter sentences vary in content, giving dialogue, single thoughts and details of the characters' actions. In this passage, then, the longest sentences describe the internal experience of the characters.

We said that the long sentences are 'loosely constructed'. In fact both of them contain lists which strive to describe and then re-describe the character's thought or feeling. In Mrs Dalloway's case she was 'so surprised . . . , so glad, so shy, so utterly taken aback'; and in Peter Walsh's mind, she had been 'mending her dress; playing about; going to parties; running to the House and back and all that'. In addition, both sentences contain parentheses. The first is inter-rupted after 'and in came' with a dash, interjecting the description of her surprise. The parenthesis never finishes, however: Peter Walsh's name is mentioned without any formal completion of the phrase 'and in came —'; and his letter is mentioned at the end of the sen-tence, in brackets. The second long sentence interrupts Peter Walsh's thoughts at a comma, and interjects a description of his mood. His thoughts continue after another comma. These two sentences, then, are very loosely constructed indeed, and are about the thoughts and feelings of characters. The sentence-structure seems to imitate the darting, bit-by-bit, loosely connected flow of thought and emotion: this is the effect Virginia Woolf wishes to convey.

When we try to follow the thought in these sentences we notice another quality they have in common. In the first, Mrs Dalloway is overcome by surprise, but completes her surprise before returning to the reason for it — that she did not read his letter. In the second, Peter Walsh reaches his dislike of her husband when he thinks of her 'running to the House and back'; but his mind shies away to a gen-eralisation about 'some women' and 'marriage' before he returns to complete his venomous thoughts about Mr Dalloway, whom he caustically calls 'the admirable Richard'. So the direction of thought includes detours and delays, in both cases; and the sentence-con-struction shows that the characters are unsuccessful at putting their thoughts together as a sequential development of ideas.

Certain other features of the passage are noticeable. There is an unusually large number of present participles, such as *thinking, giving, hearing, protecting, respecting, trembling, taking, kissing, looking, coming, putting, tilting, mending* (three times), *playing, going, running, growing, shutting, finishing*. Also, three sentences begin with 'And'. These features seem to convey a sense of a continuous present. The narrative is in the past tense, but the use of so many '-ing' endings brings actions and feelings into the present moment for the reader, and a sense of continuous flow from experience to experience is enhanced by the use of 'and' as a loose conjunction introducing new thought, speech or action.

Finally, the passage exhibits the author's use of both imagery and symbol. Mrs Dalloway tries to hide her dress 'like a virgin protecting chastity'. This simile explains a great deal about their relationship: it tells us that she does not wish to hide the dress from shame or guilt, but out of a self-protective sexual fear. The simile is important because it is the only hint that Peter Walsh represents a sexual threat or challenge to her. The symbolism in this passage resides in his knife and her scissors. Again, the implication is sexual. The pocket-knife is opened, to compensate for his embarrassment, then pointed towards her dress, and eventually snapped shut in anger because she married another man. Her scissors are then opened, dismissing his intrusion into her life, so she can continue with what she was doing. It is amusing to think of the knife as a phallic symbol, and the scissors threatening castration. However, these symbols are not as aridly precise as mere sexual labels: the two metal instruments also represent the shifting balance of domination in their relationship; and both of them use their playthings as a focus of reassurance for themselves.

We have come a long way by analysing one short passage, chosen at random. We have found that Virginia Woolf's *style* is not remarkable for 'oddness'. It has some individual features, but no more than are found in any author's work. However, when sentence-structure, verbs, imagery and symbols are looked at closely in conjunction with the content of the passage, the effect of the whole is unusual. We have learned that this author's interest is focused on a certain level of experience. She conveys a sense of her characters making their thoughts, not reporting them once they have been made; and their feelings are sudden and brief. Virginia Woolf, then, portrays a level of experience as close as possible to the chaotic and confusing present moment of life. It is more impulsive, less conscious and less logically organised than we are used to in other novels. We are used to characters – whether in the third person or the first person – expressing rationalised emotion and thinking deliberately about conscious action. Virginia Woolf surprises us, then, because the momentary flow of mental and emotional life conveyed in her narrative is not what we are used to in classical novels.

We have also learned something about the subject of the book. The imagery and symbols we noticed indicate a competitive struggle between the characters in which sexual feelings are important. On the other hand, Clarissa and Peter never mention such feelings in conversation. This suggests that primitive and instinctive feelings, at a hidden level, control Woolf's characters. Perhaps one of Woolf's interests, then, is to reveal the hidden energies which drive people; and to satirise her characters' hypocrisies and ignorance about themselves.

Thinking about the extract as a whole helps us to develop this conclusion further. Clarissa plays a feminine role in this extract: she is mending a dress, and her business is to be the hostess at a party for her and her husband's friends. Peter plays a masculine role, returning from adventure flourishing a knife. Their social roles, on the other hand, are satirised by the hidden, deeper feelings we have noticed. This suggests that Virginia Woolf is also writing about artificial and underlying issues of gender.

* * *

We have confronted a passage from *Mrs Dalloway*, and found that the style and content contribute to each other, showing Virginia Woolf's concentration on a pre-conscious level of mental experience. The next step is to try the same approach with an extract from a different novel. In *To the Lighthouse* Mrs Ramsay is saying goodnight to her two young children, Cam and James. They are quarrelling about a stuffed tusked boar's head which is fixed to their bedroom wall. The girl Cam has nightmares about it, but James wants it to stay:

> Then Cam must go to sleep (it had great horns said Cam) – must go to sleep and dream of lovely palaces, said Mrs Ramsay, sitting down on the bed by her side. She could see the horns, Cam said, all over the room. It was true. Wherever they put the light (and James could not sleep without a light) there was always a shadow somewhere.

'But think, Cam, it's only an old pig,' said Mrs Ramsay, 'a nice black pig like the pigs at the farm.' But Cam thought it was a horrid thing, branching at her all over the room.

'Well then,' said Mrs Ramsay, 'we will cover it up,' and they all watched her go to the chest of drawers, and open the little drawers quickly one after another, and not seeing anything that would do, she quickly took her own shawl off and wound it round the skull, round and round and round, and then she came back to Cam and laid her head almost flat on the pillow beside Cam's and said how lovely it looked now; how the fairies would love it; it was like a bird's nest; it was like a beautiful mountain such as she had seen abroad, with valleys and flowers and bells ringing and birds singing and little goats and antelopes. . . . She could see the words echoing as she spoke them rhythmically in Cam's mind, and Cam was repeating after her how it was like a mountain, a bird's nest, a garden, and there were little antelopes, and her eyes were opening and shutting, and Mrs Ramsay went on saying still more monotonously, and more rhythmically and more nonsensically, how she must shut her eyes and go to sleep and dream of mountains and valleys and stars falling and parrots and antelopes and gardens, and everything lovely, she said, raising her head very slowly and speaking more and more mechanically, until she sat upright and saw that Cam was asleep.

(*To the Lighthouse*, pp. 106-7)

Are the features we analysed from *Mrs Dalloway* also present in this extract? Yes, they are. First, the superficial narrative is clearly told. There is indirect speech ('Cam thought it was a horrid thing, branching at her all over the room') and direct speech ('said Cam' and 'said Mrs Ramsay' leave us in no doubt about the speaker); the characters' actions and positions are given in satisfying detail (for example, they watch Mrs Ramsay 'open the little drawers quickly one after another' and she 'laid her head almost flat on the pillow beside Cam's'). The same classical features of narrative we noticed in our first passage are also evident here.

Second, Virginia Woolf's sentences are again extremely varied in length. The shortest ('It was true') is a mere three words, while the longest (the first of only two sentences in the final paragraph) contains 119 words. Conjunctions often begin sentences, as in *Mrs Dalloway*. The passage begins 'Then', and Mrs Ramsay begins 'But' and 'Well then', while the two very long sentences of the final paragraph are strangely joined, because the second of them starts with an ellipsis as if its language begins gradually: as if the volume is gradually increased from silence to an audible level.

Finally, the structure of these longer sentences can be compared with what we found in *Mrs Dalloway*. The peculiar feature of interrupted or diverted thought, which occurred with Peter Walsh and Clarissa Dalloway, does not occur in our sample from *To the Lighthouse*. The noticeable features of the two long sentences in this extract are the lists. There are three of them, and some of the content is repeated in each, while the order changes and some new items enter each new list. Mrs Ramsay mentions a bird's nest, a mountain, valleys, flowers, bells, birdsong, goats and antelopes. In the second long sentence, the sleepy little girl Cam murmurs about a mountain, birds' nests, a garden and little antelopes; then Mrs Ramsay reinforces her statement, giving a list of mountains, valleys, stars falling, parrots, antelopes and gardens. It seems that the first list of soothing images is differently perceived by Cam: she injects the 'gardens' from her own mind, reverses the mountains and birds' nests, and makes the antelopes 'little'. She forgets about 'bells ringing' and 'little goats'. Mrs Ramsay, continuing to lull her daughter to sleep, tries to describe the tone of her voice three times, passing through 'monotonously' and 'rhythmically' before reaching 'nonsensically'. Astonishingly, when she repeats her list, Mrs Ramsay includes 'parrots' (perhaps because Cam is parroting her words), and 'stars falling'. This is rather a disturbing phrase with overtones of the end of the world, which has cropped up in Mrs Ramsay's mind because she has half-hypnotised herself with the 'rhythmically' and 'nonsensically' intoned list of images.

The lists in these two sentences make fascinating and rewarding study. They reveal the insecurity of speech and perception. Even in this simple case of a child repeating after an adult, the two minds of two people make something different of the same material: they experience different worlds. Also, thanks to the sleepy, rhythmical repetition Mrs Ramsay is engaged in, her conscious control over her words relaxes, allowing two unexpected thoughts to express themselves: parrots and falling stars. These have arrived illogically from somewhere deeper in her mind, a place where thoughts are not yet formed. Again, then, we notice that Virginia Woolf's long sentences imitate an illogical, non-conscious level of mental experience. This time, however, the author has used a different technique in order to achieve the desired effect.

One further feature of this extract deserves mention: imagery. Remember that Peter Walsh's knife and Mrs Dalloway's scissors played a supporting role as emblems of the hidden issues of power and sexuality in their relationship. In *To the Lighthouse*, the boar's head has become a significant symbolic object because of its influence over the children. When Mrs Ramsay covers it up by winding her shawl 'round and round and round', this is a sign of her normal response to discord or unpleasant realities. The head itself, a hunting trophy, is a primitive and savage object. Mrs Ramsay feels that she must transform it into something from a fairy-tale fantasy: 'bells', 'flowers', 'birds singing', and so on. This process of covering up the primitive and manufacturing a superficial prettiness in life is a constant motif in *To the Lighthouse*. The objects and images in this passage, then, have a much wider significance in our understanding of the novel as a whole. They also confirm our conclusion from *Mrs Dalloway*. Virginia Woolf's theme is primitive energies, how people attempt to hide from them and how they break through, driving people whether they understand them or not. So far, we have found a sexual power-struggle between Clarissa and Peter, and a need to transform the primitive into a fairy-tale, together with a fear of destruction, possibly of death ('stars falling'), in the two extracts we have studied.

We now think about the whole extract, and the theme of gender-roles appears again. This time the character is behaving maternally: she calms her child's fears and protects Cam from upsetting truths. Our close analysis, however, has suggested that death and the boar's head upset Mrs Ramsay as well as her daughter; and that her attempt to be motherly and 'soothe' Cam is fruitless. Virginia Woolf's subject seems to be the artificiality of social convention again – in this case a mother's role in her family.

*   *   *

A third passage should expand and confirm our developing under-standing. Here is an extract from *The Waves*:

> 'As I fold up my frock and my chemise,' said Rhoda, 'so I put off my hopeless desire to be Susan, to be Jinny. But I will stretch my toes so that they touch the rail at the end of the bed; I will assure myself, touching the rail, of something hard. Now I cannot sink; cannot alto-gether fall through the thin sheet now. Now I spread my body on this frail mattress and hang suspended. I am above the earth now. I am no longer upright, to be knocked against and damaged. All is soft, and bending. Walls and cupboards whiten and bend their yellow squares on top of which a pale glass gleams. Out of me now my mind can pour. I can think of my Armadas sailing on the high waves. I am relieved of hard contacts and collisions. I sail on alone under the white cliffs. Oh, but I sink. I fall! That is the corner of the cupboard; that is the nursery looking-glass. But they stretch, they elongate. I sink down on the black plumes of sleep; its thick wings are pressed to my eyes. Travelling through darkness I see the stretched flower-beds, and Mrs Constable runs from behind the corner of the pampas-grass to say my aunt has come to fetch me in a carriage. I mount; I escape; I rise on spring-heeled boots over the tree-tops. But I am now fallen into the carriage at the hall door, where she sits nodding yellow plumes with eyes hard like glazed marbles. Oh, to awake from dreaming! Look, there is the chest of drawers. Let me pull myself out of these waters. But they heap themselves on me; they sweep me between their great shoulders; I am turned; I am tumbled; I am stretched, among these long lights, these long waves, these endless paths, with people pur-suing, pursuing.'

> (*The Waves*, p. 15)

The classical narrative is present in this extract: we know that Rhoda removes her clothes, lies on her bed and stretches until her toes touch the bed-rail. However, it is clearly not the same kind of writing as in *Mrs Dalloway* or *To the Lighthouse*. First, the narrative is minimal, and intermingled with a metaphor-rich internal mono-logue in such a way that we do have to make an effort to distinguish physical events from mental events. Secondly, the whole passage pur-ports to be a speech by the character Rhoda, and in the opening line we read 'said Rhoda'. On the other hand, Rhoda is obviously not 'saying' it aloud: the content tells us that this is an internal account of her mental experiences, the flow of her thoughts and feelings. While the monologue continues, she begins to fall asleep, struggles into wakefulness again, then sinks back towards sleep. Rhoda herself would not be aware of most of this 'speech': it is at a level of her mind which is almost subconscious. So, this passage uses direct speech for a metaphorical purpose: as a way of giving a voice to the level of the mind between consciousness and the subconscious.

Despite this difference from the other two extracts, some features we are used to in Woolf's writing are still recognisable. For example, sentences vary in length between six words ('I am above the earth now') and the final sentence of thirty-six words. The longer sentences again occur when the content is from a deeper, less conscious level of the character's mind. In our passage from *Mrs Dalloway*, we noticed successions of phrases or lists of words which progressively modify the thought or emotion described. We commented that these lists imitate the process of thoughts being made: the character actually chooses words for thoughts as raw impressions become conscious and the brain turns them into language. This feature is prominent again in *The Waves*. There are numerous examples in our extract. Near the end, Rhoda feels 'turned', 'tumbled' and 'stretched' among 'these long lights, these long waves, these endless paths'. Clearly none of these attempts exactly describes the experience inside her, but all of them struggle to express it. In this extract, the same technique embraces whole clauses and even successions of sentences, so the sense of the mind struggling to find words for raw experience is constantly present in the narrative. For example, consider: 'Now I cannot sink; cannot altogether fall through the thin sheet now. Now I spread my body on this frail mattress and hang suspended. I am above the earth now. I am no longer upright, to be knocked against and damaged. All is soft, and bending.' The sensations of sinking, being suspended, and of lying down all contribute to Rhoda's mental landscape as she lies on her bed. Each of these sensations seems to have two or more associations in Rhoda's mind (for example, she thinks of falling as 'sink' and 'fall through this thin sheet'). In this way the whole passage circles one momentary experience, adding, qualifying, modifying expression all the time. Notice that this focus on a single 'moment' of experience is emphasised: the word 'now' appears four times.

Finally, our extract from *The Waves* reminds us of the importance of imagery in understanding Virginia Woolf. The everyday objects surrounding Rhoda are clearly significant: emotions and attitudes are frequently attached to them. For example, her mattress is 'frail' and cupboards 'whiten and bend their yellow squares'; as she is falling asleep, cupboards and looking-glass 'elongate' and 'stretch', and the flower-beds are 'stretched'. We also find imagery of nature used freely, without explanation, in the way we might expect a lyric poet to work: 'Let me pull myself out of these waters. But they heap themselves on me; they sweep me between their great shoulders'. Early in the passage, Rhoda mentions 'sink'; later on, the water-metaphor changes suddenly, and she is carried over rapids on a fast-flowing river!

Analysing extracts from three of her novels has taught us a lot about approaching Virginia Woolf's style. We are now familiar with several consistent features of her writing; and a similar approach to any other passage will therefore be effective and rewarding.

On the other hand, there does not seem to be a constant single style between the three novels. Parts of the extract from *Mrs Dalloway*, for example, could come from the pen of any classical novelist; while the extract from *The Waves* contains very little ordinary narrative and uses metaphors in the manner, and with the sudden intensity, of a lyric poem. Frankly, then, the answer to our original hypothesis is negative: Virginia Woolf does not have a very odd style. She does not have a single, distinctive *style* at all, but rather a variety of narrative flavours and techniques which she switches and flows between at will. On the other hand, investigating three extracts has been revealing. There is no single *style*, but in a broader sense there are characteristic features which will be worth looking for in any part of Virginia Woolf's writing. For example, find the longest sentences: they are the ones which convey the sense of raw mental experience being made into thoughts, and are loosely, expansively structured to imitate the flowing of a disorganised but continuous present, in the character's experience.

Both the techniques we have used to analyse these extracts, and the insights we have gained into Woolf's narrative method, are unimportant compared to our major discovery. The most useful result of this exercise is that we have an idea of one constant theme in these novels. The subject of all three extracts has been that level of mental experience which is beneath or behind our deliberate, logical thoughts. This writer focuses her attention on the place where subconscious, conscious, raw emotion, instinct and impulse meet. All of Virginia Woolf's writing – her various techniques and 'styles' – serve one aim: to explore the non-rational controlling energies in her characters' minds.

We have a working idea of Virginia Woolf's themes, therefore. The non-conscious forces we have found are to do with sex and power (*Mrs Dalloway*); are so upsetting they must be transformed into fairy-tales, and are connected to death or the end of all things (*To the Lighthouse*); are conveyed as fragmentary memories of childhood, and with the irresistible power of natural forces (*The Waves*). In all three cases, these forces could not be expressed in plain language. What we already know about Virginia Woolf's subject, then, could be summarised thus: there is something inexpressibly primitive, in control of our lives; yet we always struggle to understand, and to articulate.

In the next chapter, we will adopt a similarly empirical method, but this time looking more closely at the mental experiences and processes which are Virginia Woolf's subject. We are looking for a recognisable 'shape' in the way her characters' minds work: if we can grasp such a 'shape', we have a good chance of understanding the significance of the novels; and we can expect to find such a 'shape' reflected in the structure of ideas, whichever character or novel we have to study.

Conclusions

1. The features we have noticed point to a consistent interest: Virginia Woolf seeks to create and express mental experience at a pre-rational level. The non-conscious level of the mind is difficult

to describe. It is characteristically primitive, full of instinctive drives such as sex, power and fear.

2. Instinctive drives are not openly discussed. In *Mrs Dalloway*, Clarissa and Peter discuss polite trivia, and do not express their underlying feelings. In *To the Lighthouse*, Mrs Ramsay hides and suppresses thoughts about violent death for the children's sake. In *The Waves*, Rhoda's hidden memories begin to surface as she falls asleep. Virginia Woolf therefore has a theme of self-knowledge and self-ignorance. We can suppose that she is interested in the pressures education and society exert upon individuals, dividing them from themselves.

3. In the extracts from *Mrs Dalloway* and *To the Lighthouse*, gender roles and sexual stereotypes are a subject of the writing. Male and female roles and relationships is another theme we will explore further in later chapters.

Methods of Analysis

In this chapter we have used a standard approach to prose analysis. Our attention focused on the following:

1. Narrative of events and actions; description; direct and indirect speech (traditional features of a conventional novel).
2. Variation in the length of sentences. (Pay particular attention to the extremely short or extremely long.)
3. The structure of sentences. (Look at the clauses or groups of words, and describe how they are linked together. Find ways of describing the structure, and the effect it produces. Compare this with the progress of ideas in the sentence.)
4. Other noticeable effects of diction such as verbs, repetition, or frequent use of conjunctions.
5. Imagery, both of actual objects which are part of the narrative, and in figurative references to natural things and forces.

This amounts to observing *the way in which the passage is written* very closely, and involves an open-minded, detailed scrutiny.

Whatever you *notice* about the writing is of interest, because it must be *noticeable*, i.e. a feature of the style. Describe the feature and its effect as accurately as you can.

Having analysed passages from three novels, we are wiser about Virginia Woolf's writing. There are three features in particular which seem to be characteristic:

1. The longest sentences are very rewarding to analyse. Expect them to focus on the most intimate and deepest levels of consciousness in a character.
2. The structure of sentences, and constructions used within sentences, are often designed to imitate the actual making of thoughts from raw mental experience. So the writing often redefines or modifies experience, or shies away from the thought, digressing in mid-sentence.
3. Virginia Woolf uses the objects which figure in her stories as significant images which carry some of the story's meaning; and which attract or represent emotions and attitudes in her characters. Therefore, we can think about the *things* in Virginia Woolf's stories as symbols. There is also a great deal of reference to natural forces in imagery.

Suggested Work

At this stage, simply apply the same methods we have demonstrated to any extract selected from the work or works you are studying. This should build up your insight into and understanding of the text you have to study. Choose an extract that intrigues you, and try considering what it is about by examining the elements of the narrative, length and structure of sentences, imagery, symbols and any other noticeable features, in the kind of detail we have used in this chapter.

A more specific 'exercise' would be to analyse one of Virginia Woolf's longer sentences in detail. This will give you practice at analysing and describing the structure of the sentence, and relating that to the development of ideas. To do this, select a sentence which is more than fifty words long, from anywhere in the novel. Read enough of the narrative either side of your selected sentence, to remind you of the characters and context at that point in the book. Then analyse the sentence itself, using the same methods we have applied in this chapter.

2

Mental Processes in Virginia Woolf

We have found that Virginia Woolf is concerned with an unconscious level of experience in her characters. This means that her
characters do not always work in a logical or rational way. We
cannot expect to know what they will do, or what they feel, from
reading about their thoughts. When we read about David
Copperfield sighing for Miss Spenlow and fearfully preparing to
propose to her, in Dickens's novel *David Copperfield*, what we read is
what we get. Dickens's characterisation is traditional: David has a
feeling, interprets it, consciously calls it love, and decides to act on
this feeling. The process inside David is a direct linear progress from
original feeling to his final action: he proposes to Miss Spenlow.
There are no interruptions, blockages or detours within David on
the way, except that he is nervous and shy. In Virginia Woolf things
are much more complicated. Characters' thoughts often seem to
contradict their feelings; or their actions and speech are disconnected from or contradict their thoughts.

What can we do to help us understand such characters? In this
chapter, we will focus on the processes that take place inside Virginia
Woolf's characters between emotions and thoughts, and between
thoughts and speech or action. If we can analyse these mental
processes we may find some common principles that consistently
appear in the characterisation; and this will increase our understanding of human nature in Woolf's novels.

* * *

The first extract for us to look at comes from *Mrs Dalloway*. Peter Walsh has just left Clarissa's house, and the visit revived feelings from their love-affair long ago at Bourton. Peter is surprised at the strength of his feelings. He is walking through London:

He was not old, or set, or dried in the least. As for caring what they said of him – the Dalloways, the Whitbreads, and their set, he cared not a straw – not a straw (though it was true he would have, some time or other, to see whether Richard couldn't help him to some job). Striding, staring, he glared at the statue of the Duke of Cambridge. He had been sent down from Oxford – true. He had been a Socialist, in some sense a failure – true. Still the future of civilisation lies, he thought, in the hands of young men like that; of young men such as he was, thirty years ago; with their love of abstract principles; getting books sent out to them all the way from London to a peak in the Himalayas; reading science; reading philosophy. The future lies in the hands of young men like that, he thought.

A patter like the patter of leaves in a wood came from behind, and with it a rustling, regular thudding sound, which as it overtook him drummed his thoughts, strict in step, up Whitehall, without his doing. Boys in uniform, carrying guns, marched with their eyes ahead of them, marched, their arms stiff, and on their faces an expression like the letters of a legend written round the base of a statue praising duty, gratitude, fidelity, love of England.

It is, thought Peter Walsh, beginning to keep step with them, a very fine training. But they did not look robust. They were weedy for the most part, boys of sixteen, who might, to-morrow, stand behind bowls of rice, cakes of soap on counters. Now they wore on them unmixed with sensual pleasure or daily preoccupations the solemnity of the wreath which they had fetched from Finsbury Pavement to the empty tomb. They had taken their vow. The traffic respected it; vans were stopped.

I can't keep up with them, Peter Walsh thought, as they marched up Whitehall, and sure enough, on they marched, past him, past every one, in their steady way, as if one will worked legs and arms uniformly, and life, with its varieties, its irreticences, had been laid under a pavement of monuments and wreaths and drugged into a stiff yet staring corpse by discipline. One had to respect it; one might laugh; but one had to respect it, he thought. There they go, thought Peter Walsh, pausing at the edge of the pavement; and all the exalted statues. Nelson, Gordon, Havelock, the black, the spectacular images of great soldiers stood looking ahead of them, as if they too had made the same renunciation (Peter Walsh felt he, too, had made it, the great renunciation), trampled under the same temptations, and achieved at length a marble stare. But the stare Peter Walsh did not want for himself in the least; though he could respect it in others. He could respect it in boys. They don't know the troubles of the flesh yet, he thought, as the marching boys disappeared in the direction of the Strand – all that I've been through, he thought, crossing the road, and standing under Gordon's statue, Gordon whom as a boy he had worshipped; Gordon standing lonely with one leg raised and his arms crossed, – poor Gordon, he thought.

And just because nobody yet knew he was in London, except Clarissa, and the earth, after the voyage, still seemed an island to him, the strangeness of standing alone, alive, unknown, at half-past eleven in Trafalgar Square overcame him. What is it? Where am I? And why, after all, does one do it? he thought, the divorce seeming all moonshine. And down his mind went flat as a marsh, and three great emotions bowled over him; understanding; a vast philanthropy; and finally, as if the result of the others, an irrepressible, exquisite delight; as if inside his brain by another hand strings were pulled, shutters moved, and he, having nothing to do with it, yet stood at the opening of endless avenues, down which if he chose he might wander. He had not felt so young for years.

He had escaped! was utterly free – as happens in the downfall of habit when the mind, like an unguarded flame, bows and bends and seems about to blow from its holding. I haven't felt so young for years! thought Peter, escaping (only of course for an hour or so) from being precisely what he was, and feeling like a child who runs out of doors, and sees, as he runs, his old nurse waving at the wrong window. But she's extraordinarily attractive, he thought, as, walking across Trafalgar Square in the direction of the Haymarket, came a young woman who, as she passed Gordon's statue, seemed, Peter Walsh thought (susceptible as he was), to shed veil after veil, until she became the very woman he had always had in mind; young, but stately; merry, but discreet; black, but enchanting.

(Mrs Dalloway, pp. 43–5)

We notice the typical wide variation in the length of sentences again, in this extract. In the first paragraph, for example, the first, third, fourth, fifth and last sentences are eleven, twelve, nine, twelve and fourteen words long respectively; while the second and sixth sentences are forty-six and fifty-three words long. One short sentence narrates ('Striding, staring, he glared at the statue of the Duke of Cambridge'); the others are all written as if Peter Walsh is talking to himself. They have the tone of a conscious argument: 'He was not old, or set, or dried in the least' and 'He had been sent down from Oxford – true' both carry Peter Walsh's defensive tone of voice. Some short sentences, then, tell us that this character is having an argument inside himself. He argues against the accusation that he is old; and he makes concessions ('true') before pursuing his argument with weightier reasons: 'Still . . .'.

The two long sentences contrast with these. They meander. The first of them digresses for two parentheses and contains repetition; the second builds up a series of parallel phrases introduced by participles ('getting . . . reading . . . reading'). We remember that the long sentences are likely to imitate the character's mental process as it happens. In the first of them, the strongest statement is 'he cared not a straw', but everything else in the sentence undermines the assertiveness of this phrase. First, it is repeated, suggesting that he is insecure about it: perhaps he is only trying to convince himself, and he does care after all. Second, the part in brackets is very vaguely expressed ('some time or other' and 'to see whether Richard couldn't' are hesitant phrases), yet it expresses his dependence on the very people he claims to despise. In this sentence, then, we find Peter Walsh's insecurity, and it is not hard to conclude that he is lying to himself. He *says* that he 'cared not a straw', but the style reveals that he *really* cares a great deal and has to, because he depends on his establishment friends such as 'the Dalloways, the Whitbreads, and their set' to provide him with a job.

The second long sentence is a more complicated matter. Peter Walsh is trying to describe his idea that unconventional young men are important, because they will make the future. But Peter Walsh uses ambiguous pronouns, which may refer to his own past self, the Duke of Cambridge, or 'young men' who were either young thirty years ago or are young now. 'He' (either Peter or the Duke of Cambridge) was sent down from Oxford. 'He' (ambiguous again) was a Socialist and a failure. But young men like 'that' (which 'that?') hold the future. The most specific statement is 'young men such as he was, thirty years ago' but the pronoun 'their' which follows restores the distance between the real Peter Walsh of history, and the mythical 'young men' who are vaguely identified with him in his mind. This insistent ambiguity highlights the confusion: he does not define the age-difference between generations, and repeatedly uses the adjective 'young' to describe himself. In this sentence, then, our attention is focused on to ambiguity. That is, our attention is focused on the very thought that is absent from Peter's mind: the empty, unexplained gap in his thoughts.

Looking at sentences in the first paragraph of this extract has introduced us to three features of Virginia Woolf's style that are like signals for the reader. These features throw a spotlight upon part of the character's mind that is uneasy, or contradictory. First, repetition. We noticed repetition of 'not a straw'. We deduced that Peter Walsh is insecure about this and tries to reinforce or convince himself by means of repetition. There is another repeated phrase in the same paragraph ('The future lies in the hands of young men like that'); but there are other kinds of repetition as well. For example, Peter Walsh thinks he is 'not old, or set, or dried', using three different terms which explain 'old'; and he repeats the admission 'true' when he acknowledges his faults.

Second, we noticed an argumentative diction or tone of voice. For example, the phrase 'As for caring what they said of him' is a debater's rhetorical construction, heaping contempt on the opposition's argument. This style reads like an internal debate. We again deduced that Peter Walsh is insecure and trying to convince himself, that there is an argument taking place inside him.

Third, we noticed vagueness, ambiguity and omission. These reveal different degrees of the same mental process, so we can treat them together. Peter Walsh's vagueness about 'some time or other' asking for 'some job' reveals that he is unwilling to admit to himself that he depends on the Dalloways. His ambiguous pronouns, referring both to himself and 'young men', reveal that he would like to think of himself as young; and the gap in his thoughts where we would expect him to explain the thirty-year difference in age between himself and the 'young', reveals that he is unwilling to allow the fact of his age (that he is not young; that he has been adult for thirty years) to enter his mind. In all three of these instances, Peter Walsh seems to be sending a thought away. Vagueness makes the thought indistinct; ambiguity makes it confused; omission makes it disappear from his conscious mind. Notice how precisely Virginia Woolf uses this technique: Peter can think that he was young ('such as he was, thirty years ago'), but cannot think that he is old.

Now let us look at the rest of the passage, following up the clues we have already found. Peter Walsh's contradictory ideas about being young appear again: he is carried away by the marching 'boys', his thoughts being 'drummed . . . without his doing' so he involuntarily began to 'keep step with them'. All of these details suggest that he identifies with the boys. On the other hand, they are 'stiff', 'with their eyes ahead of them' and wear 'solemnity'. They march 'steady' and 'uniformly' and are like a 'stiff yet staring corpse'; and these details contrast with the rebellious, unconventional 'young men' he identifies with himself.

The imagery surrounding the marching boys is worth noticing. They are carrying a wreath to lay upon a tomb; in Peter Walsh's mind 'life, with its varieties, its irreticencies' was 'laid under a pavement of monuments and wreaths', and he likens the young men to a 'corpse'. This burial of life is then developed with the idea of 'renunciation', because the image-idea of walking upon 'life' is restated in a new form: 'trampled under the same temptations, and achieved at length a marble stare'. The 'marble stare' is metaphorically the expressionless gaze of the disciplined young men, and actually the stare of marble statues of 'great soldiers' Peter can see. The boys, the heroes who are now statues, and 'Peter Walsh felt he, too,' have all made the same 'renunciation'. As the marching boys disappear, Peter stands under the statue of Gordon 'whom as a boy he had worshipped' and thinks 'poor Gordon'.

The imagery, then, creates a powerful impression of hard, disciplined duty burying and trampling upon 'life'. What is Peter's response to this? We already noticed that he is carried away by the marching, tries to keep step and thinks of himself as renouncing 'life' as the boys and great soldiers do. On the other hand, he thinks himself different from them. He thinks 'One had to respect it; one might laugh'; and the marble stare 'Peter Walsh did not want for himself in the least'. Also, they 'did not look robust', but 'weedy for the most part', yet, 'I can't keep up with them, Peter Walsh thought'; and he feels that his 'renunciation' must be superior to theirs because they are so young: 'They don't know the troubles of the flesh yet, he thought . . . all that I've been through'. At this point he sees Gordon 'whom as a boy he had worshipped'. Peter seems to identify with his own childish self, and with the great 'renunciation', when he feels sorry for 'poor' and 'lonely' Gordon.

It is clear that this character's mind is a mass of contradictory feelings and thoughts. He identifies with conformist boys, or rebellious young men. He laughs at the conformists, and respects them. He has 'been through' the 'troubles of the flesh', or he 'trampled under . . . temptations' in a great renunciation. There are lists representing each side of Peter Walsh's conflict: on the one side, 'duty, gratitude, fidelity, love of England'; on the other side, 'sensual pleasure or daily preoccupations', 'life, with its varieties, its irreticences', and 'temptations'. What happens?

In the final two paragraphs Peter Walsh is said to experience a rejuvenation: and this gives rise to noticeable repetition again ('He had not felt so young for years' and 'I haven't felt so young for years! thought Peter' who 'had escaped!' and was 'escaping'). Virginia Woolf describes this change of feeling in terms that show him helpless: he no longer has control of his mind because 'down his mind went' and emotion 'bowled over him'. His mind is compared to some kind of magic light-box or camera: 'as if inside his brain, by another hand, strings were pulled, shutters moved, and he, having nothing to do with it'. This makes him feel that his future holds 'endless avenues down which if he chose he might wander', and 'like a child who runs out of doors, and sees, as he runs, his old nurse waving at the wrong window'.

There is a temptation, at this point, to speculate about Peter's childhood traumas, because the nurse waves from the 'wrong' window. When you come to the critics in Chapter 10, you will see that some of them build enormous psychoanalytical theories on to Woolf's texts. We must not do this, however: remember that this is a novel, and Peter is a literary character, not a patient on a couch.

What, then, can we legitimately say about the 'wrong window'? Simply that it is 'wrong', that there is something that is not as it should be in Peter's mind. From the order of his feelings and the narrative, we can also say that whatever is wrong coincides with a sudden feeling of freedom, potential and 'delight'; and his picture of his childhood 'nurse' motivates his next move: 'But she's extraordinarily attractive' is a thought that applies to the waving nurse of his imagination. Later in the sentence it is ambiguously transferred to the 'young woman' Peter sees and begins to follow. A quick read ahead through the next five paragraphs shows Peter living a vicarious adventure in his mind, centring on the young woman he follows. She represents excitement, enchantment, his potential for heroism and seduction. Peter has a sexual adventure in his mind, in fact, and this suggests that his desires are not satisfied: the fantasy compensates for failures in his life.

Returning to our extract, we notice that Peter describes the strange woman's character using paradoxes: she has contradictory pairs of qualities, being 'young, but stately; merry, but discreet; black, but enchanting'. We know that Peter has been attracted to Clarissa for a long time, and has just run out from a disturbing meeting with her; and we know that he is 'in love' with a young, fair-haired woman called Daisy, in India. It seems reasonable to suggest that 'stately . . . discreet . . . black' may be the restrained and cold qualities of Clarissa; and 'young . . . merry . . . enchanting' are the qualities he looks for in Daisy, which he also looked for in Clarissa before she rejected him. The young woman of his fantasy, then, is better than either the woman he lost or the woman he has won: she is a combination of the two.

We picked out the word 'wrong' in Peter's simile of the waving nurse: the word stands out since the sentence would be complete without it, and it is unexplained. Woolf achieves the same effect again, but in this list of qualities the odd-word-out is 'black'. All we know is that 'black' does not suit Clarissa (she is 'almost white') or the fair-haired Daisy; and 'black' is not the antithesis of 'enchanting'. So, our attention is focused on to one word again. We could call this effect the 'misfit word', and we should be sensitive to it. In the case of 'wrong' we suggested that it simply stood for something that was not as it should be in Peter's memories. 'Black' gives us a further lead, however. Elsewhere in the extract, the statues of great soldiers are called 'black', so Woolf seems to hint at a connection in Peter's mind between the Clarissa-side of his ideal woman, and the heroic statues which stand for renunciation and trampling 'life' underfoot. Peter's sense of his own identity, and his relationships with women, thus create a full circle: he identified the 'poor' statue of Gordon with himself, and pitied himself; now 'black' hints that he identifies Clarissa with the statues and himself, also. His attitudes, however, are always unresolved: he admires, derides and pities himself, Clarissa, and the heroic leaders.

This extract, then, has revealed a great deal about Virginia Woolf's characterisation: we can look for repetition, long sentences, internal debate, vagueness, omissions, imagery and 'misfit words', which are all signals of conflict within the character. The mental processes revealed include repression (sending unwelcome thoughts away); transferring emotion from one object to another; wish-fulfilment fantasy (building a fantasy in order to satisfy a frustrated or hidden desire), and projecting needs and desires on to others. This has told us much about how her characters are created and how they work, then; but we are still interested in finding out why Virginia Woolf writes about them: what is her subject?

To answer this question we have to see beyond the many details of Peter's character, and his momentary experiences or moods. It is helpful to construct as broad and brief a summary of the extract as possible: *Peter Walsh is emotionally carried away, marching with young soldiers and passing statues; then he is carried away following a strange woman, living a romantic seduction fantasy.* So, there appear to be two conflicting influences: convention (restraint) and rebellion (sensuality, adventure). Virginia Woolf writes about an individual who cannot resolve these two pressures, cannot settle between these two ideals. Both of the ideals are conveyed as hollow or unreal, however ('one might laugh' at the boys; and Peter's fantasy was 'made up, as one makes up the better part of life' [p. 47]); so perhaps the author is interested in the artificiality of human fantasies and self-images, and their destructive effect on our lives?

At this stage such ideas about Woolf's themes are speculative. However, we have begun the process of deducing her thematic concerns, the so-called 'message' of her writing, from a detailed analysis of one extract. These deductions will develop as we continue to study.

*   *   *

We now turn to a passage about Mrs Ramsay, from *To the Lighthouse*. Our extract is from Chapter 11 of Part I, 'The Window', and begins with Mrs Ramsay's relief that her younger children have gone to bed:

> For now she need not think about anybody. She could be herself, by herself. And that was what now she often felt the need of – to think; well not even to think. To be silent; to be alone. All the being and the doing, expansive, glittering, vocal, evaporated; and one shrunk, with a sense of solemnity, to being oneself, a wedge-shaped core of darkness, something invisible to others. Although she continued to knit, and sat upright, it was thus that she felt herself; and this self having shed its attachments was free for the strangest adventures. When life sank down for a moment, the range of experience seemed limitless. And to everybody there was always this sense of unlimited resources, she supposed; one after another, she, Lily, Augustus Carmichael, must feel, our apparitions, the things you know us by, are simply childish. Beneath it is all dark, it is all spreading, it is unfathomably deep; but now and again we rise to the surface and that is what you see us by. Her horizon seemed to her limitless. There were all the places she had not seen; the Indian plains; she felt herself pushing aside the thick leather curtain of a church in Rome. This core of darkness could go anywhere, for no one saw it. They could not stop it, she thought, exulting. There was freedom, there was peace, there was, most welcome of all, a summoning together, a resting on a platform of stability. Not as oneself did one find rest ever, in her experience (she accomplished here something dexterous with her needles), but as a wedge of darkness. Losing personality, one lost the fret, the hurry, the stir; and there rose to her lips always some exclamation of triumph over life when things came together in this peace, this rest, this eternity; and pausing there she looked out to meet that stroke of the

Lighthouse, the long steady stroke, the last of the three, which was her stroke, for watching them in this mood always at this hour one could not help attaching oneself to one thing especially of the things one saw; and this thing, the long steady stroke, was her stroke. Often she found herself sitting and looking, sitting and looking, with her work in her hands until she became the thing she looked at – that light for example. And it would lift up on it some little phrase or other which had been lying in her mind like that – 'Children don't forget, children don't forget' – which she would repeat and begin adding to it, It will end, It will end, she said. It will come, it will come, when suddenly she added: We are in the hands of the Lord.

But instantly she was annoyed with herself for saying that. Who had said it? not she; she had been trapped into saying something she did not mean. She looked up over her knitting and met the third stroke and it seemed to her like her own eyes meeting her own eyes, searching as she alone could search into her mind and her heart, purifying out of existence that lie, any lie. She praised herself in praising the light, without vanity, for she was stern, she was searching, she was beautiful like that light. It was odd, she thought, how if one was alone, one leant to things, inanimate things; trees, streams, flowers; felt they expressed one; felt they became one; felt they knew one, in a sense were one; felt an irrational tenderness thus (she looked at that long steady light) as for oneself. There rose, and she looked and looked with her needles suspended, there curled up off the floor of the mind, rose from the lake of one's being, a mist, a bride to meet her lover.

What brought her to say that: 'We are in the hands of the Lord?' she wondered. The insincerity slipping in among the truths roused her, annoyed her. She returned to her knitting again. How could any Lord have made this world? she asked. With her mind she had always seized the fact that there is no reason, order, justice: but suffering, death, the poor. There was no treachery too base for the world to commit; she knew that. No happiness lasted; she knew that. She knitted with firm composure, slightly pursing her lips and, without being aware of it, so stiffened and composed the lines of her face in a habit of sternness . . .

(*To the Lighthouse*, pp. 57–9)

In this extract we recognise several features we have noticed before. For example, the sentences vary in length between six words and ninety-five words; there are repetitions ('she knew that . . . she knew that', or 'sitting and looking, sitting and looking'); the tone of internal debate is often present ('How could any Lord have made this world? she asked'); and there are 'misfit phrases' (see 'without vanity' in the second paragraph, for example). Also, the past narrative often turns into strings of participles which create an impression of a continuous present experience in Mrs Ramsay's mind: 'knitting', 'sitting and looking', 'exulting', 'summoning', 'attaching', 'lying', and many others.

We can study these features, hoping that they will introduce us to the mental processes taking place within Mrs Ramsay. Begin by looking at the one extremely long sentence. It starts with a participle: 'Losing personality'. This sets the time of the sentence as part of a continuing process. The rhythm of the sentence is also noticeable: it is a very long sentence, so taking the number of words in each phrase as a crude measure, we may be able to see its rhythmic shape more clearly by counting each phrase, thus: 2, 4, 2, 2, 20, 2, 2, 13, 4, 5, 4, 25, 3, 4, 3. There seem to be three very long phrases, with two or three short ones in between. It is not hard to imagine the three strokes of the Lighthouse in 'the fret, the hurry, the stir'; 'this peace, this rest, this eternity'; 'the long steady stroke, the last of the three, which was her stroke'; and 'this thing, the long steady stroke, was her stroke'. The short phrases, then, are the groups of three strokes of the light; and the long phrases fill the time in between when Mrs Ramsay waits for the Lighthouse to turn around before its group of three strokes again pass across her window. Woolf has made the rhythm of the sentence as hypnotically repetitive, and as insidious in its effect on us, as the repeated groups of three strokes are for Mrs Ramsay. The sentence imitates the drowsing, pacifying effect the Lighthouse produces on Mrs Ramsay: the influence that enables her to relax and that lulls her mental defences. In her relaxed state, she can imagine something that 'curled up off the floor of the mind, rose from the lake of one's being'; and she unconsciously thinks 'we are in the hands of the Lord', the uninvited thought she is 'instantly' so annoyed about in her conscious mind.

We began by looking more closely at the outstandingly long sentence in this extract. This led us to notice a rhythm like the rhythm of the Lighthouse itself, which affects Mrs Ramsay by lulling and so relaxing her mental defences. What else contributes to lulling her, then? The fact that her children are in bed has set her free from 'all the being and the doing, expansive, glittering, vocal,' and a number of the words describing her state convey the removal of things and reduction of her life: 'evaporated', 'shrunk', 'shed', 'sank down', 'pushing aside' and 'losing'. There is also another repetitive action, her knitting, which allows her mind to 'be silent; to be alone'. Notice that the knitting continues without interfering with her thoughts ('Although she continued to knit, and sat upright, it was thus that she felt herself'). Also, when her relaxing mind is disturbed by the memory of being 'as oneself' when one does not 'find rest', her knitting suffers a similar disturbance: 'she accomplished here something dexterous with her needles'. The repetition 'sitting and looking, sitting and looking' additionally emphasises her passivity.

These details add up to a picture of Mrs Ramsay. She is subject to the monotonous regularity of the Lighthouse from outside. The monotonous regularity of her knitting and her still pose contribute further, until the state she enters is like a hypnotic trance. Woolf tells us the effect of this: 'until she became the thing she looked at – that light for example'. Meanwhile, as outside life and physical activity are reduced to limited repetition, the imagery tells another part of the story.

The imagery begins with a contrast between 'glittering' outside life, and 'a wedge-shaped core of darkness' that is her inner self. The fact that this self is 'wedge-shaped' already suggests that it may push itself further. The second image for it introduces the idea of a sea with a surface and depths: 'Beneath it is all dark, it is all spreading, it is unfathomably deep'. The artificial selves we show to others are 'apparitions', but 'now and again we rise to the surface'. 'We' must mean some solid but dark self that is normally in the 'unfathomable' depths. Mrs Ramsay now seems to be this dark self, looking across the surface because 'Her horizon seemed to her limitless'. Notice that the word 'horizon' is used partly as an abstract term, meaning something similar to 'outlook' or 'potential'; and at the same time is a development of the sea-metaphor from the preceding sentence. The 'core of darkness' is mentioned again, and its potential to rise, grow and move around is confirmed as it is described in increasingly powerful terms: it 'could go anywhere' and 'They could not stop it'. It is – in contrast to the shedding of outside life – 'a summoning together' so one finds rest as 'a wedge of darkness'. We have traced an image of darkness, then, which is progressively developed during the first half of the extract. The image-idea takes on attributes as Woolf returns to it: it begins as a 'wedge'; then we learn that it is usually 'beneath' a surface, then it comes up and looks around; and finally it – and Woolf reminds us that it is still the same 'wedge' – is unstoppable and can go anywhere. In the end it seems to be floating on the surface on some sort of metaphorical raft: 'resting on a platform of stability'.

We have analysed many and various elements of the extract. When we reached this stage with Peter Walsh, we constructed a short summary of what we had found. This helped us to simplify and clarify the situation. We use the same method with Mrs Ramsay now: *for Mrs Ramsay, outside life falls away; and a sunken, dark self rises to the surface, becoming active.* The mental process this represents is plain. Mrs Ramsay's conscious control of her mind is relaxing, and the part of her mind that is normally hidden, her unconscious, is rising to the surface. What happens next?

In her trance-like state, Mrs Ramsay allows the light, which is also herself, to lift up, repeat and add to 'some little phrase or other which had been lying in her mind'. The phrases that emerge in this way are very revealing. First, 'Children don't forget'. We know that her son James has been hurt by his father, and that he only resolves the dispute on the eventual journey to the Lighthouse years later, after Mrs Ramsay's death. Mrs Ramsay has negotiated between her husband and her son, and has tried to calm the boy's feelings; but the underlying truth she knows is that 'Children don't forget'.

Next, Mrs Ramsay says 'It will end'. Perhaps 'It', which has a capital 'I', refers to the details and duties of her everyday life. We know that Mrs Ramsay acts as the focal point for her large family and for her visitors, and takes all the pressure of their conflicts and moods upon herself. The underlying truth she knows is that this duty and labour is not eternal: 'It will end', as all activities end, with death. Mrs Ramsay's next 'little phrase' is 'It will come', which implies that death will come. We know that she has ambivalent feelings about the efforts she makes in her day-to-day life. She feels that she must continue to make these efforts, but she is weary and sometimes longs to give up. So, her dual attitude to death – both postponing it and desiring it – is aptly expressed in the two phrases 'It will end' and 'It will come'.

Finally, suddenly, she adds 'We are in the hands of the Lord'. This phrase expresses two relevant feelings. First, an absolute and passive submission to a greater power. The effect of this on Mrs Ramsay's life would be to release her from her strenuous efforts at moulding and making peace in her family. Secondly, following the two phrases which remind her of death's inevitability, the phrase suggests either religious faith or the desire for a religious faith.

This is the thought that breaks the spell. Mrs Ramsay reacts against it with annoyance. If we trace the elements we have already found through the next paragraph, the metaphors develop further. The light that helped to induce her trance is now like a searchlight. Its power is hinted in 'met the third stroke' and confirmed in 'searching' and 'purifying out of existence'. It seems that this phrase, part of the 'wedge of darkness' that she willingly encouraged, is unwelcome and must be destroyed because it is a 'lie'. Also, the Lighthouse is Mrs Ramsay looking at herself 'like her own eyes meeting her own eyes'. By the end of the passage, however, she has connected the identity she feels with the beam of light, with much softer and more natural things, 'trees, streams, flowers'; and looking into herself she no longer sees a lie being purified 'out of existence' but, 'there curled up off the floor of the mind, rose from the lake of one's being, a mist, a bride to meet her lover'. A change has clearly taken place. There was something offensive, and she turned the light on it to destroy it. A moment later, however, the light sees 'a mist' which is compared to a woman's sexual desire expressed in the language of weddings; and we know how important marriages are to Mrs Ramsay. In the middle of this process, Virginia Woolf says that she 'praised herself . . . without vanity, for she was stern, she was searching, she was beautiful'. We already commented that 'without vanity' might be a 'misfit phrase', an unexpected phrase that does not suit those around it. 'Without vanity' stands out because it is false modesty: everything else about the sentence emphasises her pride in her beauty and in her stern, honest character. This sentence, then, shows Mrs Ramsay building her ego. Meanwhile, the repetitive activity that led her into the dangerous trance in the first place, her knitting, is 'suspended'.

We can use the summary-technique again, to clarify this new process in Mrs Ramsay: *Mrs Ramsay tries to expel a thought from her mind. However, it does not disappear, but changes into something vague and attractive.* We have met characters who try to expel thoughts from their minds before, but this paragraph reveals another consequence of the process: the unwelcome thought changes into something more attractive, with romantic attributes. Thinking about Mrs Ramsay's character in the novel as a whole confirms that this process, which turns unwelcome ideas into romantic 'mist', is at the heart of her character. It helps us to understand why she imagines herself matchmaking for the Rayleys and others, and why Lily feels such pressure from her, to marry William Bankes.

In the final part of this extract, we hear the tone of internal argument. Mrs Ramsay's mind is arguing against the 'lie', the unwelcome thought, thoroughly banishing it from her mind. 'How could any Lord have made this world?' she asks, and proceeds to give reasons for her disagreement: 'the fact that there is no reason, order, justice: but suffering, death, the poor'. Repetition, on this occasion, hammers home her points as in a debate: each pessimistic fact is affirmed with 'She knew that' as if to settle it once and for all. Eventually, Mrs Ramsay has fought her way out of the relaxation of her trance, and 'without being aware of it' she knits on, 'firm', 'stiffened', and 'in a habit of sternness'.

Analysing this extract has revealed certain mental processes to us. First, Mrs Ramsay's repetitive, passive state is conveyed as a kind of trance suggested by hypnotic agents (the Lighthouse) and automatic activity (her knitting). Second, she tries to repress an unwelcome thought, diverting her mind to pleasanter subjects, boosting her ego, and arguing against the hostile idea. Third, the hostile thought undergoes a change: after it has been pushed out of her mind, it manifests itself as something else which is more attractive. We could think of this attractive 'mist' that Mrs Ramsay finally sees, as a 'screen'. It is like a screen because it has pretty pictures on the outside ('a bride to meet her lover'), and that is what the character sees; but the original horrible thought, now repressed or pushed out of sight, still hides behind it.

Analysing the extract has brought us an extraordinary subtlety of perception into the character of Mrs Ramsay, then. We admire Virginia Woolf's creative insight and the detailed naturalness, the convincing logic, of the way this character's mind works. Also, thinking about the book as a whole, we understand that this short moment explains many of the larger traits of character that are played out in the main story. However, we should not leave matters there: remember that Mrs Ramsay is not real – she is a literary character serving her author's purpose. At this stage it is important to notice the themes that make part of Mrs Ramsay's mental life: religion, death, the struggle of day-to-day existence, romantic and sexual fantasies, modern rationalism. Thinking about these themes enables us to develop our understanding of Virginia Woolf's literary aims.

First, she shows how the prominent features of a personality, particularly their most noticeable aims and dreams, have their origin in something else which has been rejected or 'repressed'. In this way, Mrs Ramsay's preoccupation with marriage is seen to arise out of her ambivalence about death, and her repressed desire for a religious faith.

Second, she is writing about modern consciousness: Mrs Ramsay's rational analysis of an unjust world, her concern for 'the poor' and her strict opposition to beliefs she considers false, make up a rational–liberal attitude that was relatively new when the novel was written. It belonged in the world that was absorbing the theories of recent thinkers, including Freud, Marx and Darwin. Virginia Woolf conveys the difficulty of living with such an attitude. There is even a suggestion that this rationalism is unnatural, that it goes against a deeper, instinctive need to believe in something. Also, Mrs Ramsay's 'we are in the hands of the Lord' expresses a desire to lay the responsibility for life elsewhere. Woolf implies that responsibility for life may be too burdensome to bear.

Finally, she writes about death. Mrs Ramsay avoids the thought of death except in rare moments, by filling her mind with duties and activities for her family. On the other hand, her weariness of constant struggle and effort is shown, suggesting that we may also desire death. It is also in the context of death that life seems without purpose, and responsibility for rationalising our existence is an unnatural burden, impossible to sustain.

These deductions about the themes of *To the Lighthouse* are broadly applicable to *Mrs Dalloway* as well. Clarissa's parties, and mending her dress, are part of an effort she devotes to maintaining her self-image as 'Mrs Dalloway', wife of Richard; and can be compared to Mrs Ramsay's duties as wife, mother and hostess. Clarissa's regrets about Peter Walsh, and her ambivalent feelings about suicide, are an undercurrent comparable to Mrs Ramsay's desire to give up, to rest; and her ambivalent attitude to death.

*   *   *

Before building further upon these conclusions, let us look at an extract from *The Waves*. Our extract comes from Bernard's attempt to 'sum up' or 'explain to you the meaning of my life', very near to the end of the novel:

> Yet some doubt remained, some note of interrogation. I was surprised, opening a door, to find people thus occupied; I hesitated, taking a cup of tea, whether one said milk or sugar. And the light of the stars falling, as it falls now, on my hand after travelling for millions upon millions of years – I could get a cold shock from that for a moment – not more, my imagination is too feeble. But some doubt remained. A shadow flitted through my mind like moths' wings among chairs and tables in a room in the evening. When, for example, I went to Lincolnshire that summer to see Susan and she advanced towards me across the garden with the lazy movement of a half-filled sail, with the swaying movement of a woman with child, I thought, 'It goes on; but why?' We sat in the garden; the farm carts came up dripping with hay; there was the usual gabble of rooks and doves; fruit was netted and covered over; the gardener dug. Bees boomed down the purple tunnels of flowers; bees embedded themselves on the golden shields of sunflowers. Little twigs were blown across the grass. How rhythmical,

and half-conscious and like something wrapped in mist it was; but to me hateful, like a net folding one's limbs in its meshes, cramping. She who had refused Percival lent herself to this, to this covering over.

Sitting down on a bank to wait for my train, I thought then how we surrender, how we submit to the stupidity of nature. Woods covered in thick green leafage lay in front of me. And by some flick of a scent or a sound on a nerve, the old image – the gardeners sweeping, the lady writing – returned. I saw the figures beneath the beech trees at Elvedon. The gardeners swept; the lady at the table sat writing. But I now made the contribution of maturity to childhood's intuitions – satiety and doom; the sense of what is unescapable in our lot; death; the knowledge of limitations; how life is more obdurate than one had thought it. Then, when I was a child, the presence of an enemy had asserted itself; the need for opposition had stung me. I had jumped up and cried, 'Let's explore.' The horror of the situation was ended.

Now what situation was there to end? Dullness and doom. And what to explore? The leaves and the wood concealed nothing. If a bird rose I should no longer make a poem – I should repeat what I had seen before. Thus if I had a stick with which to point to indentations in the curve of being, this is the lowest; here it coils useless on the mud where no tide comes – here, where I sit with my back to a hedge, and my hat over my eyes, while the sheep advanced remorselessly in that wooden way of theirs, step by step on stiff, pointed legs. But if you hold a blunt blade to a grindstone long enough, something spurts – a jagged edge of fire; so held to lack of reason, aimlessness, the usual, all massed together, out spurted in one flame hatred, contempt. I took my mind, my being, the old dejected, almost inanimate object, and lashed it about among these odds and ends, sticks and straws, detestable little bits of wreckage, flotsam and jetsam, floating on the oily surface. I jumped up. I said, 'Fight! Fight!' I repeated. It is the effort and the struggle, it is the perpetual warfare, it is the shattering and piecing together – this is the daily battle, defeat or victory, the absorbing pursuit. The trees, scattered, put on order; the thick green of the leaves thinned itself to a dancing light. I netted them under with a sudden phrase. I retrieved them from formlessness with words.'

(*The Waves*, pp. 179–81)

This part of the novel consists of Bernard, as an old man, recapitulating his life. He has retold his reaction to Percival's death, and this passage tells about his return to ordinary, day-to-day life after the shock of bereavement. *The Waves* is more difficult to get hold of than *Mrs Dalloway* or *To the Lighthouse*, because the characters tell their own mental and emotional life as a series of monologues. There is no narrator and no story apart from what the six characters happen to mention in passing. The book is therefore made up largely of reflections rather than moments of actual experience. In this extract, for example, the longest sentence (sixty-seven words long) is the one beginning 'Thus if I had a stick with which to point to indentations in the curve of being'. An analysis of this sentence tells us that there is or was a moment (the tense changes from 'I sit' to the sheep 'advanced') when Bernard sat with sheep approaching him 'remorselessly' in a 'wooden' way with 'pointed legs'; and that this moment is one when 'the curve of being . . . coils useless on the mud where no tide comes'. Also, we notice that the 'if' of the first clause is never completed: 'if I had a stick', then what? The features we have noticed in this sentence are not illuminating, however: it does not help us to know that sheep advancing are like the 'curve of being' coiled in tideless mud; and it is even less helpful for us to know that the 'if I had a stick' leads nowhere. So far, we only know that Woolf deliberately leaves the construction incomplete, so that a plausible moment from Bernard's life (sitting and watching some sheep) is likened to part of an abstract metaphor for life ('the curve of being'). This sentence is typical of Woolf's writing in *The Waves*, for it begins with the reflective metaphor (the first thirty-two words), and only then tells us anything of the character's life, as an example (the final thirty-five words).

In this situation we should build upon what we already know of the author's concerns. In *Mrs Dalloway* and *To the Lighthouse* we found a contrast between the trivial preoccupations of everyday life (Clarissa's party and dress; Mrs Ramsay's children and family duties) and their more submerged thoughts about larger, problematic issues such as death. It may be useful to ask: is this theme present in *The Waves* as well? If it is, that will give us a firm opening towards understanding the text. Then we will be able to build carefully upon that, and we have a good chance of discovering the significance of the extract.

Yes, trivial everyday details are in evidence in the second sentence.

Bernard is surprised to find people 'thus occupied' (i.e. working, earning their living – see the preceding paragraph); and on 'taking a cup of tea' he was uncertain whether to say 'milk' or 'sugar'. These details clearly belong to the external trivia of life, and Bernard seems to feel detached from them. Now, trace ordinary, everyday things through the rest of the extract. There are 'chairs and tables' in a room, and Susan's pregnancy makes Bernard think 'It goes on'; then there is a fulsome list of continuing natural processes from 'the farm carts came up dripping with hay' to 'Little twigs were blown across the grass'. All of this repetitive and pointless activity is, to Bernard, 'half conscious and like something wrapped in mist' and he finds it 'hateful' and 'cramping'. He sums up the predictable repetitiveness of ordinary life as 'this covering over'.

During the paragraph, Bernard's feelings about day-to-day existence have developed. He begins with 'some doubt, some note of interrogation' and he 'hesitated', questioning simple actions. Then he questions more fundamentally: 'It goes on; but why?' asks for a reason for the whole process of human life, including reproduction. There is a tone of contempt for the obviousness of nature in the list of processes; for example, 'the gardener dug' makes a mockery of his labour, and we hear 'the usual gabble' of birds. Eventually, Bernard's tone indicates both fear ('like a net folding one's limbs in its meshes') and resentful anger ('She who had refused Percival lent herself to this, to this covering over'). The tone asks: 'how could she?', and the repetition of 'to this, to this' conveys Bernard's spluttering outrage.

There are hints that day-to-day life and nature are stupidly repetitive, then. That is why Bernard thinks of these processes as 'rhythmical, and half conscious'; and the vague, trance-like state of Susan who has passively submitted to farming and motherhood, provokes the phrase 'something wrapped in mist'. It seems that Bernard objects to the lack of thought, the lack of intellectual clarity, when stupid repetitive routine is allowed to dominate life. This 'half conscious' state is not the same as Mrs Ramsay's, however. The overwhelming routine Bernard objects to is like her busy day of duties and tasks that she 'shed' in the extract we analysed from *To the Lighthouse*. Her passive 'trance' occurs when day-to-day activity is absent, not when it fills her mind to the exclusion of other thoughts.

Bernard then reflects that 'we submit to the stupidity of nature' and remembers two details of life's routine at Elvedon: 'the gardeners sweeping, the lady writing'. In the second paragraph of our extract, everyday routines of life become hostile: 'life is more obdurate than one had thought it'. As a child, Bernard reacted to it as to an 'enemy': 'the need for opposition had stung me'.

The sheep in the third paragraph seem to belong to the hostile, trivial routine we are tracing. The words 'wooden', 'pointed' and 'remorselessly' emphasise that their behaviour is predictably mechanical, connecting them with the trivia Bernard finds so hostile. Then Woolf introduces the image of a knife (Bernard) held to a grindstone (the trivia of life) for a long time. Life is 'lack of reason, aimlessness, the usual, all massed together' and 'odds and ends, sticks and straws, detestable little bits of wreckage, flotsam and jetsam'. The grindstone image suggests that even a blunt knife, if held to these things for long enough, will eventually spark with a 'flame' of 'hatred, contempt'; and Bernard tells us that he 'jumped up, I said, "Fight! Fight!"'.

We have traced the details of everyday life through the extract. As we did so, we found that what began as tea, milk and sugar grew to include all the efforts and activities of life, including reproduction, farming, plants, woods, birds and insects. At the same time, the character's hostility to all this has developed and crystallised. He questions, then feels contempt, fear and anger, then sees an 'enemy' and fights. Now we can ask: in this extract, what contrasts with everyday life?

In the first paragraph, Bernard contrasts 'the light of the stars falling . . . after travelling for millions upon millions of years' to questions about milk and sugar. In other words, the thought of the immensity of the universe is contrasted to trivia. In the first paragraph these thoughts of larger issues are hesitant: 'some doubt', 'interrogation', or 'a shadow flitted through my mind' which is likened to 'moths' wings'; and the hesitant thoughts only provoke the question 'but why?'

In the second paragraph, the memory of Elvedon brings Bernard to define his background thoughts more openly. He thinks of 'satiety and doom; the sense of what is unescapable in our lot; death; the knowledge of limitations'. These perceptions of futility and stupidity lead on to the image of the 'curve of being' we have already discussed. Bernard's mood belongs at the 'lowest' point on that curve, and he describes how it 'coils useless in the mud where no tide comes', which implies that it has no sense of purpose and no hope of being washed over or moved by nature. However, at the end of the passage Bernard jumps up to 'Fight! Fight!', and the remainder of the paragraph describes his battle and victory. What is the fight about?

All we can do is to select the words that describe it in the final few lines. On one side are 'shattering', 'defeat', 'scattered', 'the thick green of the leaves', and 'formlessness'. These all give an impression of chaos and purposelessness. On the other side are 'the piecing together', 'victory', 'put on order', 'a dancing light', and 'a sudden phrase' or 'words'. Clearly, Bernard fights a battle against the stupidity of everyday things and the meaninglessness of life. He fights the battle with 'words' which 'retrieve them from formlessness' or give shape and purpose to our existence. The connection between this 'Fight' Bernard still wages, and his memories of Elvedon, is obvious. Looking back to the childhood section of the novel, we remember that Bernard soothed Susan's distress saying 'let us explore', and she commented 'you rise up higher, with words and words in phrases' (*The Waves*, p. 7). The reference to Elvedon emphasises the other element described in the final lines of our extract: that the battle is 'perpetual warfare', a 'daily battle' which is 'the effort and the struggle' and 'the absorbing pursuit'.

We have managed to build upon the idea of trivial, everyday activities with which we began, and this has enabled us to interpret the extract. In doing so, we have used a number of the discoveries about Virginia Woolf's technique, already revealed in analysis of earlier passages. Notice, for example, Bernard's vehement repetition in '"Fight! Fight!" I repeated', reminiscent of Mrs Ramsay's determined 'She knew that' and Peter Walsh's argumentative 'true'. Notice also how groups of images (in this case, domestic trivia, then processes of nature, then a memory of a lady and gardeners, then 'wooden' sheep, then a grindstone and finally a number of 'odds and ends') all contribute to conveying one aspect of experience, so that it seems the metaphors are constantly modified, and the idea grows as more images are attached to it. There is one more feature of Woolf's style that appears in this extract, which is worth remarking.

In *Mrs Dalloway* we found that a subtle ironic connection was established between Peter Walsh's ideal woman, and the statue of Gordon, by the use of 'black' as a motif-word to describe both. In this case, the use of 'netted' and 'net' repays attention. It occurs three times: first as 'fruit was netted and covered over', then as a hostile image, 'hateful, like a net folding one's limbs in its meshes', and finally as Bernard's control over the formlessness of life when he 'netted them under with a sudden phrase'. This 'motif' effect is again used to hint at irony. The implication is that Bernard's creative urge to give life meaning through words is like the ancient farmer's urge to cultivate ('fruit was netted and covered'). Both of them seek to impose order upon, or throw a 'net' over, formless nature. The second mention reminds us that Bernard is himself part of the nature that is cultivated, with 'a net folding one's limbs in its meshes'.

This passage begins with slight uneasiness about life in general, and questions; but it builds up to describe a 'perpetual' warfare in the mind, an unending fight against the offensive futility and formlessness of life. This suggests that the extract is like the other two we have studied: the character's mind battles against and rejects unwelcome thoughts. However, in *The Waves* the mental process is described from a different standpoint. It is no longer tied to a single event in a narrative, an occasional experience in the character's life. In this extract the mental process is a permanent truth about human experience: we must struggle against formlessness, day after day, 'defeat or victory'.

Finally, Bernard's use of 'words' to redeem nature from the horror of its chaos raises another theme. We endow life with shape and purpose by means of art. Virginia Woolf was clearly interested in the artist's imagination, and the analogy between creating artificial life (Mrs Dalloway and Mrs Ramsay) and imaginative art (Lily Briscoe). Here, Bernard's lifelong facility with words – his ability to spin and weave fantasies with fine phrases, is his 'artistic' weapon against chaos and is subtly connected to the farmer's cultivation of fruit. So, art is connected to all human endeavours to endow a senseless nature with order, purpose or beauty. This insight will be further explored in Chapter 7.

Conclusions

We have made progress in understanding several themes of Virginia Woolf's work. These will be further developed in later chapters. Our conclusions here focus instead on characterisation and the mental processes we have been able to analyse. In the three extracts, we have found the following:

1. *Repression.* This occurs when the character's mind contains unwelcome or repugnant thoughts, and the conscious mind tries to suppress or expel these thoughts. The simplest example we found was Peter Walsh's unwillingness to admit that he is not young any more, but Mrs Ramsay's reaction to her thought about 'the Lord' is also repression.
2. *Resistance* is really an aspect of repression. It describes the conscious mind's effort to push away unwelcome thoughts: the mental energy that is used when repressing a thought.
3. A *screen.* This is the word we used to describe a prominent, attractive feature of the character's personality, which is false or deceptive, because a repugnant ('repressed') thought hides behind it. The example we found is Mrs Ramsay's preoccupation with weddings. In the extract, we saw how her religious fatalism turned into this misty image, or hid behind it.
4. Several of Woolf's characters seem to build a relationship with things outside themselves, and they do this by attributing aspects of their own character to something else. We could say that they *project* elements of themselves on to their surroundings. We have described this when Peter Walsh felt sympathy for himself, the marching boys, and Gordon, simultaneously because all three had made a 'great renunciation'. In *To the Lighthouse* we noticed Mrs Ramsay's impression that the light was her own eyes

'meeting' her own eyes, because its stern, searching qualities were the qualities she admired in herself.

5. *Passivity of mind.* We can use this phrase to describe a state of near-hypnosis, or trance, when the mind's defences are in abeyance. It seems to occur when the character's activity becomes repetitive or automatic, and makes no mental demands. For example, Peter Walsh marches in step with the boys, having his thoughts 'drummed' up Whitehall 'without his doing'; and Mrs Ramsay's monotonous knitting under the monotonous beams of the Lighthouse send her into a daze. This state of almost-sleep is important, as it creates the moments when unconscious thoughts can surface, entering the character's undefended mind. In *The Waves* the repetitive regularity of nature induces a state called 'rhythmical, and half conscious', which is an example of this effect. However, on that occasion Bernard's mental defences do not give in: he finds the misty trance 'hateful' and reacts against it aggressively.

6. In these three extracts, we have also encountered three descriptions of *moments of mental change.* These are worth remembering as they provide physical metaphors, revealing how Virginia Woolf 'saw' the inside of a character's mind. In *Mrs Dalloway*, Peter's sudden change is described: 'And down his mind went flat as a marsh . . . as if inside his brain by another hand strings were pulled, shutters moved, and he, having nothing to do with it, yet stood at the opening of endless avenues'. In *To the Lighthouse*, Mrs Ramsay looks into her mind: 'There rose . . . there curled up off the floor of the mind, rose from the lake of one's being, a mist'. In *The Waves*, Bernard describes how his memory of Elvedon came to him: 'And by some flick of a scent or a sound on a nerve, the old image – the gardeners sweeping, the lady writing – returned.' Notice that in all of these descriptions the character is passive, and the unknown, momentary nature of whatever triggers the change, gives rise to several alternative metaphors.

Beyond the particular circumstances of each character, there is a larger pattern common to all three of the novels. There seems to be a fundamental opposition between desire and reality for all three of the characters we have looked at. Life and the world are not as desire would like them to be; and this shows itself as a conflict in the minds of Woolf's characters. We have seen all three using mental energy in a struggle to push away thoughts of formlessness and futility (which include thoughts about death); and they have done so by fighting back with creative fantasies. The final few lines of our extract from *The Waves* therefore applies to all three novels: Woolf depicts a daily, perpetual struggle between the 'shattering' and 'piecing together'; between formlessness, the destructive; and form, the creative.

Methods of Analysis

1. Begin by focusing on long sentences, as these are likely to show the mental process in action, either because of their noticeable features (e.g. repetition, or a tone of internal debate) or in their structure (e.g. showing how thoughts are diverted, or the mind jumps from one thought to another). In our extract from *The Waves*, the longest sentence did not help us. When this happens, look for one of the prominent themes you can confidently expect to find in Virginia Woolf, and trace that theme as it develops through the passage you are studying.

2. Find a mental conflict. You can do this by looking for the 'signals' that highlight one of the mental processes we have focused on in this chapter. Initially, look for a character's resistance or repression as this will enable you to begin describing the mental conflict.

3. Classify the content of the extract into two opposing descriptions, and reduce these to clear summaries of the two sides. Then do the same for the mental 'actions' of the extract: what the character's mind does In this way you can define the conflict and the mental process you are studying.

4. Several *features of style* are useful pointers, helping us to locate the mental events we most want to understand:

- *Long sentences* tend to show a mental process in action either by their features or in their structure.
- *Repetition* either shows that the character is reinforcing a thought in an effort to overcome insecurity; or it is used to convey the repetitive, rhythmic state we have called 'passivity of mind'.
- *A tone of internal debate* shows the character rationalising, again reinforcing their conscious views and therefore probably resisting an unwelcome thought.
- *Misfit words* or *misfit phrases* stick out because they do not suit their context. They often help to focus our attention on a thought the character does not want to think: they are a signal pointing to unconscious thoughts.
- *The motif effect* occurs when the same word is used, apparently by chance, in different contexts. This creates an association between the different contexts and usually hints at an ironic idea about the character.
- *Imagery* – metaphors and similes – helps us to interpret the underlying meaning of Woolf's writing. However, she uses imagery flexibly, and her metaphors constantly modify themselves. The significance of imagery can often be clarified by looking at the character's attitude towards the image-idea; then you can group together all the images that are in the same relation to the character, understanding better how one aspect of the character's emotion is elaborated in the passage you are studying.

We have discovered a considerable amount about the way Virginia Woolf achieves her effects, then. However, we have also begun to depart from a strict method of analysis. Notice that the 'longest sentence' approach to our extract from *To the Lighthouse* was so successful, that we simply followed up all the clear leads that provided, without bothering to scour the extract for an exhaustive list of other 'features'. We quickly found ourselves discussing character, style and content simultaneously. As you study, you will find that your intuition about Woolf's main concerns, and your understanding of her techniques, becomes stronger, and you can afford to approach the text less mechanically. In the same way, you will become more confident when interpreting imagery as you notice 'typical' metaphors. For example, we have already found 'mist' in two different novels. In both cases it conveyed a mental delusion or vagueness. This will be an easy metaphor to understand, next time you come across it in another place.

Suggested Work

It is good practice to take a passage and carry out your own analysis. Focus on discovering and defining the mental processes taking place within characters in the following passages:

In *Mrs Dalloway*, look at pages 8–9, beginning at '"That is all," she said, looking at the fishmonger's' and studying as far as 'pushing through the swing doors of Mulberry's the florists'. Here you can see Clarissa vulnerable to uncomfortable thoughts about hating Miss Kilman.

In *To the Lighthouse*, try the passage on pages 22–3, between 'How then did it work out, all this?' and 'effusive, tumultuous, a flock of starlings'. This extract describes the development of thoughts in Lily Briscoe's mind, as she watches Mr Bankes and Mr Ramsay.

In *The Waves*, study the two paragraphs on pages 27–8, starting at '"I have won the game", said Jinny' and going as far as 'The game is over. We must go to tea now.' In this extract imagery, and descriptive words and phrases, are important; but you will also have to consider what is happening in the narrative, to explain why Jinny's experiences are as they are.

3

Male and Female in Virginia Woolf

In this chapter we analyse extracts from the novels to examine how Virginia Woolf uses sexual stereotypes and social gender-roles as a theme. This means that we want to discover how far social expectations of men and women affect the characters and their relationships with each other. We will also look for evidence of any underlying concept of 'maleness' and 'femaleness' in Virginia Woolf's novels: does she treat men and women as innately, rather than socially, distinct?

* * *

Following our usual method, we begin by analysing an extract from *Mrs Dalloway*. Our passage begins as Septimus and Rezia Warren Smith sit on a bench in Regent's Park, watching an aeroplane write an advertisement in the sky:

> So, thought Septimus, looking up, they are signalling to me. Not indeed in actual words; that is, he could not read the language yet; but it was plain enough, this beauty, this exquisite beauty, and tears filled his eyes as he looked at the smoke words languishing and melting in the sky and bestowing upon him in their inexhaustible charity and laughing goodness one shape after another of unimaginable beauty and signalling their intention to provide him, for nothing, for ever, for looking merely, with beauty, more beauty! tears ran down his cheeks.

It was toffee; they were advertising toffee, a nursemaid told Rezia. Together they began to spell t . . . o . . . f . . .

'K . . . R . . .' said the nursemaid, and Septimus heard her say 'Kay Arr' close to his ear, deeply, softly, like a mellow organ, but with a roughness in her voice like a grasshopper's, which rasped his spine deliciously and sent running up into his brain waves of sound which, concussing, broke. A marvellous discovery indeed – that the human voice in certain atmospheric conditions (for one must be scientific, above all scientific) can quicken trees into life! Happily Rezia put her hand with a tremendous weight on his knee so that he was weighted down, transfixed, or the excitement of the elm trees rising and falling, rising and falling with all their leaves alight and the colour thinning and thickening from blue to the green of a hollow wave, like plumes on horses' heads, feathers on ladies', so proudly they rose and fell, so superbly, would have sent him mad. But he would not go mad. He would shut his eyes; he would see no more.

But they beckoned; leaves were alive; trees were alive. And the leaves being connected by millions of fibres with his own body, there on the seat, fanned it up and down; when the branch stretched he, too, made that statement. The sparrows fluttering, rising, and falling in jagged fountains were part of the pattern; the white and blue, barred with black branches. Sounds made harmonies with premeditation; the spaces between them were as significant as the sounds. A child cried. Rightly far away a horn sounded. All taken together meant the birth of a new religion –

'Septimus!' said Rezia. He started violently. People must notice.

'I am going to walk to the fountain and back,' she said.

For she could stand it no longer. Dr Holmes might say there was nothing the matter. Far rather would she that he were dead! She could not sit beside him when he stared so and did not see her and made everything terrible; sky and tree, children playing, dragging carts, blowing whistles, falling down; all were terrible. And he would not kill himself; and she could tell no one. 'Septimus has been working too hard' – that was all she could say, to her own mother. To love makes one solitary, she thought. She could tell nobody, not even Septimus now, and looking back, she saw him sitting in his shabby overcoat alone, on the seat, hunched up, staring. And it was cowardly for a man to say he would kill himself, but Septimus had fought; he was brave; he was not Septimus now. She put on her lace collar. She put on her new hat and he never noticed; and he was happy without her. Nothing could make her happy without him! Nothing! He was selfish. So men are. For he was not ill. Dr Holmes said there was nothing the matter with him. She spread her hand before her. Look! Her wedding ring slipped – she had grown so thin. It was she who suffered – but she had nobody to tell.

(*Mrs Dalloway*, pp. 17–19)

We are examining this extract for the gender-roles and gender-attitudes of the two characters. There is no need to look far: 'He was selfish. So men are' leaps off the page: Rezia's explanation for Septimus's behaviour is that he is a man and therefore selfish. We can trace her views of gender-roles, starting from this clear statement. There seem to be three other elements to Rezia's attitudes, that originate in her views of male and female roles. First, she is loyal and ashamed, she 'could tell no one': even to her own mother the most she can say is a euphemistic excuse for Septimus's state of mind: '"Septimus has been working too hard"'. What does this tell us about Rezia? That she is exaggeratedly loyal to her husband, and regards his weaknesses as a secret she must guard at all costs. However, she also feels ashamed that her 'man' is not 'manly'; and invents the male virtue of overwork (sacrificing his health to provide for her is the fiction she proposes) to explain his breakdown.

Second, Rezia is puzzled by the question of courage. From her confusion about Septimus, certain stereotyped attitudes can be deduced: 'And it was cowardly for a man to say he would kill himself, but Septimus had fought; he was brave; he was not Septimus now.' First, Rezia seems to apply different standards to men and women. She thinks that it is 'cowardly' for 'a man' to threaten suicide, and this implies that it would be excusable for a woman to do the same thing. She expects men to display stoicism and perseverance, and these qualities are not expected from women. Next, she imagines only one kind of courage in a man – the courage a warrior shows in battle. Septimus's masculine courage has been proved, she reasons, because he has fought in the war. This, of course, is an extremely naïve attitude. She does not consider whether Septimus was a willing or unwilling soldier; and her picture of courage belongs to historical romances about war, not the anonymous suffering of modern warfare. However, the most revealing aspect of her attitude is again that it shows a 'man' as an unreal animal, different from herself. For most human beings (Rezia would include herself, we can be sure) 'courage' is a matter of determination overcoming fear. In other words, it is the result of a struggle, not a simple object like a jacket that you either have or do not have. Yet she imagines that Septimus's courage is either present ('[he] had fought; he was brave') or absent ('it was cowardly for a man'), as if he were not a human being at all. Virginia Woolf's comment on these attitudes is clear from the nonsensical conclusion Rezia is forced to reach because she does not understand how a man can be brave and not brave at different times. Rezia can only think: 'he was not Septimus now', which is nonsensical. Here, then, Virginia Woolf satirises the stereotyped gender-attitude by following it through to an absurd conclusion.

Third, Rezia hopes to attract Septimus's attention by means of the external trappings of femininity: 'She put on her lace collar. She put on her new hat and he never noticed'. It seems that she knows no other way of appealing to her husband than through feminine adornment; and Virginia Woolf again shows how Rezia, basing her ideas upon the shallowness of gender-stereotypes, reaches a false conclusion about Septimus: 'and he was happy without her'. We are intended to criticise the banality of this statement in its context. It means that Septimus is 'happy without her [hat]' or 'happy without her [lace collar]'.

These three aspects of Rezia's attitude towards her husband are straightforward, and Virginia Woolf reveals them with clear, critical precision. What do they have in common? They all treat 'men' as being different and incomprehensible; and they all lead to false conclusions, as we have seen. In addition, we should notice that all three contribute to Rezia's sympathy for herself. Her shame and loyalty lead her to complain 'and she could tell no one', because 'To love makes one solitary'; Septimus's lack of bravery leads her to complain that 'He was selfish'; and his failure to notice her new hat, together with everything else, leads to her self-pitying conclusion: 'It was she who suffered – but she had nobody to tell.'

When we first read Rezia's thoughts in this extract, we think her an ordinary woman with an ordinary set of attitudes, struggling to understand in a difficult situation. Our study of the extract has shown that Virginia Woolf provides a trenchant critical analysis of Rezia's attitudes at the same time. These gender-attitudes distort her relationship with her husband, hindering understanding between them and encouraging her to pity herself.

Septimus's attitude to his wife is less easy to determine from this extract. He is mad, absorbed in his hallucinations. He interprets the writing in the sky as signals meant for him ('they are signalling to me'); the trees are jumping up and down and he feels obliged to join in; and he imagines these visions to herald 'the birth of a new religion'. There are only two moments that concern us: first, as his hallucinations become wilder, 'Happily Rezia put her hand with a tremendous weight on his knee so that he was weighted down, transfixed'. For the moment, his wife's touch has a powerful effect. Her hand seems to have 'a tremendous weight' and 'he was weighted down'. Clearly her touch connects him both with reality and with the need to keep his grip on reality. Rezia's touch fights against the attraction of his hallucination and he frantically determines not to give in to unreality. 'Happily' (in the sense of 'luckily') Rezia touched his knee; otherwise 'the excitement of the elm trees . . . would have sent him mad'. In this conflict he decides in favour of Rezia, that 'he would not go mad'.

This tells us little about Septimus's attitudes towards women; but it does reveal that it is Rezia's touch that reminds him – however hazily – of some sort of obligation to avoid madness, to keep himself sane. The second moment is of the same kind. This time it is Rezia's voice that recalls him to a sense of his surroundings. When she calls his name, 'He started violently. People must notice.' It is in response to her voice, and possibly therefore on her behalf, that Septimus feels self-conscious anxiety about his public appearance.

Virginia Woolf uses the same technique as with Rezia, to show the inadequacy of Septimus's obligations to his wife. Just as her shallow stereotypes led Rezia to the absurd conclusion 'he was not Septimus now', so Septimus can only resolve the conflict between his madness and his duty to Rezia, by reaching a similarly ridiculous, impractical conclusion. He decides not to go mad, and his solution is: 'He would shut his eyes; he would see no more.' Obviously, his problem is the hallucinations, not the fact that his eyes are open; and the succeeding paragraph shows how fruitless his resolution has been. Neither of these characters can address the other's problems realistically, and both of them reach absurd conclusions. This extract shows that Rezia's and possibly Septimus's stereotyped gender-attitudes are a major barrier and hindrance between them.

We will return to Septimus and Rezia, after looking at extracts from *To the Lighthouse* and *The Waves*. Virginia Woolf's men are often preoccupied by questions and problems that seem pretentious. For example, Mr Ramsay pursues abstruse philosophical questions, and Richard Dalloway thinks of politics and the problems of society. These men seem to ignore the women in their lives, supposing their male preoccupations to be 'important' and thus an excuse. Later in the chapter, we will discuss this male freedom to ignore human relationships; and we will consider Septimus's madness as an example of this phenomenon.

*   *   *

We now turn to our second extract, from *To the Lighthouse*. It comes from the end of Part I, 'The Window'. Mr and Mrs Ramsay are alone together at the end of the evening. Mrs Ramsay has just told her husband of Paul's and Minta's engagement:

> He snorted. He felt about this engagement as he always felt about any engagement; the girl is much too good for that young man. Slowly it came into her head, why is it then that one wants people to marry? What was the value, the meaning of things? (Every word they said now would be true.) Do say something, she thought, wishing only to hear his voice. For the shadow, the thing folding them in was beginning, she felt, to close round her again. Say anything, she begged, looking at him, as if for help.
>
> He was silent, swinging the compass on his watch-chain to and fro, and thinking of Scott's novels and Balzac's novels. But through the crepuscular walls of their intimacy, for they were drawing together, involuntarily, coming side by side, quite close, she could feel his mind like a raised hand shadowing her mind; and he was beginning now

that her thoughts took a turn he disliked – towards this 'pessimism' as he called it – to fidget, though he said nothing, raising his hand to his forehead, twisting a lock of hair, letting it fall again.

'You won't finish that stocking to-night,' he said, pointing to her stocking. That was what she wanted – the asperity in his voice reproving her. If he says it's wrong to be pessimistic probably it is wrong, she thought; the marriage will turn out all right.

'No,' she said, flattening the stocking out upon her knee, 'I shan't finish it.'

And what then? For she felt that he was still looking at her, but that his look had changed. He wanted something – wanted the thing she always found it so difficult to give him; wanted her to tell him that she loved him. And that, no, she could not do. He found talking so much easier than she did. He could say things – she never could. So naturally it was always he that said the things, and then for some reason he would mind this suddenly, and would reproach her. A heartless woman he called her; she never told him that she loved him. But it was not so – it was not so. It was only that she never could say what she felt. Was there no crumb on his coat? Nothing she could do for him? Getting up she stood at the window with the reddish-brown stocking in her hands, partly to turn away from him, partly because she did not mind looking now, with him watching, at the Lighthouse. For she knew that he had turned his head as she turned; he was watching her. She knew that he was thinking, You are more beautiful than ever. And she felt herself very beautiful. Will you not tell me just for once that you love me? He was thinking that, for he was roused, what with Minta and his book, and its being the end of the day and their having quarrelled about going to the Lighthouse. But she could not do it; she could not say it. Then, knowing that he was watching her, instead of saying anything she turned, holding her stocking, and looked at him. And as she looked at him she began to smile, for though she had not said a word, he knew, of course he knew, that she loved him. He could not deny it. And smiling she looked out of the window and said (thinking to herself, Nothing on earth can equal this happiness) –

'Yes, you were right. It's going to be wet tomorrow.' She had not said it, but he knew it. And she looked at him smiling. For she had triumphed again.

(*To the Lighthouse*, pp. 114–15)

We are looking for the effect of the Ramsays' ideas of male and female, upon their relationship; and this extract consists of a detailed description of a moment of intimacy when they are alone together. What are the noticeable features of this extract?

First, the Ramsays say very little, but what they do say bears no relation to their thoughts or their feelings. When he is thinking of Scott's and Balzac's novels, and beginning to sense her 'pessimism', Mr Ramsay says 'You won't finish that stocking to-night'. Her reply, 'No, . . . I shan't finish it', comes while she thinks of Paul's and Minta's prospects of happiness. Then, while thinking that 'Nothing on earth can equal this happiness', she says: 'Yes, you were right. It's going to be wet tomorrow.' We have noticed this effect before: trivial and irrelevant dialogue is a common feature of Virginia Woolf's writing. However, in the present extract the effect is exaggerated, and the poverty of their conversation in contrast to their emotional intensity creates a powerful ironic effect: Mr and Mrs Ramsay are intensely involved with each other, and have nothing to say to each other.

The obvious question is, why do they talk so irrelevantly? Let us look at what happens more closely. First, Mrs Ramsay wants her husband to talk to her. She asks a question in her mind: 'What was the value, the meaning of things?' and then thinks 'Do say something'. However, she does not want him to answer her question. She is 'wishing only to hear his voice'. When he does speak, it is to tell her that she will not finish the stocking. 'That was what she wanted – the asperity in his voice reproving her.' Clearly, there are unspoken processes in the relationship between them; and the content of what they say to each other does not matter.

Secondly, Mr Ramsay 'wanted the thing she always found it so difficult to give him; wanted her to tell him that she loved him'. The long paragraph that makes up most of the remainder of the extract centres on Mr Ramsay's need for her to say that she loves him, and her stratagems as she avoids saying it. She cannot say that she loves him because 'she never could say what she felt' and 'she could not do it; she could not say it'. In the past, he has called her 'A heartless woman' because 'she never told him that she loved him'. This impasse is resolved when she acknowledges that she was wrong in their quarrel about the trip to the Lighthouse. 'Yes, you were right' is what she says. This takes the place of telling him that she loves him, and in Mrs Ramsay's mind 'she had triumphed again'. Looking at their needs for conversation has shown, then, that they do not say what they think or feel, but they talk in a kind of code that the other is expected to understand instinctively. We can therefore ask: what do each of their statements stand for?

When Mr Ramsay says 'You won't finish that stocking to-night', it seems to mean something like *it is wrong to be pessimistic, and I know best so you can acknowledge and rely upon my superior wisdom*. The stocking is intended for the Lighthouse-keeper's little boy, so he is also saying *See? I was right about us not visiting the Lighthouse tomorrow: we will not visit the Lighthouse tomorrow, and the stocking will not be ready anyway.* Her reply, 'No, I shan't finish it', means *you are right, I shall not be pessimistic; you are usually right and it is a relief from my own doubts to rely on your opinion. Also, I shall not make an extra effort to finish the stocking, as we probably will not visit the Lighthouse tomorrow. You are right about that as well.* Her final comment, submitting to his prediction of bad weather, is more difficult to paraphrase. It means *I love you*, or at least it is intended to convince him so that 'he knew it'. However, many of the emotional undercurrents of the day are summed up in this apparently superficial comment. For example, Mr Ramsay's pleasure in hurting his son James (see p. 4) suggested jealousy of Mrs Ramsay's attention. Her response then protected James, contradicting her husband: 'But it may be fine – I expect it will be fine' (p. 5). Her capitulation now is therefore also an acknowledgement that her husband has first claim on her attention: she will sacrifice James's happiness for Mr Ramsay's.

So far we have established that their conversation is not about their feelings, and that they talk in a code which they can interpret because of their close relationship: what they say stands for something else in their thoughts and feelings. Now we can turn our attention to what each thinks of the other, and what they demand and receive from each other.

We begin with Mrs Ramsay. She was successful in bringing Paul and Minta together, but now she is assailed by doubts: 'why is it then that one wants people to marry?' We know from elsewhere that her matchmaking activities are an insecure part of her personality: she has used them to compensate for her temptation to give in to despair, to rest in death from all her efforts to create harmony in her household. So this question is vital and dangerous for Mrs Ramsay. Any honest answer would force her to face the artificiality and futility of her life. That is why her next question is so all-embracing: 'What was the value, the meaning of things?' However, Mrs Ramsay does not wish to hear an answer: she only wishes her husband to take the question itself away, which is what he does. When he has spoken, she is grateful because he is 'reproving her', and she accepts his opinion. Apparently she is relieved that she does not have to continue thinking for herself.

Mr Ramsay apparently wants attention: he wants to know that she loves him, or, he wants her avowal that he is the most important person to her, more important than anyone else including their son James. The author tells us that he was 'roused' by 'Minta and his book, and its being the end of the day and their having quarrelled'. We know, from the dinner scene, that Mr Ramsay was roused by Minta: 'For he, her husband, felt it too – Minta's glow; he liked these girls, these golden-reddish girls, with something flying, something a little wild' (p. 92), and that he had felt 'astonishing delight and feeling of vigour' from reading Scott (p. 111). These two excitements are sexual, and in both cases he cannot express his desires directly to his wife. We know this because of Mrs Ramsay's comment that Minta's attractive quality was something 'she herself had not' (p. 92) and from Mr Ramsay's decision not to 'bother' his wife again because 'The whole of life did not consist in going to bed with a woman, he thought, returning to Scott and Balzac' (p. 112). So, Mr Ramsay wants attention: he seeks a response to his sexual desire.

Mrs Ramsay cannot give what he asks. She tries rather desperately to find something else that will satisfy him, and her first attempt shows that she runs to a gender-role: 'Was there no crumb on his coat? Nothing she could do for him?' Here, she offers the subservient care of a housewife to her man. However, he continues to want something from her, and she continues to feel his pressure.

What, then, is the significance of the admission she eventually gives to him? Remember that she has already acknowledged that the Lighthouse trip is off, by agreeing that she will not finish the stocking. Now she goes further: not only is Mr Ramsay's knowledge superior to her own; but his predictions of the future are infallible as well! In agreeing that he could predict tomorrow's weather, she confers upon him the status of a prophet: the all-knowing, all-wise. This is the concession that enables her to avoid responding to his desire, so that 'she had triumphed again'.

In summary, the intimate details of this passage fit what we know of their relationship, and can be described in terms of a deal. She will bolster and feed his greedy and insecure ego; and in return he will worship her 'beauty' and ascribe to her the wife's role. She needs his support in maintaining her role as wife, hostess and mother, because his self-righteousness takes responsibility and helps to keep her own sense of futility at bay. His brittle ego and rage for admiration need her support to keep his doubts about his own brilliance at bay. In making this deal, both of them accept gender-roles for themselves: he accepts his arbitrary male right to dictate, and acts out his duty to worship her beauty from afar like a courtly lover. She submits to his superior knowledge and wisdom, and acts out her own beauty and helplessness.

As in the passage we analysed from *Mrs Dalloway*, Virginia Woolf structures her analysis of sex-roles within a framework that implies serious criticism. Both of the Ramsays are living up to artificial, even rather ridiculous ideas of themselves; and their marital relationship sustains both of them in their denial of plain truths. The extract we have analysed shows how the gender-roles they manipulate enable them to deny their own and each other's true feelings. The irony – that in getting what they want they frustrate what they need – is so powerful that their relationship takes on tragic overtones. Their behaviour to each other is like an inescapable web of fate, so strongly and tightly woven that the Ramsays, mere confused individuals, are helplessly entangled. There is, in particular, a bitterness of fatalism in 'she looked at him smiling. For she had triumphed again', that suits the mood of tragedy rather than social comedy.

The influence of gender-stereotyping, then, is shown to be perni-

cious. Gender-roles are seen to be false-masculine and false-femi-
nine. Is there anything else about male and female in this extract? Is
there any sign that Virginia Woolf distinguishes genuine masculinity
and genuine femininity from each other? This is a difficult question,
and only speculative ideas are available. The only firm evidence we
have is of social sexual roles; and these are so deeply ingrained in the
characters that they occasionally seem to derive from instinct. For
example, Mr Ramsay's display of gaiety and teasing at the dinner-
table, for Minta's benefit, is the mating-ritual of a male animal. This
subtlety of treatment simply reminds us that stereotyped male and
female behaviour is as old as the hills: men have been showing off to
girls for millennia. The only clear distinction that exists in both of
the extracts we have looked at is between thinking about other
things and thinking about life. Septimus and Mr Ramsay seem able
to concentrate on non-living things (Septimus's hallucinations, the
novels of Scott and Balzac), while Rezia and Mrs Ramsay are preoccupied with life and their relationships. However, this is only a suggestion of different preoccupations; and could equally be the result
of socialisation. We must remember that the social background is a
tradition where men learn things and do things, while women
merely exist. Woolf does not necessarily suggest that there is something innately different between the minds and hearts of men and
women.

*   *   *

In *The Waves*, Neville and Bernard, then Susan and Rhoda, describe
their arrival at school:

> 'After all this hubbub,' said Neville, 'all this scuffling and hubbub, we
> have arrived. This is indeed a moment – this is indeed a solemn
> moment. I come, like a lord to his halls appointed. That is our
> founder; our illustrious founder, standing in the courtyard with one
> foot raised. I salute our founder. A noble Roman air hangs over these
> austere quadrangles. Already the lights are lit in the form rooms.
> Those are laboratories perhaps; and that a library, where I shall
> explore the exactitude of the Latin language, and step firmly upon the
> well-laid sentences, and pronounce the explicit, the sonorous hexame-

ters of Virgil, of Lucretius; and chant with a passion that is never obscure or formless the loves of Catullus, reading from a big book, a quarto with margins. I shall lie, too, in the fields among the tickling grasses. I shall lie with my friends under the towering elm trees.

'Behold, the Headmaster. Alas, that he should excite my ridicule. He is too sleek, he is altogether too shiny and black, like some statue in a public garden. And on the left side of his waistcoat, his taut, his drum-like waistcoat, hangs a crucifix.'

'Old Crane,' said Bernard, 'now rises to address us. Old Crane, the Headmaster, has a nose like a mountain at sunset, and a blue cleft in his chin, like a wooded ravine, which some tripper has fired; like a wooded ravine seen from the train window. He sways slightly, mouthing out his tremendous and sonorous words. I love tremendous and sonorous words. But his words are too hearty to be true. Yet he is by this time convinced of their truth. And when he leaves the room, lurching rather heavily from side to side, and hurls his way through the swing-doors, all the masters, lurching rather heavily from side to side, hurl themselves also through the swing-doors. This is our first night at school, apart from our sisters.'

'This is my first night at school,' said Susan, 'away from my father, away from my home. My eyes swell; my eyes prick with tears. I hate the smell of pine and linoleum. I hate the wind-bitten shrubs and the sanitary tiles. I hate the cheerful jokes and the glazed look of everyone. I left my squirrel and my doves for the boy to look after. The kitchen door slams, and shot patters among the leaves when Percy fires at the rooks. All here is false; all is meretricious. Rhoda and Jinny sit far off in brown serge, and look at Miss Lambert who sits under a picture of Queen Alexandra reading from a book before her. There is also a blue scroll of needlework embroidered by some old girl. If I do not purse my lips, if I do not screw my handkerchief, I shall cry.'

'The purple light,' said Rhoda, 'in Miss Lambert's ring passes to and fro across the black stain on the white page of the Prayer Book. It is a vinous, it is an amorous light. Now that our boxes are unpacked in the dormitories, we sit herded together under maps of the entire world. There are desks with wells for the ink. We shall write our exercises in ink here. But here I am nobody. I have no face. This great company, all dressed in brown serge, has robbed me of my identity. We are all callous, unfriended. I will seek out a face, a composed, a monumental face, and will endow it with omniscience, and wear it under my dress like a talisman and then (I promise this) I will find some dingle in a wood where I can display my assortment of curious treasures. I promise myself this. So I will not cry.'

(*The Waves*, pp. 17–19)

In this extract two boys and two girls give their first impressions of school. We can begin by noting that the two institutions – a boys' school and a girls' school – are not contrasted. The boys both mention 'Old Crane' the headmaster; and the girls mention 'Miss Lambert'; Neville describes the statue of their 'founder' and Susan mentions 'a picture of Queen Alexandra'; the building in the boys' school is institutional and grand ('these austere quadrangles' and 'those are laboratories perhaps') while in the girls' school 'there are desks with wells for the ink'; and both descriptions emphasise order, discipline and uniformity. The boys see their masters, who 'lurching rather heavily from side to side, hurl themselves also through the swing-doors' after the Headmaster; and the girls are 'all dressed in brown serge' with 'cheerful jokes and the glazed look of everyone'.

So far, then, the boys' and girls' experiences are similar. But the extract gives a strong impression of contrast between boys and girls, and our aim is to analyse and define this contrast. We will begin by picking out the most powerful words from each section, starting with the boys. Neville uses 'solemn', 'appointed', 'illustrious', 'salute', 'noble', 'austere', 'exactitude', 'firmly', 'well-laid', 'explicit', 'sonorous', 'never obscure or formless', 'towering'. Bernard is clearly less impressed by the school, but he uses 'tremendous and sonorous' and 'heavily' and 'hurl' twice.

The boys' accounts give a clear picture of their relationship with the school. Neville imagines 'I come, like a lord to his halls appointed.' This statement is sonorous and classical in style, the pompous 'I come' leading to an archaic inversion 'halls appointed'. Neville's language emphasises that he has a destined place at school: he immediately fits in and his actions conform to the formality of the place: 'I salute'. When he imagines his life in the school, he imagines himself as part of it. What he learns will be 'exactitude' and 'explicit'; and he will learn 'firmly' with a passion that is 'never obscure or formless'. His private happiness will also be provided by the school as he lies 'with my friends' under the benign and grand influence of 'the towering elm trees'. Neville's aspirations, then, are all towards clearly defined and exact knowledge that is not hidden or implied, but 'explicit'; and he expects to find the same qualities in his emotions, hoping for a 'passion' about the 'loves' of Catullus as exact and clear as Latin grammar! Neville is perceptive enough to notice the ridiculous in the Headmaster, but his reaction is to regret this: 'Alas'.

Bernard's observations are more independent: he too gives a critical picture of 'Old Crane' and his descriptions are irreverent, amusing. On the other hand, Bernard is like Neville in feeling immediately at ease. Notice that he includes himself with the other boys naturally when Crane addresses 'us'; and he acknowledges the same attraction to 'tremendous and sonorous words' as Neville feels. In Bernard's case there is criticism (the words are 'too hearty to be true') tempered with an understanding of their subjective validity ('yet he is by this time convinced of their truth'); and although he is aware of the ridiculous when the staff follow the Headmaster, he is not critical.

We can conclude that the boys immediately consider themselves as members of the institution; and that they are attracted by the formal and traditional trappings of school. Their reservations occur because the Headmaster does not quite live up to their ideal of what a Headmaster should be: they detect that he is an imitation. So we can say that both of the boys have a positive ideal or stereotype of conformity, education and school.

Now let us look at the girls' relationship with their school. First, Susan mentions 'my father' and 'my home', and she thinks of 'my squirrel' and 'my doves', remembering the patter of shot when 'Percy fires at the rooks'. Rhoda promises herself that she will 'find some dingle in a wood' and lay out her 'curious treasures'. Both of the girls, then, feel the need to keep a private, personal place in their minds: both think of a place of their own, and neither feels that she fits in at the school. The school, to Susan, is 'the smell of pine and linoleum' which she hates. It is 'false', and 'meretricious'. Rhoda feels 'herded' with the other girls and that 'I am nobody. I have no face' because uniformity has 'robbed me of my identity'. The girls are all 'callous, unfriended'. Susan and Rhoda are both distressed by their contact with uniformity: 'If I do not screw my handkerchief, I shall cry', and 'I promise myself this. So I will not cry.'

The girls, then, hate an institution. They feel threatened and take steps to preserve themselves from it; while the boys, by contrast, join it without a qualm. Where the boys feel that the purpose of the institution is the same as their own, the girls immediately sense that its purpose is to destroy their individuality and make them become 'callous, unfriended'. We have found that the girls' feelings contrast to those of the boys. Do the girls contrast in other ways as well?

We noticed how 'explicit' and 'never obscure' Neville expects to be; and Virginia Woolf highlights the contrast between boys and girls by emphasising the secrecy of Susan's and Rhoda's private feelings: Susan must 'purse [her] lips' and 'screw [her] handkerchief', actions that are designed to be as invisible as possible and to help her to hide her tears; while Rhoda will wear her private feelings 'under [her] dress like a talisman' and find a 'dingle in a wood' – clearly an isolated, private spot – where she will be able to be her true self.

We found that Neville is keen to participate in the purpose of school. He mentions 'laboratories' and the 'library', and fantasises about his future studies. The details of the girls' thoughts again provide a contrast. Neither of the girls thinks of what they will study, and Virginia Woolf is careful to keep the girls' emphasis on physical things, not abstractions. For example, the building comes down to 'the smell of pine and linoleum' and 'brown serge' for Susan. For Rhoda, the significant detail of their 'exercises' is that they will write 'in ink' because the desks have 'wells for the ink'; and she also mentions 'brown serge'. Rhoda's paragraph mentions wider learning in the form of maps; but its extent seems too large, beyond her mental scope, as she describes 'the entire world' with awe. Meanwhile, Rhoda's imagery contrasts with Neville's. She finds the light of Miss Lambert's ring 'vinous' and 'amorous', two words which, when put together with her 'talisman' and 'dingle in a wood', subtly suggest a pagan sexual fantasy developing in her. We should be aware of the cultural suggestion Woolf inserts by means of this subtle motif. In contrast to Christianity, Rhoda's desires associate with natural folk religions; in terms of classical mythology, her fantasy relates to Dionysus, the sensually indulgent antithesis of stern stoicism. Neville, in contrast, admires the 'noble Roman' (i.e. stoic) air of the 'austere' quadrangles; and mentions the Headmaster's 'crucifix'.

In this series of light touches, Virginia Woolf has established a connection between the contrasting reactions of two girls and two boys, and contrasting cultural traditions stretching back through the history of Christianity to pre-Christian times and the Classical world. This element in the extract implies that the children's feelings relate to something ancient, something permanent, and therefore represent two different sides of life.

At the start of this chapter, one of our stated aims was to discover any distinction there may be between Virginia Woolf's use of gender-stereotypes as a theme, and her concepts of masculine and feminine in nature. We were not able to draw any firm conclusion about Woolf's concepts of masculine and feminine in nature after analysing the extracts from *Mrs Dalloway* and *To the Lighthouse*. Rezia's stereotypes belong to her upbringing and social background. Mr and Mrs Ramsay's relationship suggests overtones of something fixed and long-running in marital relations, as if men and women have 'always' been caught in these stereotypes. Our extract from *The Waves* takes us further. We have found, in the boys and girls of this passage, a masculine tendency towards the abstract and a feminine tendency towards the concrete; masculine conformity and ideals of clarity and openness as against a feminine emphasis on individuality and things that are hidden below the surface; and masculine heroic self-denial in contrast to feminine sensual indulgence. Virginia Woolf has added delicate cultural and mythological references to this picture, which suggest that 'male' and 'female' tendencies, described in this way, have always existed.

This does not mean that men and women are born with essentially different characters, of course. Virginia Woolf does not suggest that. What she shows is that gender-roles began to be formed in primitive times, and that they are now so deeply embedded in tradition, so pervasive and powerful that they are almost indistinguishable from 'nature'. The imagery of Neville's and Rhoda's paragraphs hints at a further idea: that gender-roles have been so powerful throughout prehistory and history, that they account for fundamental dualities and conflicts in cultural and religious development. For example, she hints that 'male' and 'female' principles were at work in the struggle between the Greek pantheon and Dionysus; and in the thousand-year struggles between Christianity and the 'Old Religions' or nature-worships of Northern Europe. Clearly, we cannot exaggerate Virginia Woolf's view of the power and importance, throughout the history of humanity, of sexual attitudes.

Conclusions

1. We have found that sexual stereotyping affects the attitudes and behaviour of all the characters who appear in our extracts. This happens on an evident level, as for example when Rezia equates male courage with fighting in a war and is confused by anything more complex; or when Mr Ramsay demands his wife's admiration. If we are usually sensitive to the influence of gender-roles on social conventions, we will discern such stereotypes at work throughout Virginia Woolf's novels.

2. Woolf's analysis of male and female stereotypes is in harmony with the main tenets of twentieth-century feminism. For example, the depiction of Mr Ramsay's demanding ego, and his need for his wife's praise imply a criticism of man's traditional assumption of superiority. Rezia's confusion over courage exposes male military bravado. Mrs Ramsay's presumption of a 'courtly' role with her husband, and her matriarchal responsibilities, follow a feminist analysis of courtship and family roles, and family structure.

3. The relationship between characters and their gender-role is ambivalent. On the one hand, the gender-role inhibits the individual character from expressing himself or herself, or from forming honest emotional relationships. So, the gender-role inhibits and frustrates the individual. For example, much of Mr Ramsay's drive to be 'brilliant' and famous is due to his need for Mrs Ramsay's admiration, in their courtly-love relationship. The

natural Mr Ramsay suffers agonies of insecurity as a result. On the other hand, the gender-role tempts and attracts characters who use it as a safe haven: it helps them to avoid their fears. Many of Virginia Woolf's characters are anxious and insecure about their identities, when they confront infinities such as nature and death. When confronting the awful or the formless, characters find relief in adopting a nice, safe gender-role. In this way, Mrs Ramsay shelters under her husband's supposed superior wisdom, rescuing herself from 'pessimism' or despair.

4. So Virginia Woolf shows sexual stereotypes as presenting a tragic dilemma. They prevent us from reaching true fulfilment or self-expression; yet they are seductive and tempting, possessing almost insurmountable power over the individual who is terrified by the futilities of nature and death. Incidentally, this also applies to those who struggle to become truly creative, such as Lily Briscoe in *To the Lighthouse*. Her painting is a 'treasure' she remembers suddenly, countering the suggestion that she should pity and marry William Bankes (see *To the Lighthouse*, p. 79).

5. Virginia Woolf uses cultural and classical references, and natural imagery, to suggests that there is a connection between gender-roles and human development throughout history. She suggests that these roles originated in primitive times. This enhances our appreciation of the enormous tragic power of these stereotypes, and we realise how deeply embedded they are in the human psyche. The fact that Woolf creates gender-roles as possessing such power, rather than treating them as artificial contemporary 'add-ons' that are easily criticised, contributes to the sympathy we feel for her characters, as they are almost all caught within the meshes of these stereotypes.

6. Virginia Woolf's descriptions of sexual attitudes, and their connection to cultural trends, go beyond a critique of social conventions, and suggest that 'masculine' and 'feminine' are so deeply embedded that they actually constitute different experiences of life. For example, the distinction between the boys' affinity for abstraction, and the girls' observation of physical detail, we noticed in *The Waves*, begins to delineate two ways of living that correspond to 'masculine' and 'feminine'.

7. Our sample of three extracts has shown that Virginia Woolf is quite even-handed. She is capable of treating Septimus, Mr Ramsay, Rezia, Mrs Ramsay and the four boys and girls from *The Waves* with the same degree of understanding. The author's critique of sexual stereotypes does agree with the main perceptions of feminism; but her creative treatment shows both men and women equally contributing to and dependent on their continuance, and equally in need of liberation from them.

Methods of Analysis

1. *Getting started:* in this chapter we were looking for a specific theme: the gender-roles and relationships of men and women. Our first insight into each extract relied on using our common sense. With *Mrs Dalloway*, as soon as we read the extract, we noticed an obvious example: Rezia generalises about men being selfish. Having noticed this, we analysed by asking why and how she came to use such a gross generalisation. With *To the Lighthouse*, we knew that the extract is about a married couple. We were struck by the poverty of their conversation, a feature of Woolf's writing that we first noticed in Chapter 1, and we began the analysis by investigating the relationship between spoken words and thought in each character. With *The Waves*, we knew that half of the extract is about boys and half is about girls. Therefore we carried out a standard analysis of each half, expecting to define the difference or contrast between them. So, when you begin to study an extract in order to focus on gender attitudes, you can make a start by using your common sense in these two ways:

   • Look for any generalisation where a character reasons that 'all men' or 'all women' have a certain characteristic, or that a character is like that 'because' they are male or female.

   • Select the male and female character(s) and use our usual methods of analysis on each separately, then compare and contrast what is revealed by your analyses of the 'male' and 'female' in the passage you are studying.

2. Look at references to the cultural context, or to mythology and religion. Treat these in the same way as you would treat imagery. There is a connection between what is being described in the text, and the culture or mythology referred to. For example, we noticed that Neville described his school using the phrase 'noble Roman', and we deduced that there was a connection in his mind between the school and a tradition of stoicism.

Suggested Work

We have found that 'masculine' and 'feminine' stereotyping is a major theme in Virginia Woolf's writing. We could therefore select almost any passage and learn more about this theme from detailed study. Here are three suggested extracts that you can study, one from each of the novels, which will reward studying with the special focus on gender-stereotypes that we have adopted in this chapter.

In *Mrs Dalloway*, look at pages 103–5 beginning at 'But why should she invite all the dull women in London to her parties' and studying as far as '"An hour's complete rest after luncheon," he said. And he went.' This passage makes an interesting comparison with our extract about Mr and Mrs Ramsay, as Richard Dalloway arrives home determined to tell Clarissa that he loves her, but then leaves without doing so.

In *To the Lighthouse*, study pages 84–6, from 'There is a code of behaviour she knew' until 'She had not been sincere.' In this passage Lily finds herself pressured into acting a 'feminine' role to soothe Mr Tansley, much to her own annoyance.

In *The Waves*, look at pages 132–3, beginning where Louis begins '"I come back from the office," said Louis. "I hang my coat here,"' and analysing as far as where he writes: 'to have been born without a destiny, like Susan, like Percival, whom I most admire.' The relationship between Louis's private character, and the conventional trappings of male commercial power, makes an interesting study in this extract.

4

Social Commentary and Satire

All three of the novels we are studying are set in Virginia Woolf's own time. Septimus's friend Evans died in the First World War and Clarissa exclaims with relief that 'it was the middle of June. The War was over' (*Mrs Dalloway*, p. 2). So, the Bourton memories in *Mrs Dalloway* belong before the First World War, but the day of the narrative itself is a June day in 1923. *To the Lighthouse* also bridges the First World War. 'The Window' takes place on a summer day before the war; 'Time Passes' refers to events and deaths of the war itself; and some of the original actors return years after the end of the war, during the 1920s. *The Waves* is less specific in its date and setting; but some internal references (deaths in action among the 'boasting boys' for example) show that the time-span of this novel also bridges the First World War.

The setting is unmistakably within the English middle class. Clarissa Dalloway lives in Mayfair and her husband is a minor minister in the government; Mr Ramsay is a university teacher and although his family and guests have a bohemian style of living, they are educated, professional or artistic people. The six characters of *The Waves* are brought up in country houses and go away to boarding schools. Louis, the Australian, becomes a City businessman; otherwise there is only vague reference to work (Bernard works, but we do not know what he does) and none of them lacks money.

There are characters from a lower class, but the two treated in any detail, Septimus Warren Smith and Miss Kilman from *Mrs*

Dalloway, both belong among the educated, aspiring, lower middle class. Working people and servants are mere names and presences, figures rather than characters. Even the rolling Mrs McNab who cleans the house in *To the Lighthouse* is a caricature as 'she creaked, she moaned. She banged the door'; and her observations about the Ramsays and the house are like char-lady dialogue from an Ealing comedy: 'Suppose the house were sold (she stood arms akimbo in front of the looking-glass) it would want seeing to – it would.'

Virginia Woolf, then, has this in common with Jane Austen: she writes about her own class and time. She writes of an England overshadowed by tradition, the fading of Empire, the social problems of an industrial society, and the First World War. She was a precise observer and analyst of her society, also like Jane Austen, and this chapter focuses on her analysis and observations.

*   *   *

Our first extract, from *Mrs Dalloway*, comes from the opening part of the novel, when Clarissa is out visiting Mulberry's, a flower shop in Bond Street:

> The motor car with its blinds drawn and an air of inscrutable reserve proceeded towards Piccadilly, still gazed at, still ruffling the faces on both sides of the street with the same dark breath of veneration whether for Queen, Prince, or Prime Minister nobody knew. The face itself had been seen only once by three people for a few seconds. Even the sex was now in dispute. But there could be no doubt that greatness was seated within; greatness was passing, hidden, down Bond Street, removed only by a hand's-breadth from ordinary people who might now, for the first and last time, be within speaking distance of the majesty of England, of the enduring symbol of the state which will be known to curious antiquaries, sifting the ruins of time, when London is a grass-grown path and all those hurrying along the pavement this Wednesday morning are but bones with a few wedding rings mixed up in their dust and the gold stoppings of innumerable decayed teeth. The face in the motor car will then be known.
>
> It is probably the Queen, thought Mrs Dalloway, coming out of Mulberry's with her flowers; the Queen. And for a second she wore a

look of extreme dignity standing by the flower shop in the sunlight while the car passed at a foot's pace, with its blinds drawn. The Queen going to some hospital; the Queen opening some bazaar, thought Clarissa.

The crush was terrific for the time of day. Lords, Ascot, Hurlingham, what was it? she wondered, for the street was blocked. The British middle classes sitting sideways on the tops of omnibuses with parcels and umbrellas, yes, even furs on a day like this, were, she thought, more ridiculous, more unlike anything there has ever been than one could conceive; and the Queen herself held up; the Queen herself unable to pass. Clarissa was suspended on one side of Brook Street; Sir John Buckhurst, the old Judge on the other, with the car between them (Sir John had laid down the law for years and liked a well-dressed woman) when the chauffeur, leaning ever so slightly, said or showed something to the policeman, who saluted and raised his arm and jerked his head and moved the omnibus to the side and the car passed through. Slowly and very silently it took its way.

Clarissa guessed; Clarissa knew of course; she had seen something white, magical, circular, in the footman's hand, a disc inscribed with a name, – the Queen's, the Prince of Wales's, the Prime Minister's? – which, by force of its own lustre, burnt its way through (Clarissa saw the car diminishing, disappearing), to blaze among candelabras, glittering stars, breasts stiff with oak leaves, Hugh Whitbread and all his colleagues, the gentlemen of England, that night in Buckingham Palace. And Clarissa, too, gave a party. She stiffened a little; so she would stand at the top of her stairs.

The car had gone, but it had left a slight ripple which flowed through glove shops and hat shops and tailors' shops on both sides of Bond Street. For thirty seconds all heads were inclined the same way – to the window. Choosing a pair of gloves – should they be to the elbow or above it, lemon or pale grey? – ladies stopped; when the sentence was finished something had happened. Something so trifling in single instances that no mathematical instrument, though capable of transmitting shocks in China, could register the vibration; yet in its fulness rather formidable and in its common appeal emotional; for in all the hat shops and tailors' shops strangers looked at each other and thought of the dead; of the flag; of Empire. In a public house in a back street a Colonial insulted the House of Windsor which led to words, broken beer glasses, and a general shindy, which echoed strangely across the way in the ears of girls buying white underlinen threaded with pure white ribbon for their weddings. For the surface agitation of the passing car as it sunk grazed something very profound.

(*Mrs Dalloway*, pp. 13–14)

We notice that there are some very long sentences in this extract, so we can begin by looking closely at the first of them. It begins 'But there could be no doubt that greatness was seated within' and ends 'innumerable decayed teeth'. Rereading this sentence we are struck by two elements in its phrasing. In the first half of the sentence Woolf sets short additional phrases between commas, which are placed to split the verb. So 'hidden' splits 'passing/down', and 'for the first and last time' splits 'who might now/be'. This technique introduces a hesitation in the middle of the actions, creating suspense and excitement in the manner of a music-hall master of ceremonies or a fairground barker. The tone of this part of the sentence is thus exaggerated and we hear the ironic amusement in the author's 'voice', pointing out the silliness of public awe. The interjected phrases themselves enhance this effect. The first, 'hidden', seems incongruous: would 'greatness' not be great if not 'hidden'? The second, 'for the first and last time', is exaggeration. Limousines regularly ferry royalty and politicians through the West End: people may often find themselves close to 'greatness'. The second outstanding structural feature of this sentence is the thirty-seven-word single phrase with which it ends. This ensures that the sentence, which has jerked and gasped its way to the grand ironic phrase 'the majesty of England', rushes headlong to its end. The subject of the long final phrase is time, ruin and death; and the hurtling rush of the sentence aptly emphasises the acceleration of time in our minds, as Woolf rushes us beyond the end of English civilisation, into an unrecognisably distant future. The deliberate effect of this is to undermine 'greatness' and public admiration of 'greatness' even further. So the first half of this sentence ridicules 'greatness', and the second half uses Time, Death and its own breakneck speed to shatter its significance.

In the third paragraph, a sentence of seventy-three words occurs, beginning 'Clarissa was suspended on one side of Brook Street'. The structure of this sentence is similar to that of the one we already looked at. The situation waits while we are told Clarissa's, the Judge's and the car's positions, and something of the Judge's character, in five phrases of fairly even length. Then the main clause comes: 'the chauffeur . . . said or showed something to the policeman'. This is interrupted by a descriptive phrase 'leaning ever so slightly', which further prolongs the moment. Finally, a single phrase of twenty-two words rolls uninterrupted to the end of the sentence. Notice that nothing happens until the verb 'said', which is the forty-fifth word of the sentence; then the policeman 'saluted', 'raised his arm', 'jerked his head', 'moved the omnibus', and the car 'passed', giving five action verbs in the final third of the sentence. The effect is that the sentence hangs still, extending the moment when the car with 'greatness' inside is stuck, so that it seems to last an interminable time; then, when the magic pass is shown, it passes away very quickly. The power of the magic pass, or whatever the chauffeur said to the policeman, is exaggerated by this sentence-structure. Virginia Woolf is clearly aiming at the same kind of effect as she achieved in the first sentence we looked at: the importance of the car, and the power of whoever is inside, is conveyed as mysterious and magical, and is exaggerated so that the effect of people's awe seems overblown and absurd. She then adds some absurdities to what she writes, underlining the silliness of the whole event. For example, the Judge 'liked a well-dressed woman' and the policeman 'jerked his head'. There are other touches that contribute to the effect of the sentence, so that everything works together towards the creation of contrasting speeds and times, and the sense of absurdity. For example, Clarissa and the Judge are said to be 'suspended', and the word evokes the elongated stillness we noted before the chauffeur leans towards the policeman. Also, the chauffeur 'leaning ever so slightly' contrasts with the sudden, energetic movements of the policeman, implying that as power reduces the need for physical activity, subservience increases it.

The last paragraph of our extract develops sentence-structure to depict before the moment, the moment, and afterwards. So, before the car appeared people had been 'choosing a pair of gloves'; then 'ladies stopped' and something 'had happened'. The moment of the car is described in paradoxical terms: it is 'something' and 'so trifling' that the most sensitive equipment could not detect it as a 'vibration'; yet it has 'fulness' and is 'formidable' and 'emotional'. The effect of the car is that 'strangers looked at each other and thought of the dead; of the flag; of Empire', and that the pub brawl 'echoed strangely' in the ears of girls who were buying wedding-clothes. So, this paragraph paints a picture of something vague, which none the less brings people together for a moment, across the barriers of class (the common people in the pub are noticed by middle-class girls buying trousseaux in fashionable shops) and social privacy (strangers 'looked at each other'). Woolf tells us what the moment was, because the pub brawl is about patriotism and people think of 'the flag; of Empire'. So the moment of the car is about glory and patriotism, which is presented as having an exaggerated impressiveness that Woolf treats ironically in a cheeky tone. Yet at the same time, she highlights another element in patriotism and monarchy, a more human and complex effect.

One hint of this is given in the list of what people think about: 'death' goes with the flag and Empire. Here, Virginia Woolf seems to hint at a truth: that patriotism is the father of war, and the English have just endured the loss of millions in the name of love of one's country. Death and national glory go hand in hand, then. The other complication of patriotic feeling occurs in the paragraph describing Clarissa's own response.

The satirical effect is strong: Clarissa's vanity (she 'guessed', she 'knew of course') is pathetic; and her patriotic mind-pictures are ridiculous ('glittering stars, breasts stiff with oak leaves, Hugh Whitbread and his colleagues, the gentlemen of England'). These stereotyped images come to her mind, inspired by a traffic pass: 'something white, magical, circular, . . . a disc inscribed with a name'. On this level, then, Clarissa's reaction is laughable.

Some elements of the paragraph hint at a deeper involvement, however. For example, Clarissa remembers a Palace party in the middle of her gushings about stars and oak leaves: 'that night in Buckingham Palace'. She associates the Queen's party with her own and she 'stiffened', thinking 'so she would stand at the top of her stairs'. On one level this is amusing: Clarissa is dreaming of being a Queen, like any pretentious social climber. On another level, it is essential to understanding her character. We know that she gives her parties in order to belong to Richard Dalloway's exclusive, establishment world; that she aspires to be 'very dignified', 'slow and stately' like her idol Lady Bexborough; and that she yearns to be invited to Lady Bruton's lunches. We also know that the entire fabric of Clarissa's society life is manufactured to compensate for her regretful memories of Peter Walsh, Sally Seton and Bourton. In this paragraph, Clarissa manages to think of her own party as belonging to the same heroic, glorious enterprise that the monarchy and the government lead: the just and righteous enterprise of the British nation!

In this extract, then, Virginia Woolf depicts nationalism with a poignant mixture of sharp satire and understanding. She sees and conveys the absurdities of awe, power, ceremony and pretentiousness; yet she also shows that there is a deep human need to belong to the tribe; and that the national experience connects people on an emotional, human level (for example through their common fear of death), who have otherwise been divided by society. The final sentence sums up the dual insight Woolf transmits: it is as trivial as 'the surface agitation of the passing car'; yet it 'grazed something very profound'.

*   *   *

In *To the Lighthouse*, Mr Ramsay, Cam, James, and two fishermen sail to the lighthouse:

> Mr Ramsay opened the parcel and shared out the sandwiches among them. Now he was happy, eating bread and cheese with these fishermen. He would have liked to live in a cottage and lounge about in the harbour spitting with the other old men, James thought, watching him slice his cheese into thin yellow sheets with his penknife.
>
> This is right, this is it, Cam kept feeling, as she peeled her hard-boiled egg. Now she felt as she did in the study when the old men were reading *The Times*. Now I can go on thinking whatever I like, and I shan't fall over a precipice or be drowned, for there he is, keeping his eye on me, she thought.

At the same time they were sailing so fast along by the rocks that it was very exciting – it seemed as if they were doing two things at once; they were eating their lunch here in the sun and they were also making for safety in a great storm after a shipwreck. Would the water last? Would the provisions last? she asked herself, telling herself a story but knowing at the same time what was the truth.

They would soon be out of it, Mr Ramsay was saying to old Macalister; but their children would see some strange things. Macalister said he was seventy-five last March; Mr Ramsay was seventy-one. Macalister said he had never seen a doctor; he had never lost a tooth. And that's the way I'd like my children to live – Cam was sure that her father was thinking that, for he stopped her throwing a sandwich into the sea and told her, as if he were thinking of the fishermen and how they live, that if she did not want it she should put it back in the parcel. She should not waste it. He said it so wisely, as if he knew so well all the things that happened in the world, that she put it back at once, and then he gave her, from his own parcel, a gingerbread nut, as if he were a great Spanish gentleman, she thought, handing a flower to a lady at a window (so courteous his manner was). But he was shabby, and simple, eating bread and cheese; and yet he was leading them on a great expedition where, for all she knew, they would be drowned.

(*To the Lighthouse*, pp. 194–5)

Let us start by remembering what we know: the first extract showed that Woolf is concerned with society on two levels simultaneously: as an unjustifiable structure appropriate for satire; and as a powerful, profound influence that the individual needs. Remember our conclusions about gender-stereotypes: does society present a similar dilemma? Is society's offer of a 'role' also frustrating and comforting to the individual?

There are two longer sentences in this extract, both of which focus on Mr Ramsay. The first (from 'And that's the way I'd like my children to live' to 'back in the parcel') simply completes the relationships that are present in the boat, explaining that Cam imagines what her father is thinking, and describing his actions. The second (from 'He said it so wisely' to '(so courteous his manner was)') is more revealing. We notice the same technique of a delaying phrase interjected to increase bathos when Mr Ramsay gives Cam 'from his

own parcel, a gingerbread nut'. The final part of the sentence introduces a simile that removes us from the boat entirely, into a glam-
orous world of romance, before the parenthesis at the end links the
two worlds. Clearly, Woolf has made us fly from the prosaic 'gingerbread nut' into a world of 'Spanish' gentlemen, flowers and ladies,
and back again to Mr Ramsay's 'courteous' manner, because that is
the journey travelled by Cam's thoughts. Can we develop this contrast between prosaic and romantic worlds?

Yes: it is presented several times in the extract. Cam distinguishes
between fantasy and reality when she realises that she can think
'whatever I like' while 'there he is'. Then they seem to be doing 'two
things at once', one the prosaic matter of eating sandwiches, the
other being in a fantastical adventure. So she is 'telling herself a
story' while 'knowing . . . the truth'. The duality of fantasy and
reality finally embraces Mr Ramsay himself: he is 'shabby, and
simple, eating bread and cheese' and at the same time he is 'leading
them on a great expedition'. The content of the imagery shows some
progression. The first image compares Cam's feeling of security when
Mr Ramsay is happy, now, with being in the study 'when the old
men were reading *The Times*'. The second simile is that of the
'Spanish' romance. It is also applied to Mr Ramsay's influence, but
the image tells us that this has now grown to fill the much wider and
wilder reaches of Cam's imagination. Woolf's imagery thus provokes
us to associate Cam's feeling of security with both the social establishment ('old men reading *The Times*') and her highly coloured
fantasy.

What are the relationships between these threads in Cam's mind?
The first occasion is clear. She thinks: *if* the old men are reading *The
Times* (and Mr Ramsay is 'there . . . keeping his eye on' her), *then*
she can indulge her fantasies. Later, this is modified to: *because* his
manner is courteous, *therefore* he is like a romantic fantasy. These
details convey how far Cam depends on her father for security: the
extract gives versions in which he protects her, he becomes her
fantasy, and finally he presides over both as simultaneously 'shabby,
and simple' and 'leading them on an expedition'.

We have found a significant focus on security and her father in
this extract about Cam. However, we still do not know why Virginia

Woolf highlights this process so insistently. Yes, Mr Ramsay provides a feeling of security to his daughter; but how does this relate to the novel's wider themes?

There are several references to danger and violent death in the extract. First, Cam knows that she 'shan't fall over a precipice or be drowned' while her father is there; then, indulging her morbid fantasy, she imagines them 'making for safety' and asks herself whether they will die of thirst or starvation. In the background, she still has the luxury of knowing 'what was the truth'. Finally, truth and fantasy are only joined by the paradox 'yet': Mr Ramsay presides over both, and 'for all she knew, they would be drowned'. This progression of ideas tells a story of the development of Cam's fantasy, gradually revealing its significance. Clearly, Cam is playing with thoughts about death; and the security she absorbs from Mr Ramsay encourages her to let her fears of death become increasingly real, until, 'for all she knew', they might come true.

We have already found that Mrs Ramsay was unconsciously tempted by death. It is reasonable to deduce that Cam is here exercising similar feelings – the combined desire and horror that thoughts of death inspire. Here, Virginia Woolf's insight shows how a combination of her father, and the social stability he is associated with, enable Cam to cope with these feelings. If we conflate Mr Ramsay and the old men reading *The Times*, as Cam does, we can call the resulting conglomerate a 'paternal establishment'. This establishment does not help by banishing thoughts about death, as we might expect. On the contrary, it encourages them in a vicarious, luxurious context of safety. By showing the process of Cam's fantasy here, Virginia Woolf is also, by implication, analysing the popular appeal of horror-stories and tales of violence. She suggests that they all have their roots in a common perplexity about death, which consists of fear and desire; and that they are a fantasised indulgence of these dangerous feelings within the safe framework of a 'paternal' establishment.

We are reminded of the people in *Mrs Dalloway*. Their thoughts of death are similarly indulged within the context of an establishment they admire, when the car passed and they 'thought of the dead; of the flag; of Empire'. In both of these cases, Woolf has succeeded in conveying a close relationship between glory and glamour on the one hand, and death on the other.

Before we leave this extract, we should note that the social situation is more complex than Cam's thoughts alone. Mr Ramsay's behaviour in this episode is socially remarkable. James realises that his father 'would have liked' to 'lounge' around 'spitting with the other old men'; and Cam realises that the simple fishermen's life is what Mr Ramsay wants for his children, that he is 'shabby, and simple, eating bread and cheese'. In much of the rest of the book Mr Ramsay has been an impossibly tortured soul, striving after brilliance and fame, and made miserable by his need to be Mrs Ramsay's admired hero. It is remarkable that he is so contented with the fishermen, then; and in the next paragraph the extent of his change is underlined: when they pass the site of a wreck he acts as if thinking: 'But why make a fuss about that? Naturally men are drowned in a storm, but it is a perfectly straightforward affair' (p. 239). The class distinction of his education and aspirations seems to have disappeared, then. Ironically, this enables Mr Ramsay, finally, to become for his daughter the 'Spanish gentleman', or courtly fantasy, that all his striving could never make him for his wife.

The evolution of social themes is thus continuous, complex and ironic in this novel. Virginia Woolf's play upon class, social attitudes and the establishment is always present. So, although we have highlighted Cam's thoughts and fantasies from this extract, other significant contributions to an analysis of society and social behaviour are continuing simultaneously.

*   *   *

Our third extract in this chapter is taken from Bernard's long summing-up towards the end of *The Waves*:

> 'I rose and walked away – I, I, I; not Byron, Shelley, Dostoevsky, but I, Bernard. I even repeated my own name once or twice. I went, swinging my stick, into a shop, and bought – not that I love music – a picture of Beethoven in a silver frame. Not that I love music, but because the whole of life, its masters, its adventurers, then appeared in

long ranks of magnificent human beings behind me; and I was the inheritor; I, the continuer; I, the person miraculously appointed to carry it on. So, swinging my stick, with my eyes filmed, not with pride, but with humility rather, I walked down the street. The first whirr of wings had gone up, the carol, the exclamation; and now one enters; one goes into the house, the dry, uncompromising, inhabited house, the place with all its traditions, its objects, its accumulations of rubbish, and treasures displayed upon tables. I visited the family tailor, who remembered my uncle. People turned up in great quantities, not cut out, like the first faces (Neville, Louis, Jinny, Susan, Rhoda), but confused, featureless, or changed their features so fast that they seemed to have none. And blushing yet scornful, in the oddest condition of raw rapture and scepticism, I took the blow; the mixed sensations; the complex and disturbing and utterly unprepared for impacts of life all over, in all places, at the same time. How upsetting! How humiliating never to be sure what to say next, and those painful silences, glaring as dry deserts, with every pebble apparent; and then to say what one ought not to have said, and then to be conscious of a ramrod of incorruptible sincerity which one would willingly exchange for a shower of smooth pence, but could not, there at that party, where Jinny sat quite at her ease, rayed out on a gilt chair.

'Then says some lady with an impressive gesture, "Come with me." She leads one into a private alcove and admits one to the honour of her intimacy. Surnames change to Christian names; Christian names to nicknames. What is to be done about India, Ireland or Morocco? Old gentlemen answer the question standing decorated under chandeliers. One finds oneself surprisingly supplied with information. Outside the undifferentiated forces roar; inside we are very private, very explicit, have a sense indeed, that it is here, in this little room, that we make whatever day of the week it may be. Friday or Saturday. A shell forms upon the soft soul, nacreous, shiny, upon which sensations tap their beaks in vain. On me it formed earlier than on most. Soon I could carve my pear when other people had done dessert. I could bring my sentence to a close in a hush of complete silence. It is at that season too that perfection has a lure. One can learn Spanish, one thinks, by tying a string to the right toe and waking early. One fills up the little compartments of one's engagement book with dinner at eight; luncheon at one-thirty. One has shirts, socks, ties laid out on one's bed.

'But it is a mistake, this extreme precision, this orderly and military progress; a convenience, a lie. There is always deep below it, even when we arrive punctually at the appointed time with our white waist-coats and polite formalities, a rushing stream of broken dreams, nursery rhymes, street cries, half-finished sentences and sights – elm trees, willow trees, gardeners sweeping, women writing – that rise and sink even as we hand a lady down to dinner. While one straightens the fork so precisely on the table-cloth, a thousand faces mop and mow. There is nothing one can fish up in a spoon; nothing one can call an event. Yet it is alive too and deep, this stream. Immersed in it I would stop between one mouthful and the next, and look intently at a vase, perhaps with one red flower, while a reason struck me, a sudden revelation. Or I would say, walking along the Strand, "That's the phrase I want", as some beautiful, fabulous phantom bird, fish or cloud with fiery edges swam up to enclose once and for all some notion haunting me, after which on I trotted taking stock with renewed delight of ties and things in shop-windows.'

(*The Waves*, pp. 169–71)

In this extract, Bernard reflects upon the beginning of his adult life after he finished his education. It is not easy to define what the extract is about, because he describes several stages of his experience in abstract or metaphorical terms. For example, when Bernard feels like 'the one appointed to carry it on', he comments 'The first whirr of wings had gone up, the carol, the exclamation'. A little later he says that he 'took the blow' which has something to do with 'the impacts of life'. Later still he describes how 'a shell forms upon the soft soul, nacreous, shiny' but soon exclaims 'But it is a mistake, this extreme precision . . . a convenience, a lie' because it hides beneath it 'a rough stream of broken dreams'. Finally, he talks of a 'phantom bird, fish or cloud with fiery edges' enclosing a 'notion haunting me' while he walks down the Strand. Metaphors are used as definite ref-erences, and we are supposed to follow what Bernard means (see, for example, 'the first whirr of wings had gone up'), new images con-stantly appear (see the 'silences . . . as dry deserts, with every pebble apparent', or the sudden 'smooth shower of pence'), and are elabo-rated (see, for example, that the 'shell' on Bernard's soul is then tapped by the 'beaks' of 'sensations'). How can we find a consistent story of Bernard's experience in all this? Look at the images he uses more closely, asking whether they have anything in common. The images include a beak tapping a shell, dry deserts, a whirr of wings, a rushing stream, elm trees, willow trees, a thousand faces that 'mop and mow', and a fabulous 'bird or fish or cloud' that swims up. These all bring a sense of natural wildness.

The extract is also filled with numerous references to ordinary objects and everyday actions. These are 'my stick', 'shop', 'picture of Beethoven in a silver frame', 'swinging my stick', 'I walked down the street', 'its objects, its accumulations of rubbish, and treasures displayed upon tables', 'tailor', 'at that party', 'on a gilt chair', in the first paragraph. The second paragraph contains 'private alcove', 'decorated under chandeliers', 'this little room', 'Friday or Saturday', 'carve my pear', 'dessert', 'string', 'engagement book', 'dinner at eight; luncheon at one-thirty', 'shirts', 'socks', 'ties', 'one's bed'. In the final paragraph, we find 'white waistcoats and polite formalities', 'dinner', 'the fork', 'table-cloth', 'spoon', 'mouthful', 'a vase', 'walking down the Strand', 'ties and things in shop-windows'. This collection shows that the passage is full of references to eating, shopping, clothes and furniture.

We have found two contrasting elements in the passage, then. On the one hand there is a vein of wild and natural imagery; on the other hand, there are numerous references to the trivialities of urban life. What is the relationship between these two parts of the experience Woolf describes? This question leads us into closer detail, so we will look at the extract paragraph by paragraph, rather than all in one go.

The picture of Beethoven that Bernard buys is a symbol of all great people of the past, and his word 'miraculously' tells us that he felt elation at his sense of belonging to a tradition. This elation must be the 'first whirr of wings had gone up, the carol, the exclamation'. His image relates to dawn, as of birds rising and singing the dawn chorus. Then, however, 'one goes into the house', which must symbolise entering adult life and society, and brings with it all of the everyday objects mentioned in the paragraph. The only other natural imagery in this paragraph describes the interior of the house and embarrassing social silences as 'dry' and 'glaring as dry deserts'. This only makes sense as a description of the sterility of everyday life; so this image belongs with the material objects, in contrast to the birds, trees and streams evoked elsewhere in the extract. A further pair of metaphors contrasts his rigid 'ramrod' of sincerity with the soft 'shower' of money. This again is explicit, and implies that he would like to be rich but cannot bring himself to be a hypocrite. In this first paragraph, then, Bernard first identifies his natural elation with an object (the picture of Beethoven). As soon as he enters adult society, however, he is overwhelmed by trivial and banal details which – in terms of natural imagery – make a 'dry desert'.

In the second paragraph, Bernard brings the multitude of everyday details under control, by distinguishing between 'outside' (where 'the undifferentiated forces roar') and 'inside', where he feels that he and 'some lady' make their own reality. The image for this process is that 'a shell forms upon the soft soul' and the outside 'sensations' are unable to be sensed through this shell. By the end of this paragraph Bernard uses the known details of his day-to-day life, the 'inside' that he can control, to keep at bay the 'undifferentiated forces' and 'sensations' of too many, overwhelming and senseless details, which are kept 'outside'. The natural imagery evokes something protective of tender life – a shell – and the word 'nacreous' likens it to mother-of-pearl, the hard substance which forms around an irritation on the shell, creating a smooth and comfortable surface next to the soft creature inside. In this paragraph, then, Bernard copes with the excess detail of life by narrowing his experience to what he can control, and shutting out everything else.

The third paragraph sets the controlled, artificial life Bernard lives, day by day, against natural images for his private memories and thoughts. His memories and private thoughts are 'always deep below' the 'extreme precision' of his surface life, which is therefore a 'lie'. They are 'a rushing stream', 'alive' and 'deep' and he can become 'immersed' in them at any time. Notice also that the 'stream' he refers to includes his earliest memories, for the 'gardeners sweeping, women writing' are mentioned again: we know that Bernard continually returns to this memory, which dates back to Elvedon (see *The Waves*, p. 8). The contrast between his surface life and deeper being is clear: deeper thoughts can bring 'a sudden revelation' or 'some beautiful, fabulous phantom bird, fish or cloud with fiery edges' to 'enclose once and for all some notion haunting me'. Meanwhile, his surface life is 'between one mouthful and the next' and 'walking down the Strand'. The words 'revelation', 'fabulous', 'phantom' and 'haunting' give mystical overtones to Bernard's deeper being, in contrast to the banality of eating and walking. Finally, the effect of contact with his inner 'stream of broken dreams' is refreshing: he takes stock of 'ties and things' with 'new delight'. In this paragraph, then, Bernard seems to have learned how to live a dual life. He uses his childhood memories and private, hidden thoughts as a means of reviving his pleasure in the artificial emptiness of life's outer details. There is a suggestion in 'bird . . . with fiery edges' that Bernard's deeper being revives like a phoenix (the 'fabulous' bird that is consumed by fire and rises from its ashes after a thousand years); but this may be following interpretation too far.

Once we realise that there are two contrasting elements in this extract, then, we are able to construct a commentary. This tells us Bernard's 'story', the stages he went through as he entered adult society. It is helpful to summarise what we have discovered as briefly and clearly as possible: *Bernard's mind and soul are both elated at the beginning, but his first contact with adult social life is hurtful and overwhelms him with sterile details. He gains control by restricting his life to a familiar, controllable range and shutting out the rest; but this restricted life is a lie, and Bernard must be periodically refreshed by contacting his buried, deeper self, to sustain his happiness and his interest in day-to-day details.*

Society appears as a vast accumulation of meaningless artificiality in this extract. Virginia Woolf highlights eating and table manners, social occasions, shops and clothing as particularly representative of the sterile, gratuitous multiplicity of details in modern urban life. Her account of Bernard's progress shows us his deluded eagerness at first; but most of the extract impresses us with the pain and difficulty he experiences, trying to accommodate his natural self to an artificial outside 'shell'; and in defending himself against the infinite meaninglessness ('the undifferentiated roar') of society. In this sense, then, our extract from *The Waves* focuses on the same dilemmas highlighted in *Mrs Dalloway* and *To the Lighthouse*: the friction between an individual's natural self, on the one hand; and external demands on them or their social existence, on the other.

We have, then, found a consistent concern about the individual in society in these three extracts. However, it is important not to make too many assumptions when going on to look at further extracts from other parts of the novels. Remember that Clarissa Dalloway enlists society's mores to help bury her natural memories and regrets; Mr Ramsay only finds social ease when relieved of his artificial courtly aspirations; and Bernard searches his hidden natural self to help make social living tolerable. In other words, these characters reach very different accommodations with society, although Woolf's concern with individuals in relation to society remains constant.

In all three of the extracts there is satire directed at the banal or empty pursuits of society. In *Mrs Dalloway*, patriotism and admiration of 'greatness' is mocked; in *To the Lighthouse*, the 'paternal' establishment is analysed, and Woolf is sadly ironic about an ordinary man who was bedevilled by the masculine need to be extraordinary; in *The Waves*, a multiplicity of table-manners, clothes and shops stifles humanity.

However, our understanding is an important key: throughout her writing, Virginia Woolf shows society opposing all of an individual's efforts to face the infinite truths of the human condition. She focuses on different aspects of society, and her characters respond differently, at different times; but the fundamental dilemma between personal and social living remains the same.

We remarked that the novels are set in middle-class society on both sides of the First World War. There is therefore a sense of society in a process of change. The values of pre-war society, the Conservative establishment, Empire and patriotism, and formal manners, are receding; and social problems, the frightening facts of war and death, and egalitarian ideas, are growing. However, this contrast should not be over-interpreted. In *Mrs Dalloway*, the experience of war has certainly contributed to the disturbing truths surrounding Septimus's suicide. On the other hand, in *To the Lighthouse* the change in mood between 'The Window' and 'The Lighthouse' is due in large part to Mrs Ramsay's and other characters' deaths, and the passage of time; and the influence of the war is not stressed. In

The Waves, death arrives as a colonial accident to Percival, and the First World War, with its consequent social changes, has less prominence than this one private event.

Conclusions

1. Social, national and political pressures are both a reassurance and a problem for the individual. They support individuals' superficial efforts to manufacture a role and a purpose for themselves, and so they help people to avoid confrontation with disturbing thoughts about death, and the futility in their own lives. On the other hand, they frustrate people's deeper desire to express themselves more naturally.

2. Virginia Woolf takes a satirical approach to class divisions and snobbery, English patriotism and the establishment, and ideals such as Empire. She uses irony, sarcasm and hyperbolic style to reveal the absurd emptiness of society's mores. In the structure of the novels she ironically sets these against more permanent truths, such as the effects of the First World War and the frustrated desires of characters.

3. The demands and temptations of society are shown to have enormous power in Virginia Woolf's novels. For example, in *Mrs Dalloway* we found that a glimpse of 'greatness' could bring a divided society together in patriotic emotion, for a moment; and in *The Waves* we found that Bernard must defend himself and seek an accommodation with the bombardment from innumerable trivia.

4. Although her methods are predominantly ironic and satirical, Virginia Woolf's vision of society is potentially tragic. This is analogous to her use of gender-roles. Social demands and temptations are shown to prevent individuals from achieving their potential.

Methods of Analysis

1. In this chapter we employed the same initial approach we developed in Chapter 1: find the longest sentences and carry out a detailed analysis of them. In *Mrs Dalloway* the sentence-structure was particularly revealing, and we built the remainder of our analysis from the insight this provided. In *To the Lighthouse*, the second long sentence we looked at displayed the contrast between romantic fantasy and prosaic reality that provided us with a key to Cam's thoughts.

2. In *The Waves*, however, it was necessary to follow a different initial approach.

   • Thinking about the extract as a whole, we noticed two prominent features. First, the confusing images Bernard uses. Second, that trivial details of clothing, food and shopping abound in the extract.

   • Next, we divided the extract into more manageable sections. We concentrated on the three paragraphs in turn, and this enabled us to write a detailed commentary, interpreting the different stages in Bernard's relationship with his life in urban society.

3. Interpreting natural imagery is helpful. For example, realising the contrast between 'dry deserts' and a 'rushing stream' enabled us to see that the former does not belong with the rest of the nature-imagery, but applies to the sterile artificiality of society instead.

4. The extracts enabled us to deduce certain specific conclusions about the way Virginia Woolf portrays society; however, we also discern an underlying pattern which is a consistent feature in her presentation of society and individuals, and lies behind her particular depictions of society in different contexts. This underlying 'pattern' can be used as a key that can be applied to any extract. Therefore, you can begin by understanding how an extract conveys the conflict between the individual and a powerfully attractive yet hostile society. This will enable you to grasp more quickly how the theme is being used.

Suggested Work

Study another episode from the text you are working on, that focuses on society. You can begin by asking how the relationship between individual and society is conveyed, or works, in the episode you are looking at. This may provide you with the insight to set your analysis in motion. Or, you may choose to focus on close analysis of long sentences, the initial approach we have found to be consistently revealing.

In *Mrs Dalloway*, the episode covering Peter Walsh's return to his hotel and him eating supper would richly repay analysis, beginning on page 138 at 'But it would not have been a success, their marriage' and continuing as far as page 142, 'What did the Government mean – Richard Dalloway would know – to do about India?' In this episode the interplay between subjective and external views of Peter Walsh is worth investigating.

Another, equally suitable episode is that where Miss Kilman and Elizabeth sit in the tea-room of a department-store. Begin on page 114, at 'She had passed the pillar-box, and Elizabeth had turned into the cool' and study as far as 'and at last came out into the street' on page 117. In this extract, you may find that analysing the imagery applied to the two characters is useful.

In *To the Lighthouse*, any part of the dinner scene (which is Chapter 17 of Part I, 'The Window', pages 96–130) would repay detailed analysis. I suggest the opening, which begins with Mrs Ramsay asking herself 'But what have I done with my life?' (p. 77), and proceeding as far as 'The thought was strange and distasteful' (p. 82). In these few pages Mrs Ramsay overcomes the pessimism of her opening mood; and Lily succumbs to social pressure to soothe Mr Tansley.

In *The Waves*, the characters' responses to their schooling, and their expectations from life, are the focus for all six personalities on pages 32–8, between '"I have torn off the whole of May and June," said Susan' and 'It is the first day of the summer holidays.'

5

Imagery and Symbol

Imagery: Similes and Metaphors

Images are comparisons between something the writer describes, and an idea the writer imagines for the sake of the comparison. For example, as Peter Walsh walks up Whitehall in *Mrs Dalloway*, Virginia Woolf writes 'a patter like the patter of leaves in a wood came from behind'. This describes the footsteps of the marching boys by comparing them to 'the patter of leaves in a wood'. The footsteps of the marching boys are there in the story, they really happen: that is the **literal** side of the comparison. The leaves falling in a wood are not there, they are an image-idea Woolf imagines as a comparison for the footsteps: that is the **figurative** side of the comparison. In this example, the author explains that there was 'a patter *like* the patter of leaves'. The word 'like' tells us that there is a comparison, so we call this image a **simile**. Later in the same extract Peter follows a woman whose cloak 'blew out with an enveloping kindness, a mournful tenderness'. This time the way the cloak blows (the **literal** side of the comparison) is compared to 'kindness' and 'tenderness' (the **figurative** side); but none of the words tell us that it was 'as if' the cloak felt kindness or tenderness. Woolf simply writes that the kindness and tenderness were there: it blew out 'with' these feelings. This kind of image is called a **metaphor**.

Virginia Woolf uses imagery extensively in her novels, and we have already analysed several instances. For example, we noticed a contrast between the quality of dryness in Bernard's 'desert' image (see our extract from *The Waves*, Chapter 4) and wetness in the later images of his underlying self as a 'stream'. This led us to deduce the ideas of sterility and fertility respectively from the dryness and wetness of the image-ideas. Explaining what we did makes it sound like a complicated process, but at the time the connection between desert–dry–sterile and stream–wet–fertile seemed natural and self-evident. The point is that we respond to and interpret imagery naturally, all the time.

Imagery: Symbolism

When something that is there in the narrative (something **literal**) takes on added significance, we call it a **symbol**. This happens with the boar's skull, a hunting trophy fixed to the wall of the children's bedroom in *To the Lighthouse*. What do we mean by 'takes on added significance'? We mean that it starts to mean more than just what it is. The boar's skull begins by being important, because James and Cam have strong feelings about it (he 'screamed if she touched it' and Cam 'couldn't go to sleep with it in the room'). Also, Mrs Ramsay is exasperated by it. She wonders 'what had possessed Edward' to send it, and it is 'horrid'. She was 'foolish' to put it in their room. She is angry with Mildred who, 'of course, had forgotten' to get rid of it (all quotations are from p. 106).

Virginia Woolf, then, draws our attention to this object by surrounding it with a cluster of strong emotions. It stands out for us, because it is obviously more important than the chest of drawers or the pillow, or any of the other things in the room which are mentioned in passing. This provokes us to think about the skull: what is it like? It is animal, primitive, and it died a violent death. Soon, and quite naturally, we are thinking of the skull as a sign of the nastier, savage side of life. This means that we connect the thing itself (the skull) with an idea (savagery in life in general). The boar's head has become a symbol as soon as we make this connection.

From this moment onwards, Woolf can make use of the boar's head as a 'symbol'. So, when Mrs Ramsay puts her shawl over it to hide it, we understand that she covers up the savage or 'horrid' side of life. This action reminds us of other moments, such as her soothing remarks to James, which calm him down after his father has antagonised him. By now, the action 'covering the boar's head' is another way of saying 'Mrs Ramsay's struggle against chaos, destructiveness, and thoughts about death'.

Imagery in the Novels

In this chapter we look at imagery and symbols we have already noticed within extracts, and trace Virginia Woolf's use of them more widely through the novel in which they appear. We start with the extract from *Mrs Dalloway* we studied in Chapter 2. Here is one paragraph from that extract again:

> A patter like the patter of leaves in a wood came from behind, and with it a rustling, regular thudding sound, which as it overtook him drummed his thoughts, strict in step, up Whitehall, without his doing. Boys in uniform, carrying guns, marched with their eyes ahead of them, marched, their arms stiff, and on their faces an expression like the letters of a legend written round the base of a statue praising duty, gratitude, fidelity, love of England.
>
> (*Mrs Dalloway*, p. 44)

The two similes in this paragraph account for fifty-one of the seventy-nine words, which is a high proportion of imagery. The first one begins 'like the patter of leaves in a wood'; then 'rustling' develops the idea into a power which 'drummed' his thoughts up Whitehall. The second begins 'like the letters of a legend' and leads to the idea of a list of virtues: 'duty, gratitude, fidelity, love of England'. Both similes travel a long distance from the first comparative idea (leaves, an inscription) to the final idea (a drumming power, patriotic virtues). This happens because Virginia Woolf does not stop when she has compared two things. She goes on, and writes about the figurative idea in ever-increasing detail until she has reached something else, different from but derived from the first idea. So, footsteps compared with leaves become a power that takes control of Peter's mind; and faces like writing on a statue become the patriotic and heroic virtues. In other words, Woolf transforms a concrete idea (leaves, an inscription) into something abstract (a power, patriotic virtues).

A third example helps to reveal why she does this. Later in the extract, the boys march 'as if one will worked legs and arms uniformly, and life, with its varieties, its irreticences, had been laid under a pavement of monuments and wreaths and drugged into a stiff yet staring corpse by discipline'. This simile follows the same pattern as the others we have analysed. First, the group marching is compared to a single animal with 'one will'. Then we are told several further details in succession: (a) that 'life' had been buried by this creature; (b) where it was buried – 'under a pavement'; (c) what was on the pavement – 'monuments and wreaths'; (d) how it was suppressed – 'drugged'; (e) the effect of the drug – 'into a stiff yet staring corpse'; (f) who drugged it – 'discipline'. The 'one will' which is imagined at the start of this has the abstract name 'discipline' by the end. So, as she elaborates her idea, Virginia Woolf steadily moves us further from the concrete, external reality of the story, and towards abstract, internal and theoretical events.

Virginia Woolf's similes are often like this. Characteristically, the initial idea is no more than a comparison that we might find in any piece of descriptive writing. It gains its particular effect from being elaborated. These similes provide a direct link between the concrete world in which external actions and events occur, and the non-physical world of inner, mental events. In other words, the image is like a bridge that leads us into the inner world of the character's mind, which is where, as we found in Chapter 1, the significant story in Virginia Woolf's novels takes place.

* * *

Now we can look at another kind of imagery we have noticed in *Mrs Dalloway*: everyday objects that become significant. In Chapter 1, we noticed Peter Walsh's pocket-knife and Clarissa's scissors, and commented that these objects: 'represent the shifting balance of domination in their relationship; and both of them use their playthings as a focus of reassurance to themselves'. To study Virginia

Woolf's exploitation of such objects, simply find other places where they are mentioned. Then try to explain the object's function, in each different context. We will do this for Peter Walsh's pocket-knife.

It is first mentioned on page 1. Clarissa remembers Peter, 'his eyes, his pocket-knife, his smile'. 'Eyes' and 'smile' are natural features, with the knife between them, and this emphasises that it is part of his character. The knife's next appearance is in the extract we studied, and it reappears again on page 37:

> and he took out his knife quite openly – his old horn-handled knife which Clarissa could swear he had had these thirty years – and clenched his fist upon it.
>
> What an extraordinary habit that was, Clarissa thought; always playing with a knife.

This time, Peter is spurred to take out his knife by thinking angrily about Clarissa's smug, artificial life, then about his own life of 'journeys; rides; quarrels; adventures; bridge parties; love affairs; work; work; work!' The inclusion of 'bridge parties' in this list, and the repetition of 'work', reveal his insecurity. His own life feels futile despite all the activity, and he takes out the knife as a reassurance. This time, Clarissa's reaction is to take up her needle. At the same time, her mind summons 'to her help the things she did; the things she liked; her husband'. Peter and his knife make her feel 'frivolous; empty-minded' and she is like a 'Queen . . . left unprotected', so she concentrates on the details of her life, symbolically taking up her needle as a weapon in order to 'beat off the enemy' (p. 38).

Later in the visit Clarissa asks Peter what he will do about his current affair with Daisy, who is married. He replies in an off-hand manner, 'And he actually pared his nails with his pocket-knife' (p. 39). We know that Peter is very unsure of himself. People in India have tried to persuade him not to marry Daisy; now in England, his feeling for Clarissa has surprised him with its power. His knife is again set to work to reassure him: he pares his nails with it to shore up the falsely casual tone of what he says. Clarissa's reaction to the knife is more violent this time. 'For Heaven's sake, leave your knife alone! she cried to herself in irrepressible irritation', and she thinks 'at his age, how silly!' On this occasion, the knife becomes the focus for all her vexation at Peter: it is a sign of his immaturity and stings her to fury against him.

In the next paragraph he is 'running his finger along the blade of his knife' as he thinks of Clarissa 'and Dalloway and all the rest of them' with defiance, before suddenly breaking down in tears. This is the final mention of the knife before he leaves the house.

Notice that the significance of Peter's knife grows new branches for both of the characters, throughout the scene. Peter's behaviour is natural: he is sexually uncertain and immature, and the knife is a boyish reassurance. Clarissa's reactions are natural: she is first amused, then threatened, then irritated by the knife, because it represents the threat of sexual arousal; but also quite naturally because it reminds her of his insecurity. Clarissa knows that she is responsible for his not having grown up. He has never recovered from the revenge she took on him by rejecting him, thirty years ago. For this reason, his habit of fiddling with the knife seems to blame her, making her angry. It is an intolerable reminder that she must summon all her defences to suppress. So, the knife represents the unfulfilled desires and regrets Clarissa struggles to suppress throughout the novel. Yet it remains an utterly convincing part of the narrative, throughout the scene.

The knife continues to represent aspects of Peter, as the novel proceeds. For example, the next time it is mentioned is when he diverts his romantic desires into the fantasy of pursuing a strange woman through London. Peter is half-aware that his fantasy is 'made up' and so he fingers his pocket-knife 'stealthily' (see pp. 45–7). Later, when Peter acknowledges the shallowness of his emotion for Daisy as 'jealousy which survives every other passion of mankind', he '[held] his pocket-knife at arm's length'; and finally, on stating his complaint against Clarissa ('realising what she might have spared him, what she had reduced him to – a whimpering, snivelling old ass'), Peter dismisses women: 'But women, he thought . . . don't know what passion is' while 'shutting his pocket-knife' (see p. 70). Even on page 170 Sally notices that Peter 'was thinking only of Clarissa, and was fidgeting with his knife'.

So, Peter Walsh's knife represents several aspects of his romantic life: his memory of desire, his fantasies, continuing proof of the damage Clarissa's rejection wrought. For her it resurrects the same events but in a different guise: a sexual threat, his permanent immaturity, a reproachful reminder of her loss and the viciousness of her revenge against him. In this way, the knife reminds Clarissa of the side of her own nature that she decided to suppress when she accepted Richard Dalloway. In fact, each time it appears, it brings into our minds the entire complex of memories and emotions associated with Bourton. Virginia Woolf frequently uses ordinary objects in this way.

Clarissa has two weapons of her own in the scene with Peter Walsh: her scissors and her needle. We have already commented that they are a part of the artificial life – with husband, politics, parties and society – that keeps Clarissa busy and helps to keep her from dwelling too much on memories of Bourton. In the scene with Peter, she 'summoned' these things to help her to 'beat off the enemy', simultaneously 'taking up her needle'.

*   *   *

Some elements in Woolf's novels seem to carry a larger and more baffling significance. As an example of this, we will examine the symbolic role of the lighthouse itself, from *To the Lighthouse*. We already met the pervasive power of its light as it falls on Mrs Ramsay with hypnotic regularity, in the extract we analysed in Chapter 2. In this chapter we look at other passages where the lighthouse becomes significant, hoping to draw conclusions about its function in the novel as a whole.

The first line of the novel is Mrs Ramsay's conditional promise to James, that they will go to the lighthouse: 'Yes, of course, if it's fine to-morrow.' The description of James's excitement that follows is the first influence of the lighthouse itself:

> the wonder to which he had looked forward, for years and years it seemed, was, after a night's darkness and a day's sail, within touch. Since he belonged, even at the age of six, to that great clan which

cannot keep this feeling separate from that, but must let future prospects, with their joys and sorrows, cloud what is actually at hand, since to such people even in earliest childhood any turn in the wheel of sensation has the power to crystallize and transfix the moment upon which its gloom or radiance rests, James Ramsay, sitting on the floor cutting out pictures from the illustrated catalogue of the Army and Navy Stores, endowed the picture of a refrigerator as his mother spoke with a heavenly bliss. It was fringed with joy.

(*To the Lighthouse*, p. 3)

In this extract the lighthouse has already gained greater significance than its mere physical existence. There are three stages in this growth. First, we know that James longs to go to the lighthouse, so it is an object of desire to him. The second stage begins with Mrs Ramsay's promise, because this makes it possible that his desire will come true. His reaction reveals that there is a separation between his dream of happiness (going to the lighthouse), and his dull, everyday experience of life. The lighthouse (prosaically) is a real thing; yet James did not expect it ever to become real for him, because he had made it into an unattainable dream, in his mind. The 'extraordinary joy' he feels arrives because of the prospect that his fantasy and reality worlds might be 'within touch' of each other and might actually come together. Both of these stages in the development of the lighthouse idea centre upon James's subjective experience.

The third stage comes with Virginia Woolf's own sardonic interpretation. James, she writes, was one of those people who 'must let future prospects . . . cloud what is actually at hand', being unable to 'keep this feeling separate from that'. There are interesting implications in this comment. First, Woolf reminds us that fantasies and reality are 'this' and 'that', so any hope that they might unite is an illusion in the minds of people who wilfully confuse their feelings. Second, she writes of 'future prospects' as intruding and preventing us from seeing the present clearly: they 'cloud' present reality, causing it to become vague and obscure. This suggests that confused 'prospects' are a major cause of the evasions and hopeless longings we will meet in so many of the characters in the book. Finally, the imperative 'must' hints at an emotional compulsion. This hint of compulsive idealism foreshadows various characters' struggles with ideals and reality, and reality's habit of shifting out of view, or turning into something else, in the novel.

We can now examine what the lighthouse idea leads to, from both James's and the reader's point of view. First, James is in a crisis because there is a prospect that his ideal world and the real world will become the same (he will go to the lighthouse). The wondrous aura of the lighthouse therefore attaches itself to ordinary, everyday things: James endowed the picture of a refrigerator with 'a heavenly bliss. It was fringed with joy.' This implies that our fantasies can bring us relief from the dullness of everyday life, as long as there is a prospect that they will come true. Virginia Woolf has chosen her example well: a picture of a refrigerator from the Army and Navy Stores catalogue is a particularly trivial thing; and cutting it out is a futile activity, passing time but leading nowhere.

The fact that James is one of 'that great clan' who live for the future, encourages the reader to make other deductions. If future ideals 'cloud' our view of reality, what will happen when they become real? Even this early passage implies that achieving one's desire presents a danger: I've done that. What next? The danger is that there would be nothing left to live for. On the other hand, people must have some hope of achieving their ideal; and they are plunged into acute mental pain when it seems out of reach.

This insight is widely relevant to other scenes and characters. Notice Mr Ramsay's agony when he thinks that his books will be forgotten: 'He must have sympathy. He must be assured that he too lived in the heart of life; was needed; not here only, but all over the world' (p. 35). Think about Mrs Ramsay's fixation with marriage and matchmaking: notice for example how the thought of life's repetitive dullness ('And even if it isn't fine to-morrow, . . . it will be another day') leads to her 'Smiling, for an admirable idea had flashed upon her this very second – William and Lily should marry' (p. 24). So, there is a necessary relationship between a character's purpose or dream, and their ability to cope with life and avoid despair.

We have deduced a great deal about the significance of the lighthouse from its appearance in the narrative on the first page. All our deductions have one feature in common: they can all be put in two different ways. For example, we have remarked that the lack of an

ideal brings pain; but we could also conclude that pain brings the
need for an ideal.

Virginia Woolf's significant symbols characteristically express
paradoxical ideas in this way. We cannot say 'the lighthouse represents an idealised fantasy' because it is a real lighthouse at the same
time as being James's childhood dream. Instead, we can think of the
lighthouse as more like a trigger. It provokes us to think about the
human tendency to live for a future fantasy, together with all the
paradoxical emotions Virginia Woolf conveys as associated with that
tendency.

Now let us look at the lighthouse's growing and shifting significance in its other appearances during the novel. On page 29, Mr
Ramsay says that 'There wasn't the slightest possible chance that
they could go to the Lighthouse to-morrow', and Mrs Ramsay's
reaction brings forward a new set of ideas provoked by the lighthouse:

> To pursue truth with such astonishing lack of consideration for other
> people's feelings, to rend the thin veils of civilization so wantonly, so
> brutally, was to her so horrible an outrage of human decency that,
> without replying, dazed and blinded, she bent her head as if to let the
> pelt of jagged hail, the drench of dirty water, bespatter her unrebuked.
> There was nothing to be said.
>
> (*To the Lighthouse*, pp. 29–30)

The argument is still the same: is James's dream possible to achieve,
or impossible? First, the language of Mrs Ramsay's thoughts sets
'consideration' and 'truth' as opposites, so she seems to accept that
James's dream will not come true. Yet she is clearly on the side of
'civilization', 'decency' and 'consideration' (all positive words), pre-
ferring to maintain a lie because 'truth' is so cruel. Secondly, she uses
the violent verb 'rend', intensified by adverbs 'wantonly' and 'bru-
tally' to describe her husband's action; the metaphor 'thin veils of
civilization' is added. The overtones of this language are of rape:
'thin veils' cover modesty and beauty, and the violent man will 'rend'
them 'wantonly'. Telling the truth is therefore an unforgivable sin:
'so horrible an outrage of human decency'. Finally, the destructive

effect of the truth is likened to the violence of winter: 'the pelt of jagged hail, the drench of dirty water'.

We already knew that the lighthouse presents a problem: the relationship between people and their fantasies has to be maintained in a delicate balance so that they neither lose hope, nor suffer disappointment by running out of dreams. Now, by extension, Mrs Ramsay suggests that this delicate balance is 'civilization', which is sustained by false hopes. The imagery in this passage connects with other parts of the novel as well. A 'thin veil' which is rent by Mr Ramsay's 'truth' like 'the pelt of jagged hail' reminds us of Mrs Ramsay's shawl that is placed over the pig's head, and which falls away fold by fold, attacked by the hostile winter weather described in 'Time Passes'. So the significance of the lighthouse is extended by connection with 'civilization' and 'truth', and is connected to other themes by means of the 'veil' and 'hail' images used here and elsewhere.

There is not enough space in this chapter to trace the influence of the lighthouse throughout the book. We analysed its influence on Mrs Ramsay in Chapter 2, where the 'stroke' of its three beams made a familiar, repetitive caress that combined with her knitting to soothe her in an almost hypnotic way. In that passage, remember, the lighthouse beam was typically ambivalent. On the one hand, it has the monotonous regularity of an outside 'truth' that dispels the trivial details of her day-to-day life and allows her subconscious thoughts of death to surface. On the other hand its beam brings forth a 'mist' and ideas of beauty – 'trees, streams and flowers' – that are like 'tenderness' and help to restore her equanimity. Also, it is both external, looking at her, and her own eyes, gazing at herself. Now we will look at the end of James's involvement with the lighthouse:

> Indeed they were very close to the Lighthouse now. There it loomed up, stark and straight, glaring white and black, and one could see the waves breaking in white splinters like smashed glass upon the rocks. One could see lines and creases in the rocks. One could see the windows clearly; a dab of white on one of them, and a little tuft of green on the rock. A man had come out and looked at them through a glass and gone in again. So it was like that, James thought, the

Lighthouse one had seen across the bay all these years; it was a stark tower on a bare rock. It satisfied him. It confirmed some obscure feeling of his about his own character. The old ladies, he thought, thinking of the garden at home, went dragging their chairs about on the lawn. Old Mrs Beckwith, for example, was always saying how nice it was and how sweet it was and how they ought to be so proud and they ought to be happy, but as a matter of fact James thought, looking at the Lighthouse stood there on its rock, it's like that.

(To the Lighthouse, p. 193)

First, the words applied to the lighthouse here contrast with its description on the novel's opening page. Here, it 'loomed' 'stark' and 'straight', all 'black' and 'white' on its 'rock'. The rock is 'bare', but there is a 'dab' of 'white' in a window and a 'tuft' of 'green' on the rock. All of these are one-syllable, plain words. They are not qualified or weakened in any way, but are 'stark' and 'straight' words, like the lighthouse they describe. The opening page of the novel, by contrast, has 'extraordinary', 'wonder', 'cloud', 'gloom' and 'radiance'. The stark language of this description emphasises James's sudden realisation that the lighthouse, which was once a 'fabled land' (p. 4) for him, is actually a plain, real object.

Secondly, the sentence-structure is repetitive. 'One could see' and 'one had seen' occur four times; phrases begin 'there it loomed', 'so it was', 'it was', 'It satisfied', 'It confirmed' and 'it's like that'. Such repeated use of impersonal and neuter pronouns removes the sense of an individual character, again emphasising that James now sees the same 'stark tower' as everybody else. Only two sentences contrast with this repeated form: when James thinks of 'The old ladies', the sentence becomes less direct. Two phrases ('he thought, thinking of the garden at home') slow the sentence down before the verb, which is a participle, 'dragging', a less definite form of the verb than a simple past like 'loomed' or 'was'. The next sentence is similar. 'Old Mrs Beckwith' has 'for example' put in before the continuous verb 'was always saying', which introduces four clauses without punctuation, imitating her endless rambling speech: 'how nice it was and how sweet it was and how they ought to be so proud and they ought to be so happy'. The second half of this double sentence, introduced by 'but', also delays, emphasising the short finality of the three-word main clause: 'it's like that'. This brings us sharply back to the plain, stark reality of the lighthouse. These two vague and rambling sentences among short, stark ones, create the sense that a lot of woolly, comforting nonsense goes on and on forever (the 'old ladies' and 'Mrs Beckwith'), trying to hide the short, plain fact that life is 'like that'.

How does this passage develop the lighthouse's significance from earlier in the novel? The same contrast between 'truth' and 'civilization' is here; but James differs from Mrs Ramsay: he does not find truth 'horrible' or 'an outrage'. He is 'satisfied' because he had an 'obscure' feeling that the truth would turn out this way, which is now 'confirmed'. The old ladies and their meaningless, soothing conversation provide us with another version of 'civilization': now it is an evident silliness, made up of 'sweet' and 'nice' platitudes.

The story this passage tells about James is straightforward. At the beginning he had a wonderful illusion; now he sees the bare reality. He had unconsciously (an 'obscure feeling') expected to be disillusioned, so the event is satisfying and reveals to him the silliness of people with their soothing evasions. This simple story also embraces the various feelings and illusions different characters have attributed to the lighthouse during the book. In particular, it lends a clear insight into Mrs Ramsay's subtle and ambivalent feelings of desire, hostility and unity in relation to the lighthouse. Remember, however, that we are analysing the lighthouse as a symbol: if we now ask: 'What does it symbolise?', the answer is that it symbolises all that we have discussed. Virginia Woolf has thus created a symbol which is rather like James's insight into life itself: it defies simple definition, and all we can say is: 'it's like that'.

The lighthouse is a prominent symbol, then, which touches various characters and has a complex, shifting influence upon emotions and thoughts throughout the narrative. Its effect is to bring together several elements of this rambling, almost plotless novel, providing a unifying focus through which we can increase our understanding of the author's concerns.

*   *   *

As her style developed, so did Woolf's use of imagery. We
have analysed similes from *Mrs Dalloway* that are introduced
by 'seemed', 'like' and 'as if', so that the reader is led into the
character's mental world. In later novels Woolf uses metaphors
more freely, often without any transitional image. In some
passages the literal fades into an intermittent background, and the
abstract, figurative vision is given in vivid detail. The following
extract from *The Waves* displays this kind of metaphorical writing
clearly:

> 'They vanish, towards the lake,' said Rhoda. 'They slink away over the
> grass furtively, yet with assurance as if they asked of our pity their
> ancient privilege – not to be disturbed. The tide in the soul, tipped,
> flows that way; they cannot help deserting us. The dark has closed
> over their bodies. What song do we hear – the owl's, the nightingale's,
> the wren's? The steamer hoots; the light on the electric rails flashes;
> the trees gravely bow and bend. The flare hangs over London. Here is
> an old woman, quietly returning, and a man, a late fisherman, comes
> down the terrace with his rod. Not a sound, not a movement must
> escape us.'
> 'A bird flies homeward,' said Louis. 'Evening opens her eyes and
> gives one quick glance among the bushes before she sleeps. How shall
> we put it together, the confused and composite message that they send
> back to us, and not they only, but many dead, boys and girls, grown
> men and women, who have wandered here, under one king or
> another?'
> 'A weight has dropped into the night,' said Rhoda, 'dragging it
> down. Every tree is big with a shadow that is not the shadow of the
> tree behind it. We hear drumming on the roofs of a fasting city when
> the Turks are hungry and uncertain tempered. We hear them crying
> with sharp, staglike beaks, "Open, open." Listen to the trams
> squealing and to the flashes from the electric rails. We hear the beech
> trees and the birch trees raise their branches as if the bride had let her
> silken nightdress fall and come to the doorway saying "Open, open".'
> 'All seems alive,' said Louis. 'I cannot hear death anywhere tonight.
> Stupidity, on that man's face, age, on that woman's, would be strong
> enough, one would think, to resist the incantation, and bring in
> death. But where is death tonight? All the crudity, odds and ends, this
> and that, have been crushed like glass splinters into the blue, the red-

fringed tide, which, drawing into the shore, fertile with innumerable fish, breaks at our feet.'

'If we could mount together, if we could perceive from a sufficient height,' said Rhoda, 'if we could remain untouched without any support – but you, disturbed by faint clapping sounds of praise and laughter, and I, resenting compromise and right and wrong on human lips, trust only in solitude and the violence of death and thus are divided.'

'For ever,' said Louis, 'divided. We have sacrificed the embrace among the ferns, and love, love, love by the lake, standing, like conspirators who have drawn apart to share some secret, by the urn. But now look, as we stand here, a ripple breaks on the horizon. The net is raised higher and higher. It comes to the top of the water. The water is broken by silver, by quivering little fish. Now leaping, now lashing, they are laid on shore. Life tumbles its catch upon the grass. There are figures coming towards us. Are they men or women? They still wear the ambiguous draperies of the flowing tide in which they have been immersed.'

(*The Waves*, pp. 153–4)

In this passage, the actual story is clear: 'They vanish, towards the lake' tells us that the other four leave Rhoda and Louis alone. The author mentions two or three people they see: an old woman, a stupid man, a late fisherman; and they notice details of the London landscape such as the 'flare' above the city, trees that 'bow and bend', squeals from trams and flashes from railway lines. Finally, 'There are figures coming towards us', and the other four return. There is enough of the physical narrative, then, to make clear that Louis and Rhoda stand looking out over the scene while Jinny, Bernard, Neville and Susan go for a walk under the trees towards the lake.

On the other hand, parts of the writing seem to describe Louis and Rhoda as standing on a different, metaphorical shore. The transition begins with Louis's question: 'But where is death tonight?' He begins to answer with generalised phrases for the details of life, 'crudities, odds and ends, this and that', which are crushed 'like glass splinters' into 'the blue, the red-fringed tide'. Notice that the first idea was simply 'odds and ends', which are then compared to 'glass splinters'. However, the picture is incomplete until the main metaphor of a sea appears in 'the blue, the red-fringed tide'. Soon, Louis and Rhoda are pictured on a symbolic shore where a gory, fish-filled 'tide' is coming in. The description has travelled, via a simile, to a descriptive metaphor for their situation. Woolf does not explain to us how this comes about, by saying that they stood 'as if' on a wider shore. The simile of life's 'odds and ends' like 'glass splinters' is enough to let in a wider metaphor for their situation, without any further explanation.

The second time we are taken into a metaphorical landscape is even more abrupt. The author carefully reminds us of the physical reality – 'now look, as we stand here' – before launching into inner, metaphorical vision, without any preparation: 'a ripple breaks on the horizon. The net is raised higher and higher. It comes to the top of the water. The water is broken by silver, by quivering little fish. Now leaping, now lashing, they are laid on shore. Life tumbles its catch upon the grass.' All of this is metaphor: in external reality they are at Hampton Court – the small lake they see does not stretch to a 'horizon'. The vast net Louis imagines full of tiny silver fishes, as 'Life tumbles its catch upon the grass', is clearly only in his mind. Immediately following the metaphorical picture, and again with no indication from the author to warn us that we are leaving metaphor and returning to the narrative, Louis observes: 'There are figures coming towards us.' These figures are the other four characters, in external reality. The striking feature of this writing, then, is Virginia Woolf's refusal to prepare us for transitions from naturalism into metaphor and symbol, and back again.

Notice, also, that the second excursion into metaphor is a continuation of the first: the 'tide . . . fertile with innumerable fish' is still there when 'the water is broken by silver, by quivering little fish' which, 'now leaping, now lashing', are turned on to the shore, and the idea of a vast 'net' breaking the horizon is added. So we assume that Louis's inner vision develops continuously in his mind, despite the fact that he heard what Rhoda said. This point is underlined at the end of the paragraph. The 'figures coming towards us' are real: they turn out to be the other four characters. However, Louis sees them still wearing the 'flowing tide in which they have been immersed'. Of course, they have not been literally underwater: they

went for a walk by the lake. So Louis's mind seems able to see in two
different ways at once. On the one hand he sees external reality, and
hears what Rhoda says; on the other hand, his inner metaphorical
vision continues all the time. Virginia Woolf conveys this by the way
she slips into and out of metaphor without warning, and by giving
continuity to both outer and inner visions.

We should also notice that the metaphor is a simplified version of
their situation. Louis and Rhoda really stand on a terrace outside a
restaurant, with trees before them and various people walking, then
the edge of a small lake with a steamer upon it, beyond which they
can see London with its flare and the electric flashes. The metaphor
contrasts with this: there is a shore, a horizon, a net and some fish.
All the rest of the scene has disappeared. The metaphor removes the
clutter of real life, and presents a symbolic vision of simple, basic elements such as shore and sea.

Why does Virginia Woolf use imagery in this startling way? And
what does Louis's vision mean? The answers to these questions are
related.

Louis answers the question 'where is death?' with a metaphor of
the tide breaking on a shore. 'Odds and ends, this and that' and
fishes are carried on this tide. When the others appear, Louis imagines that they have been 'immersed' in the tide, so there is a connection between people, the fish, and the 'crudities, odds and ends' of
life. As an answer to his question, Louis's vision is ambiguous: We
cannot say that 'death' is the sea, the things in the sea, or the net
which catches them. Instead, the suggestion seems to be that 'death'
is expressed throughout the vision Louis presents, of a tidal sea,
shore, net and fish. It is the whole metaphor and the story (the net
rising, and fish landing on shore) that expresses 'death'.

This helps to explain Virginia Woolf's purpose. She conveys her
characters' experience of life as two continuous perceptions. First,
they are continuously aware of the external reality surrounding
them. So, Louis notices when the figures of his friends reappear
from the darkness under the trees. Secondly, an inner perception of
life in metaphorical terms is also continuous. The characters are
always struggling to understand their place and purpose on earth.
So, in this inner perception, they ponder the big forces: birth, life,

death, nature. Louis's inner vision of life and death is expressed by the sea and shore metaphor we have been looking at.

*   *   *

In the final discussion of this chapter, we look at Virginia Woolf's use of a natural element as symbolic. The sea and water figure prominently in both *To the Lighthouse* and *The Waves*. Again, we do not expect to interpret these symbols thoroughly, only to introduce analysis of them by focusing on their significance in a few arbitrarily selected passages. In this way, we can suggest how to find their significance in any extract you have to study.

In Part I, 'The Window', from *To the Lighthouse*, Mrs Ramsay's mood undergoes a change during the family dinner. Chapter 17 begins with her wondering 'But what have I done with my life?' and thinking 'it's all come to an end'. She sees 'no beauty anywhere' and feels that 'the whole effort of merging and flowing and creating rested on her' (all quotations are from pp. 77–8). Then she pities William Bankes, and her recovery begins. Virginia Woolf uses this image to describe the beginnings of Mrs Ramsay's recovery:

> in pity for him, life being now strong enough to bear her on again, she began all this business, as a sailor not without weariness sees the wind fill his sail and yet hardly wants to be off again and thinks how, had the ship sunk, he would have whirled round and round and found rest on the floor of the sea.
>
> (*To the Lighthouse*, p. 78)

The image is that her life is a voyage in a ship, and the stark choice between carrying on with all her social and family efforts, and giving up, resigning herself to death, is presented as a choice between sailing on, or sinking beneath the sea. In this image, Mrs Ramsay imagines herself in the only safe, man-made place, surrounded by infinite chaotic water. She is not secure, for the ship could have 'sunk'; her feelings are ambivalent because she is 'not without weariness' and 'hardly' wants to continue, while drowning would send her 'whirling round and round' but eventually allow her to find 'rest'.

The image conveys Mrs Ramsay's conflict, then, between her commitment to maintaining their family life, moment by moment; and her weary desire for death.

As the narrative of the meal continues, further touches are added to the significance of water in Mrs Ramsay's thoughts. An example is Mrs Ramsay's memory of 'the Mannings' drawing-room at Marlow twenty years ago' (p. 86). She finds the memory comforting because it is 'like reading a good book again, for she knew the end of that story'. In other words, she is reassured by the limited predictability of her memory, in contrast to the life of that moment which was unpredictable and too difficult to control. Here again, the contrast between a safe, organised thought (her memory) and the chaos of actual experience (the present) is conveyed in terms of water:

> life, which shot down even from this dining-room table in cascades, heaven knows where, was sealed up there, and lay, like a lake, placidly between its banks.
>
> (*To the Lighthouse*, p. 86)

Contrasting images of wild water 'shot . . . in cascades' and tame water 'sealed up there . . . like a lake, placidly between its banks' express Mrs Ramsay's constant desire to mould the rough, raw material of life into a limited form, and to control it. Ironically, the image also reveals the poverty and artificiality of her achievement. Later in the evening, when the candles are lit, she begins to feel that she has achieved her aim: she has imposed order and shut out the chaotic sea and night:

> for the night was now shut off by panes of glass, which, far from giving any accurate view of the outside world, rippled it so strangely that here, inside the room, seemed to be order and dry land; there, outside, a reflection in which things wavered and vanished, waterily.
>
> Some change at once went through them all, as if this had really happened, and they were all conscious of making a party together in a hollow, on an island; had their common cause against that fluidity out there.
>
> (*To the Lighthouse*, p. 90)

The image comparing the room to 'dry land' and outside to a place where things vanish 'waterily', continues the idea of sea/chaos and a desire for an ordered haven, that we have already found. However, if we think carefully, a complex irony is added. The image is not actually a simple contrast between inside and outside: it is a contrast between inside and the 'reflection' of inside on the windows, in candlelight that 'rippled'. The distinction between order and chaos has thus become more subtle: it is between the mood of unity and camaraderie Mrs Ramsay has created around the dining-table; and another image of that mood. This figurative idea, then, ironically reveals that Mrs Ramsay's illusion of creating order around herself is just that: an illusion. Her 'triumph' in the *Boeuf en Daube*, in the engagement of Minta and Paul that she has brought about, in reviving her husband's youth and her own jealousy of him: all the successes she achieves during the meal are revealed to be synthetic. Several cynical comments come to mind. Mrs Ramsay did not cook the *Boeuf en Daube*; Minta's and Paul's marriage fails; Mr Ramsay is revived by Minta's attractions; Mrs Ramsay's jealousy is kindled by herself (she manipulated Minta into the position of younger rival, and so aroused her husband's gallantry). The irony that watery chaos is the image of the diners themselves, not some outside force, is thus subtly developed by this slight modification of water and sea imagery during the narrative of the meal.

In *The Waves*, the title of the novel alerts us to the symbolic significance of the sea. A series of nine descriptive passages, printed in italics, interrupts the narrative at intervals. Each of these passages mentions the waves and the sea as part of a symbolic landscape, passing through the different lights, moods and weathers of a day. We will look at one of these passages:

> *The sun rose higher. Blue waves, green waves swept a quick fan over the beach, circling the spike of sea-holly and leaving shallow pools of light here and there on the sand. A faint black rim was left behind them. The rocks which had been misty and soft hardened and were marked with red clefts.*
>
> *Sharp stripes of shadow lay on the grass, and the dew dancing on the tips of the flowers and leaves made the garden like a mosaic of single sparks not yet formed into one whole. The birds, whose breasts were specked canary and rose, now sang a strain or two together, wildly, like*

skaters rollicking arm-in-arm, and were suddenly silent, breaking asunder.

The sun laid broader blades upon the house. The light touched something green in the window corner and made it a lump of emerald, a cave of pure green like stoneless fruit. It sharpened the edges of chairs and tables and stitched white table-cloths with fine gold wires. As the light increased a bud here and there split asunder and shook out flowers, green veined and quivering, as if the effort of opening had set them rocking, and pealing a faint carillon as they beat their frail clappers against their white walls. Everything became softly amorphous, as if the china of the plate flowed and the steel of the knife were liquid. Meanwhile the concussion of the waves breaking fell with muffled thuds, like logs falling, on the shore.

(*The Waves*, p. 16)

Before this interlude, the characters describe childhood together in a country house; afterwards, they are sent away to school. The nine descriptive passages are clearly written to describe different stages in the characters' lives as well as different times in a day. So the opening paragraph here shows that the growing light begins by making the world clearer: 'The rocks which had been misty and soft hardened and were marked with red clefts.' In this light, the waves 'swept a quick fan'. They leave 'shallow pools' behind, and 'A faint black rim'. At the start of this passage, then, the viewpoint is one that can clearly see these waves; and is beginning to be aware that the tide leaves a sediment. The waves bring something – dirt, weed, the passage does not specify what – and leave it on the beach as the 'faint black rim'.

By the end of the passage the situation has changed. There is a description of flowers opening, and the increasing reproductive activity of the garden. Then everything becomes 'softly amorphous'. After this, the waves have somehow become a background noise, no longer seen; and their rhythm is heavy and sinister: a 'concussion' of 'muffled thuds, like logs falling'.

So far, this analysis tells us that the waves are described differently, and that this is intended to convey some sort of development. We can speculate that the children have achieved a clear view of their childhood lives, so at the start of the passage they see the beach clearly. By the end of the passage, however, the viewpoint shifts to the growing and multiplying activity in the garden, and as the children turn their attention to a new, disturbing and confusing future away from their original home, the waves become a background rhythm pounding on behind them. However, the passage itself does not give us sufficient evidence to interpret symbols with confidence. In these circumstances, we must look back at the preceding description, and forward to the next one, hoping to find an understandable continuity between them. Here are descriptions of the waves from the preceding passage:

> *The sea was indistinguishable from the sky, except that the sea was slightly creased as if a cloth had wrinkles in it . . . barred with thick strokes moving, one after another, beneath the surface, following each other, pursuing each other, perpetually.*
>
> *As they neared the shore each bar rose, heaped itself, broke and swept a thin veil of white water across the sand. The wave paused, and then drew out again, sighing like a sleeper whose breath comes and goes unconsciously.*
>
> (*The Waves*, p. 1)

Our theory seems to be supported by this passage. The simile in the final sentence compares the sea to a sleeper breathing 'unconsciously', and the opening description brings a gradual but dim perception of waves 'pursuing each other' in a vague but perpetual motion. Our theory is now stronger: this passage suggests the beginning of the characters' consciousness, their first awareness of a sea or of waves moving across that sea.

The next 'interlude', after our extract, contains these evocations of the waves:

> *Their quivering mackerel sparkling was darkened; they massed themselves; their green hollows deepened and darkened and might be traversed by shoals of wandering fish. As they splashed and drew back they left a black rim of twigs and cork on the shore and straws and sticks of wood, as if some light shallop had foundered and burst its sides . . .*
>
> *. . . The waves drummed on the shore, like turbaned warriors, like turbaned men with poisoned assegais who, whirling their arms on high, advance upon the feeding flocks, the white sheep.*
>
> (*The Waves*, pp. 46–8)

Our theory is now confirmed: the language has become more threat-ening and sombre ('darkened', 'massed themselves', 'deepened', 'darkened'), and the 'black rim' is now seen more clearly to consist of 'twigs and cork', 'straws and sticks of wood'. These in turn hint at the possibility of a disaster: 'as if some light shallop had foundered and burst its sides'. The sound of the waves has also developed, becoming more threatening in military images of a foreign invasion: the 'concussion' of 'muffled thuds' is more distinct as waves 'drummed', and they are like 'turbaned warriors'. Their weapons are 'poisoned' and they threaten the innocent, defenceless creatures on land, the 'feeding flocks'. It is evident from this passage that the world has become a much more dangerous, complicated and threat-ening place now that the characters are leaving school and about to enter adulthood.

We can corroborate our theory by looking at another element of the three descriptions. In the first, 'The birds sang their blank melody outside' (p. 2); in the second, 'The birds, whose breasts were specked canary and rose, now sang a strain or two together' (p. 16); and in the third, 'Fear was in their song, and apprehension of pain, and joy to be snatched quickly now at this instant' (p. 46). There is now no doubt that the descriptions of nature in these passages emulate the growing children's perception of the world. In early childhood birdsong is 'blank': it is there, unexplained. As the chil-dren grow, they take in more details, such as the colours 'specked canary and rose'. At the beginning of adulthood, the characters understand danger and desire, and perceive feelings and motives, including cruelty and pain, in the birds.

Now we are confident that the waves are described in a way that reflects the life-experience of the characters. Virginia Woolf uses the nine repeated descriptions to chart her characters' passage through life; and the use of the waves as a symbol helps to provide an explanatory unity and continuity running from end to end of the novel. Details in these descriptions also help us to interpret the char-acters' experiences. So, in the passage we analysed first, the change of viewpoint turning from the original sea towards the teeming garden, with the noise of the waves becoming simultaneously less distinct and heavier, helps us to follow the children's changing perspective as

they turn from self-absorbed play and exploration of their imme-
diate home, and begin to face an unfamiliar future in which they
will travel to school.

On the other hand, we are no wiser about the actual significance
of this symbol. We know that Virginia Woolf conveys her views of
life in the way she describes the waves; but what *are* they? As we
have called them a 'symbol', we should be able to describe their significance as well as their function and effect. We can approach this
question by looking at the beginning and the end, as the 'shape' of
Woolf's ideas is likely to appear more clearly in this way, than if we
attempt to follow the small developments in between.

We have already looked at the opening passage, which suggests
that at the beginning of life the characters become dimly aware of
the sea and the waves, and the first light appears on the sea's horizon.
If we turn to the final descriptive passage (pp. 157–8: for convenience, I discount the final six words of the novel), we find that 'Sky
and sea were indistinguishable' again, as at the start; and there is a
description of 'Darkness' rolling 'its waves' over the land, 'engulfing'
and 'blotting out' everything in its path – people, trees, buildings
and mountains.

The repetition of a complete formula, 'The sun had not yet risen.
The sea was indistinguishable from the sky' (p. 1) becoming 'Now
the sun had sunk. Sky and sea were indistinguishable' (p. 157) is
striking, and clearly deliberate. Virginia Woolf must be telling us
that life is a cycle, beginning and ending in 'indistinguishable' darkness. The waves were there at the start, however, and cover everything in the end. Therefore, we can deduce that the sea represents
both birth and death, the origin and ultimate end of our lives. This
interpretation calls to mind a number of traditions. In particular, the
unformed darkness of the opening, followed by a division between
sea and sky, recalls Genesis's description of the Creation; and the sea
as a maternal 'origin' figures in Darwin's theory of evolution and in
Freudian interpretations of dreams. The waves themselves beat,
strike, drum, and so on throughout the characters' lives; and they
stand for something more ambiguous and paradoxical. Their energy
drives both creation and growth, and destruction and death. We can
suggest, then, that the waves broadly stand for the rhythm of life

itself, which necessarily contains both birth and death. Like generations of birds, flowers and people, they are 'moving, one after
another, beneath the surface, following each other, pursuing each
other, perpetually' (p. 1).

Virginia Woolf, then, has simply taken an archetypal force – the
sea – and by means of a series of suggestive and developing descriptions, she has attached implications and associations to it. The result
is a significant expressive symbol, standing for something as abstract
and all-inclusive as the rhythm of life. She uses this, in turn, as a
means to define and explain the characters' progress and experiences.

Conclusions

1. Virginia Woolf uses a great deal of imagery. Her similes often
   begin as a straightforward comparison, which is then elaborated
   at length. Elaboration moves the ideas steadily away from the
   physical reality of the narrative and towards mental events, emotions and ideas. Similes thus provide a 'bridge' between the story
   and the level of life-experience Woolf is most interested in.
2. Imagery is sometimes used purely to convey internal experience
   or abstract ideas, particularly in Woolf's later writing. The effect
   is that there is a real and solid inner life of thoughts and emotions, which is created by means of physical metaphors. Often,
   the characters' thoughts alternate between a metaphorical 'inner'
   story and a real 'outer' one. In these cases we can trace an image-
   idea as it develops in intermittent passages, in order to help us
   understand the character's inner life.
3. Virginia Woolf's purpose in using such imagery seems to be to
   create the impression of simultaneous, equally valid and 'real'
   inner and outer experiences of life.
4. Small, everyday objects are used as significant motifs. The contexts in which they appear, and the characters' feelings and
   thoughts about them, build up their significance further each
   time they are mentioned. They often seem to be an external manifestation of some aspect of character (as Peter Walsh's knife is an
   external sign of his insecure masculinity in *Mrs Dalloway*); but

they can also grow a larger significance and become like a trigger which calls a particular experience, together with the character's attendant feelings, into our minds.

5. Virginia Woolf endows some objects with added and more complicated significance. An example of this is the lighthouse in *To the Lighthouse*. These objects attract the attention and emotions of so many characters that they act like a reflector of various different subjective perceptions. As 'symbols' they are difficult to interpret, often remaining ambiguous; but they stand for so many things to different characters that they grow a related complex of meanings as the novel progresses. These objects also act as a focus, so they are structurally important, having a unifying effect in almost plotless novels.

6. Virginia Woolf makes free use of 'archetypal' natural images such as the sun, sea, flowers, storms, mountains, moon, night and day, and so on. These often refer to the cycles of life and death in the traditional manner.

7. In the 'symbolic descriptions' that occur in later works, these forces of nature provide a continuous link between incidental imagery and a wider symbolic structure in the novel; and the variations in their description help us to interpret and understand the characters' experiences in relation to life as a whole. Part II, 'Time Passes', from *To the Lighthouse*, and the nine symbolic passages printed in italics in *The Waves*, are symbolic descriptions of this kind.

Methods of Analysis

1. To analyse a particular simile or metaphor, choose one and begin by defining its literal and figurative sides. Analyse the way in which it is elaborated by comparing the image-idea at the beginning with the idea that is finally reached. Describe the effect this development of ideas has upon the reader.

2. Find further instances of the same or comparable imagery/symbolism, beginning with the passage you are studying, and spreading to other parts of the novel from there. Describe the

function and development of the image-idea and consider its
relation to characters and themes. Remember that an image-idea
or a significant object may:

- appear at different times and in different contexts throughout
  the novel (Peter Walsh's knife in *Mrs Dalloway* is like this);
- appear occasionally within an episode, developing with one
  character's experiences (water-images in Mrs Ramsay's thoughts
  are like this, during the meal in *To the Lighthouse*);
- appear and develop intermittently but frequently in a short
  episode, making an 'inner' metaphor for a particular experience (Louis's vision of the shore and a net of fish, from *The
  Waves*, is like this).

3. Be flexible and open-minded in your interpretation of images
   and symbols. Remember that Virginia Woolf often uses imagery
   to convey the difference between different characters' perceptions
   of the same object or event. The nature of the image often seems
   to change radically, because she writes from the characters' subjective points of view. Most of Woolf's imagery and symbolism
   does not have a single, defined significance. Expect to find an
   ambiguous or complex meaning which contains different but
   related ideas.

Suggested Work

This chapter has found several different kinds of imagery in Virginia
Woolf's novels. It is worthwhile to practise analysing three kinds
which are typical features of her writing.

1. **An object used as an external manifestation of either an unac-
   knowledged aspect of character or a part of life-experience.**
   Choose any recurrent object from the text you are studying, and
   trace its story by analysing each of its appearances during the narrative, e.g. the boar's head or Mrs Ramsay's shawl (*To the
   Lighthouse*); the flowers or Clarissa's green dress (*Mrs Dalloway*);
   the sound of a bell (*The Waves*).
2. **A symbolic object, giving rise to multiple and changing perceptions.** In this connection it would be worthwhile to look at the

aeroplane writing in the sky (*Mrs Dalloway*); the island and headlands (*To the Lighthouse*); and Hampton Court (*The Waves*).

3. **A natural element used as symbolic.** The use of nature in *Mrs Dalloway* is more incidental and less developed than in either of the other two novels. However, the sky has significance that will repay investigation. In *To the Lighthouse*, the wind and its effects would be a revealing study; and in *The Waves*, either mountains or wind are worth looking at.

Studying a symbolic natural element is a lengthy and voluminous task, as it involves combing the text for numerous references. Some of these are detailed and will be found quickly; but others may be passing, incidental phrases. You can begin by analysing the first and last appearance of the symbol you are studying. In this way you can quickly gain an 'overview', an insight into the symbol's significance in the text as a whole.

6

The Significance of Nature

The significance of the sea and waves as a symbol in *The Waves*, and the water-images in Mrs Ramsay's thoughts from *To the Lighthouse*, were discussed in the last chapter. We were mainly interested in how Woolf uses symbols, however. Our conclusions about the sea's implications, and its function in the novels' structure, were therefore only cursory.

In this chapter we look at nature and natural forces as a major theme in all three novels. We begin by reminding ourselves of what we already know, as a platform on which to build further ideas. Three insights from earlier chapters are worth recalling. First, we found that Virginia Woolf uses natural forces symbolically. Sometimes they are described in separate 'symbolic' passages, divorced from the characters and the surrounding narrative. Clearly, then, we can expect to find a philosophical statement of some sort, from analysing such explicit symbolic writing.

Second, we noticed that Mrs Ramsay struggles to maintain a limited, orderly human life around herself which she calls 'civilization'. This is contrasted with the 'fluidity' of nature outside. Mrs Ramsay views natural forces as chaotic, and sees them as the enemy in her struggle to protect 'order and dry land'. She imagines the Ramsay family and their guests at dinner making 'common cause against that fluidity out there' (*To the Lighthouse*, p. 90). We can expect, therefore, to study a conflict between nature and human society, and the characters' struggles in this conflict.

Third, in Chapters 2 and 4 we found that the underlying or subconscious thoughts in Bernard's mind were expressed using imagery of nature. Remembering his childhood, he comments on bees, twigs, flowers in the garden: 'How rhythmical, and half conscious and like something wrapped in mist it was; but to me hateful' (*The Waves*, p. 179). In adulthood Bernard describes his subconscious ('deep down below' his everyday surface life, which is a 'lie') as 'a rushing stream of broken dreams', and its visions are of 'bird, fish or cloud' (p. 171). Woolf regularly uses natural imagery to describe the shadowy subconscious areas of the mind, then. There is a very clear example in *Mrs Dalloway*, which confirms that Woolf consistently connects the subconscious and nature-imagery. The conflict between Clarissa's natural but unconscious emotions, and her conscious wish to control her life, is powerfully evoked. Her subconscious is represented as a primitive jungle with a wild beast stirring:

> It rasped her, though, to have stirring about in her this brutal monster! to hear twigs cracking and feel hooves planted down in the depths of that leaf-encumbered forest, the soul; never to be content quite, or quite secure, for at any moment the brute would be stirring, this hatred, which, especially since her illness, . . . made all pleasure in beauty, in friendship, in being well, in being loved and making her home delightful rock, quiver and bend as if indeed there were a monster grubbing at the roots . . .
>
> (*Mrs Dalloway*, p. 9)

There is clearly a struggle within Clarissa between her surface, conscious existence, and her repressed subconscious urges, which are expressed using a metaphor of nature. These examples show that Woolf sees the conflict between civilization and nature in two ways: first, between an orderly sanctuary and the wildness outside (see Mrs Ramsay's dining-room); secondly, between the conscious mind and the wild, natural subconscious, within a character. Our investigation of nature in this chapter begins, then, with the knowledge that Woolf portrays a struggle where human civilization, human aims and ideals struggle against nature both in the world and within individuals.

*   *   *

Our first extract is from *Mrs Dalloway*. Clarissa's party is in full swing, and Lady Bradshaw has just mentioned Septimus's suicide. Clarissa walks away from her guests into a side room:

Then (she had felt it only this morning) there was the terror; the overwhelming incapacity, one's parents giving it into one's hands, this life, to be lived to the end, to be walked with serenely; there was in the depths of her heart an awful fear. Even now, quite often if Richard had not been there reading the *Times*, so that she could crouch like a bird and gradually revive, send roaring up that immeasurable delight, rubbing stick to stick, one thing with another, she must have perished. She had escaped. But that young man had killed himself.

Somehow it was her disaster – her disgrace. It was her punishment to see sink and disappear here a man, there a woman, in this profound darkness, and she forced to stand here in her evening dress. She had schemed; she had pilfered. She was never wholly admirable. She had wanted success, – Lady Bexborough and the rest of it. And once she had walked on the terrace at Bourton.

Odd, incredible; she had never been so happy. Nothing could be slow enough; nothing last too long. No pleasure could equal, she thought, straightening the chairs, pushing in one book on the shelf, this having done with the triumphs of youth, lost herself in the process of living, to find it, with a shock of delight, as the sun rose, as the day sank. Many a time had she gone, at Bourton when they were all talking, to look at the sky; or seen it between people's shoulders at dinner; seen it in London when she could not sleep. She walked to the window.

It held, foolish as the idea was, something of her own in it, this country sky, this sky above Westminster. She parted the curtains; she looked. Oh, but how surprising! – in the room opposite the old lady stared straight at her! She was going to bed. And the sky. It will be a solemn sky, she had thought, it will be a dusky sky, turning away its cheek in beauty. But there it was – ashen, pale, raced over quickly by tapering vast clouds. It was new to her. The wind must have risen. She was going to bed, in the room opposite. It was fascinating to watch her, moving about, that old lady, crossing the room, coming to the window. Could she see her? It was fascinating, with people still laughing and shouting in the drawing-room, to watch that old woman, quite quietly, going to bed alone. She pulled the blind now. The clock began striking. The young man had killed himself; but she did not pity him; with the clock striking the hour, one, two, three, she did not pity him, with all this going on. There! the old lady had put out her light! the whole house was dark now with this going on, she repeated, and the words came to her, Fear no more the heat of the sun. She must go back to them. But what an extraordinary night! She felt somehow very like him – the young man who had killed himself. She felt glad that he had done it; thrown it away while they went on living. The clock was striking. The leaden circles dissolved in the air. But she must go back. She must assemble. She must find Sally and Peter. And she came in from the little room.

(Mrs Dalloway, pp. 164–5)

Begin by looking at the longest sentences. The first two sentences are forty-six and forty-two words long, respectively. Clarissa had felt something 'only this morning' which is defined three times in the first sentence, as 'the terror', 'the overwhelming incapacity' and 'an awful fear'. This feeling relates to 'life' and the very fact of being born brings it on ('one's parents giving it into one's hands, this life'). The sentence is built from short phrases including the sudden reminiscence in brackets, and each short phrase expresses a thought related to the 'awful fear' she is describing. Notice that the sentence is heavy with 'fear', 'terror', 'incapacity', 'until the end' (i.e. death), so that the word 'serenely' is in utter contrast to the rest. 'Serenely' is ambiguous. We know that Clarissa tries, consciously, to walk through life 'serenely' (like, for example, Lady Bexborough); so the word arrives as her conscious determination fighting back against the overwhelmingly negative feeling she expresses. On the other hand, in the context of the sentence, 'serenely' is so out of place that it implies an extra burden: living is hard enough, but to top it all you have to do it 'serenely' as well!

The second sentence re-states the power of these negative feelings. The main clause ('Even now . . . she must have perished') encloses a long interjection describing the security Richard gives her by being conventional (he is 'there reading the *Times*'). The struggle, then, is between the establishment represented by Richard reading *The Times* and her social duty expressed in 'serenely'; and the 'awful fear' inspired by birth, life and death. In other words, nature inspires a fear so great that it leads to despair and suicide unless Clarissa can keep it away by filling her life with the security of the establishment, and superficial social duties.

This conflict is developed in the next paragraph. Clarissa's social duty has now become both an unwelcome burden: 'she forced to stand here in her evening dress'; and something that morally disgusts her: 'She had schemed; she had pilfered. She was never wholly admirable.' Nature is still presented as the fear of death ('to see sink and disappear here a man, there a woman, in this profound darkness'); yet it now also includes Clarissa's moment of bliss: 'she had walked on the terrace at Bourton'.

The other long sentence of this extract, in the third paragraph, again encloses the artificial detail of Clarissa's life within a natural feeling; but this time the natural experience is her intense pleasure on the terrace at Bourton. 'No pleasure could equal', she thinks at the start; and at the end it is 'a shock of delight, as the sun rose, as the day sank'. In between, Clarissa straightens a chair and some books, and thinks of being lost in 'the process of living'.

So far, we have taken the basic boundaries of life – birth and death – to be representative of 'nature' in this extract; and we find them in conflict with the artifice of civilisation. In two of the sentences, this conflict is structurally expressed, as nature surrounds civilisation. However, the sentence we have just looked at introduces a further paradoxical truth. When Clarissa thinks of 'losing herself in the process' she does this 'to find it', 'it' being the sudden delight she felt at Bourton. So the relationship is not a straightforward conflict. Somehow, Clarissa feels that immersing herself in day-to-day trivia (she straightens a chair, for example) is a way to experience sudden delight in nature. She elaborates this idea by remembering that she used to choose a time 'when they were all talking' to go and look at the sky. So, now, it is at the height of her elaborate party that she walks to the window to look out.

In the final paragraph of the extract, nature figures as the sky Clarissa sees. Before seeing it, Clarissa thinks it 'held . . . something of her own in it'. However, she feels a double shock when she parts the curtains. First, the old lady opposite appears to be looking straight at her. Secondly, the sky is not as she had imagined. She expected 'a dusky sky, turning away its cheek in beauty'; but instead she sees it 'ashen, pale, raced over quickly by tapering vast clouds. It was new to her.' 'Ashen, pale' has overtones of death, reminding us of Septimus's death which prompted Clarissa to go aside into this little room. In contrast to the seductive, feminine sky Clarissa imagined, the description 'Tapering vast clouds' and the fact 'The wind must have risen' are uncompromising. The old woman's actions are also plain and truthful. Woolf presents them in bald, short sentences that seem to lead Clarissa's mind back to the bald fact about Septimus: 'going to bed alone. She pulled the blind now. The clock began striking. The young man had killed himself.'

How does this develop our understanding of nature and civilisation, then? The contrast between Clarissa's party, and the view outside the window, is emphasised throughout the paragraph. Clarissa finds it 'fascinating, with people still laughing and shouting in the drawing-room, to watch that old woman'; and as her thoughts about Septimus develop, she repeats the phrases 'with all this going on', 'she did not pity him', and mentions the clock striking, like a chant. It is as if her position, standing at the window, symbolically between the bubble of social life behind her and the uncompromising view of nature and truth outside, allows her to exist at the focal point of the contrast. Virginia Woolf builds a repetitive chant of Clarissa's thoughts as she stands there; and the upshot is a single, unexpected, new thought: 'and the words came to her, Fear no more the heat of the sun.'

This process may remind us of Mrs Ramsay being lulled into a trance-like state by the repetitive 'strokes' of the Lighthouse and her repetitive action, knitting. In her trance, she suddenly thought, 'We are in the hands of the Lord' and was immediately angry with herself for having thought it (see Chapter 2). Clarissa is in a similar situation: she thinks repetitively of the clock, the party, and her lack of pity for Septimus. Her position between two great conflicting forces induces her mind to circle, or swing, in this way. While she is in this state the unexpected thought surfaces. The words themselves are a quotation from Shakespeare's *Cymbeline*, from a funeral song that celebrates death as relief and release from life, and stresses death's inevitability:

Golden lads and girls all must,
As chimney-sweepers, come to dust.

(Shakespeare, *Cymbeline*, IV, ii. 262–3)

For the remainder of the paragraph, Clarissa continues to be pulled in the two directions. 'She must go back' to the party; 'but what an extraordinary night!', 'But she must go back', although 'the leaden circles [of the clock striking] dissolved in the air'. In this state, she feels 'somehow very like him' and 'glad' that Septimus committed suicide, that he 'had done it; had thrown it away'; and she returns to the party because 'she must assemble'.

'Assemble' suggests putting herself back together, as if her journey to the window had partly dismantled her social self 'forced to stand here in her evening dress', and there is now a need to put her outer shell back on. To sum up, there is a powerful attraction towards the outside, which is full of implications of darkness and death; but there is an insistent duty ('She must') towards her social life and the party. There is more than an implication in all this that Clarissa makes use of Septimus's suicide in place of her own: that she could have jumped through her window, but she is 'glad' that he has already 'done it' for her. His suicide enables her to feel like him without actually jumping; so her duty can win, she can 'assemble' and return to her ordinary life.

It is not possible to describe in full how Virginia Woolf has achieved these effects. However, we can notice the contrast between romanticised imagery (the 'dusky' sky 'turning away its cheek in beauty', for example) and bald statements, which conveys the shock of the actual sky; and the use of several repeated phrases to build a growing sense of Clarissa's swinging thoughts. Notice also the subtle implications conveyed by modulations of Clarissa's tone. For example, we become aware that she is socially distancing herself from Septimus, when she thinks of him as 'the young man'; and that she does not wish to define her feelings when she thinks the old lady 'fascinating' or the night 'extraordinary', in her thoughtless luncheon-party vocabulary.

Analysing this extract has taught us a great deal about Clarissa's feelings, but how has our understanding of nature progressed? In this extract, the struggle between nature and civilisation has become a more complicated issue because a paradox is introduced, suggesting that it is more than a battle that one side wins or loses. The interaction of the two within a character brings significant experience: within an individual, the conflict produces something else, a potential insight into the whole question of living. Clarissa's realisation of this insight is incomplete. She feels 'like' Septimus; but her duty reassembles her and she returns to the party. The night is 'extraordinary', but she has experienced the shock of an 'ashen' sky, which dashed her romantic illusions of nature, without quite realising its effect. None the less, a potentially higher, more all-embracing vision of life appeared for a moment out of the interplay of civilisation's demands, and her response to the sky. The suggestion is that understanding the conflict itself may release a further vision of the shape of things, that has some higher significance, unlike nature on its own, which is merely formless, and leads only to death.

*   *   *

Our extract from *To the Lighthouse* is drawn from the descriptive Part II, 'Time Passes'. This section of the book describes the gradual decay of the Ramsays' holiday home on Skye, over several years of neglect. Eventually, the cleaning-lady Mrs McNab is asked to make the house ready for occupation again. Our extract describes the house's most neglected days:

> What power could now prevent the fertility, the insensibility of nature? Mrs McNab's dream of a lady, of a child, of a plate of milk soup? It had wavered over the walls like a spot of sunlight and vanished. She had locked the door; she had gone. It was beyond the strength of one woman, she said. They never sent. They never wrote. There were things up there rotting in the drawers – it was a shame to leave them so, she said. The place was gone to rack and ruin. Only the Lighthouse beam entered the rooms for a moment, sent its sudden stare over bed and wall in the darkness of winter, looked with equanimity at the thistle and the swallow, the rat and the straw. Nothing now withstood them; nothing said no to them. Let the wind blow; let the poppy seed itself and the carnation mate with the cabbage. Let the

swallow build in the drawing-room, and the thistle thrust aside the tiles, and the butterfly sun itself on the faded chintz of the armchairs. Let the broken glass and the china lie out on the lawn and be tangled over with grass and wild berries.

For now had come that moment, that hesitation when dawn trembles and night pauses, when if a feather alight in the scale it will be weighed down. One feather, and the house, sinking, falling, would have turned and pitched downwards to the depths of darkness. In the ruined room, picnickers would have lit their kettles; lovers sought shelter there, lying on the bare boards; and the shepherd stored his dinner on the bricks, and the tramp slept with his coat round him to ward off the cold. Then the roof would have fallen; briars and hemlocks would have blotted out path, step, and window; would have grown, unequally but lustily over the mound, until some trespasser, losing his way, could have told only by a red-hot poker among the nettles, or a scrap of china in the hemlock, that here once someone had lived; there had been a house.

If the feather had fallen, if it had tipped the scale downwards, the whole house would have plunged to the depths to lie upon the sands of oblivion. But there was a force working; something not highly conscious; something that leered, something that lurched; something not inspired to go about its work with dignified ritual or solemn chanting. Mrs McNab groaned; Mrs Bast creaked. They were old; they were stiff; their legs ached. They came with their brooms and pails at last; they got to work. All of a sudden, would Mrs McNab see that the house was ready one of the young ladies wrote: would she get this done; would she get that done; all in a hurry. They might be coming for the summer; had left everything to the last; expected to find things as they had left them. Slowly and painfully, with broom and pail, mopping, scouring, Mrs McNab, Mrs Bast stayed the corruption and the rot; rescued from the pool of Time that was fast closing over them now a basin, now a cupboard; fetched up from oblivion all the Waverley novels and a tea-set one morning; in the afternoon restored to sun and air a brass fender and a set of steel fire-irons. George, Mrs Bast's son, caught the rats, cut the grass. They had the builders. Attended with the creaking of hinges and the screeching of bolts, the slamming and banging of damp-swollen woodwork, some rusty laborious birth seemed to be taking place, as the women, stooping, rising, groaning, singing, slapped and slammed, upstairs now, now down in the cellars. Oh, they said, the work!

(*To the Lighthouse*, pp. 132–3)

We can make use of our previous knowledge to set this extract in context. Remember that the house was a haven of 'order' and 'dry land' struggling against the 'fluidity out there', during the dinner scene. We are used to Mrs Ramsay's idea that the house represents order and civilisation in contrast to the wild darkness of 'outside' and the sea. So, this extract is typical of the nature-theme as we have found it before: there is a struggle between the house, a now-deserted haven of civilisation, and nature, which threatens to over-whelm it.

Now we can begin to study the passage itself. There is liberal use of metaphor, and the writing is dense with incidental details of animals, birds, plants, furniture and housewares. Also, the style is as rich and fast-changing as we have come to expect from Virginia Woolf. Despite this richness, we have a good idea of the meaning from a first reading: an old house is decaying, until the cleaning-ladies are sent in to rescue it. We should confirm this, however: it is important to ensure a precise understanding of the meaning to begin with. This can be obtained by breaking the passage down into sections, and writing a brief sentence summarising the content of each section.

The first section, which asks and answers a question and continues in Mrs McNab's indirect speech, lasts as far as 'to rack and ruin'. The second section completes that paragraph. The second paragraph, beginning 'For now had come that moment', begins a new idea which continues through the second paragraph and as far into the third paragraph as 'sands of oblivion', where Woolf imagines nature's complete victory. 'But' begins a new movement, because the feather which, 'if' it fell, would have sunk the house, did not fall, and the rescuing force is described as far as 'solemn chanting'. The final section of the passage, beginning 'Mrs McNab groaned', describes the work of restoring the house. We have divided the extract into five sections, then. Here are five short sentences, briefly summarising each section:

1. What power can prevent nature from taking over (not Mrs McNab, who gave up because it was too much work)?

2. Nothing now prevents nature's takeover: let nature overwhelm the house.
3. A moment comes when the tiniest additional push from nature would obliterate the house.
4. But a primitive, half-conscious power begins to work against nature.
5. Miss Ramsay writes asking Mrs McNab to reopen the house, so she and several other local people work hard to make it habitable again.

Reading these five sentences makes the meaning of the extract appear straightforward. Indeed, the overall 'shape' of the extract leaps out at us in the form of a question and answer:

Q. What power will prevent nature's takeover?
A. A primitive, half-conscious power does.

So far, our work on this extract has reduced it to its barest essential content; but this final, shortest question-and-answer form highlights the unexpectedness of Virginia Woolf's statement. We expected to find a struggle between civilisation and nature. Instead, there is a struggle between nature and something 'not highly conscious; something that leered, something that lurched' – a primitive force quite the opposite of what we expect from 'civilisation'. The elaborate story is convincing, with its rich detail of rats, chintz, china, thistles, cupboards and Waverley novels: we easily understand how decay and cleaning-ladies struggle against each other in an old house; but our summaries have highlighted the surprising point we might otherwise have missed.

Now we want to work out what Virginia Woolf means: why is the force of civilisation described as so primitive? We need fuller understanding of the extract before we can answer this question. Our next task, then, is to analyse both of the opposed forces, nature and civilisation, in detail.

First, nature appears as 'thistle', 'swallow', 'rat', 'straw'; 'wind', 'poppy', 'carnation', 'cabbage', 'butterfly' and things 'tangled over with grass and wild berries'. The next stage of nature's attack includes 'briars and hemlocks', 'a red-hot poker among the nettles'. When Mrs McNab and the others begin work, they fight 'the corruption and rot', 'rats', 'grass' and 'damp'. Such a list of the natural things mentioned confirms that there is considerable detail; but their actions are also revealing. These natural things 'blow', 'seed', 'mate', 'build', 'thrust aside'; then the butterfly will 'sun itself' and grass 'tangle over' things. Plants would have 'blotted out' parts of the house and garden, and 'grown . . . lustily'. All of these denote energetic, positive actions: the writing conveys nature as powerful, fertile and busy. After Mrs McNab begins work, by contrast, nature becomes the object of actions: the rot was 'stayed', rats were 'caught' and the grass 'cut'. In the final section, then, nature becomes passive and the energetic verbs 'stooping, rising, groaning, singing, slapped and slammed' belong to people. So the crucial moment when the balance tipped towards people is built into Woolf's writing as a moment of change when the constructions suddenly turn the other way around. This moment is like a fulcrum: afterwards, everything swings the other way.

The details of nature – rats, grass and so on – contribute to a single overall force which is described several times. First, there is 'the fertility, the insensibility of nature'; then we read of the house 'sinking' into 'the depths of darkness'; next we read of a house that 'plunged to the depths to lie upon the sands of oblivion'. People rescued the house 'from the pool of Time that was fast closing over them' and 'from oblivion'. These descriptions build one continuous metaphor: nature is a sea, and if you sink into it there is darkness and oblivion. At the start, there are also 'fertility' and 'insensibility', which suggest a mindless, blind force, darkly unaware of anything other than its procreative drive. If we think back to the imagery we have previously studied, it is clear that nature is described in terms associated with the unconscious.

This insight adds to our understanding of Clarissa Dalloway: it is clear that her movement away from her 'civilised' party and towards the window was also a move towards the darkness of the unconscious; so the emergence of her unwanted thought 'Fear no more the heat of the sun' is a natural outcome of this move, in the scheme of things presented by Virginia Woolf.

Now we can examine the opposing force, which we have continued to call 'civilisation', for want of a better word. At the start of the extract, 'Mrs McNab's dream of a lady, of a child, of a plate of milk soup' (which is a sentimental memory of Mrs Ramsay) is ineffective, since it only 'wavered' and then 'vanished'. Mrs McNab's idea is treated as silly, and 'dream' implies that it was never real, anyway.

The real force that tips the balance against nature is described as 'something not highly conscious', 'something that leered, something that lurched'; and Woolf carefully specifies that it has nothing to do with civilised rituals: 'something not inspired to go about its work with dignified ritual or solemn chanting'. Apart from the word 'leered', which implies a sexual lust, this description of the rescuing force is borne out and elaborated in the remainder of the extract: the cleaners work 'slowly and painfully', 'stooping' and 'groaning'; noises include 'creaking', 'screeching', 'slamming' and 'banging'. The change they bring about is a 'rusty laborious birth'. All of these words emphasise rough work and coarseness, and are appropriate to the characters Mrs McNab and Mrs Bast.

But Mrs McNab alone does not explain Virginia Woolf's idea of 'a force working'. The force is clearly associated with basic and primitive aspects of humanity, including the sex drive in 'leered'. Woolf seems to be saying that all 'high' civilisation, including social forms ('dignified ritual') and religious ceremonies ('solemn chanting'), rests and depends upon coarse work and primitive human drives. So, all the highest achievements of civilisation – the monuments, books, operas, Mr Ramsay's philosophy and so on – are reduced to this: they are produced by something 'not highly conscious' which 'leers' and fights coarsely to preserve itself against the oblivion of nature. This appears to be Virginia Woolf's message, and it is in harmony with the general tenets of Freudian theory, which sees even the highest of human endeavours as driven by primitive drives such as sex and power.

This surprising message provokes us to an ironic conclusion. The struggle only superficially appears to involve the artifice of 'civilisation'. Essentially, it is between non-human nature, and the basic nature of humanity; and it is a classic struggle for survival between these two 'natural' enemies.

Before leaving this extract, there is one amusing subtlety to remark upon. In the third paragraph there is indirect quotation from Cam's letter to Mrs McNab. The Ramsays 'expected to find things as they had left them'. In the context of the surrounding descriptions of time and decay, this casual phrase shows a monumental ignorance of nature, and provides a passing critique of social class. We realise that the coarse Mrs McNab has to battle against nature; while middle-class Cam, in her clean and comfortable surroundings, is utterly unaware of the work that sustains her. This is a light, ironic touch from Virginia Woolf, similar to the ease with which Mrs Ramsay 'triumphs' in the *Boeuf en Daube* which was cooked by the servants (see pp. 76 , 93–4).

This extract has given us an insight beneath the superficial appearance of a struggle between nature and some kind of artificial 'civilisation'. The apparent orderliness of human society is revealed to be merely a superstructure dependent upon primitive human drives for sex and power: drives which 'leer' and 'lurch' and are 'not highly conscious'. The struggle, then, is finally between two kinds of nature: human nature which fights for its own survival and builds its own havens of order, to protect itself; and the 'insensibility' of external nature – a mindless, negative force that brings a catastrophic flood of darkness and death.

*   *   *

We now turn to *The Waves*. The following passage is the final symbolic interlude:

> *Now the sun had sunk. Sky and sea were indistinguishable. The waves breaking spread their white fans far out over the shore, sent white shadows into the recesses of sonorous caves and then rolled back sighing over the shingle.*
>
> *The tree shook its branches and a scattering of leaves fell to the ground. There they settled with perfect composure on the precise spot where they would await dissolution. Black and grey were shot into the garden from the broken vessel that had once held red light. Dark shadows blackened*

the tunnels between the stalks. The thrush was silent and the worm sucked itself back into its narrow hole. Now and again a whitened and hollow straw was blown from an old nest and fell into the dark grasses among the rotten apples. The light had faded from the tool-house wall and the adder's skin hung from the nail empty. All the colours in the room had overflown their banks. The precise brush stroke was swollen and lop-sided; cupboards and chairs melted their brown masses into one huge obscurity. The height from floor to ceiling was hung with vast curtains of shaking darkness. The looking-glass was pale as the mouth of a cave shadowed by hanging creepers.

The substance had gone from the solidity of the hills. Travelling lights drove a plumy wedge among unseen and sunken roads, but no lights opened among the folded wings of the hills, and there was no sound save the cry of a bird seeking some lonelier tree. At the cliff's edge there was an equal murmur of air that had been brushed through forests, of water that had been cooled in a thousand glassy hollows of mid-ocean.

As if there were waves of darkness in the air, darkness moved on, covering houses, hills, trees, as waves of water wash round the sides of some sunken ship. Darkness washed down streets, eddying round single figures, engulfing them; blotting out couples clasped under the showery darkness of elm trees in full summer foliage. Darkness rolled its waves along grassy rides and over the wrinkled skin of the turf, enveloping the solitary thorn tree and the empty snail shells at its foot. Mounting higher, darkness blew along the bare upland slopes, and met the fretted and abraded pinnacles of the mountain where the snow lodges for ever on the hard rock even when the valleys are full of running streams and yellow vine leaves, and girls, sitting on verandahs, look up at the snow, shading their faces with their fans. Them, too, darkness covered.

(*The Waves*, pp. 157–8)

As with *To The Lighthouse*, the overall sense of this extract is plain: as night comes, darkness covers everything. However, it is worthwhile to follow the same method we employed before, to obtain a precise summary of the content. First, then, what sections can we find in this extract?

The first paragraph describes sea and shore. Then, in the second paragraph, we move on to land and the garden is described, as far as 'among the rotten apples'; and the second half of the paragraph, beginning 'The light had faded from the tool-house wall', describes the house. The third paragraph is a further section, focusing on the country around the house including the 'cliff's edge' and the 'hills'. In the fourth and last paragraph the author's viewpoint moves on, rolling over the world with the darkness; and description includes towns, countryside, and the highest mountain peaks as the darkness is 'mounting higher'. The extract can be divided into five sections, then. Here are five sentences, each attempting to summarise a section:

1. It is so dark that sky and sea cannot be told apart.
2. Blackness is added to darkness all over the garden, where things rot and creatures retreat.
3. In the house, everything melts together into one 'huge obscurity'.
4. The surrounding country is largely dark and silent, land and sea air meet and mingle at the cliff's edge.
5. The darkness from the sea pushes forward, covering everything including civilisation, people, and the highest mountains.

These summaries help us by adding some detail to our first impression. They show that the author's eye is moving, from sea, to garden, house, land, world, throughout the extract; and that there is a moment of balance on the 'cliff's edge', before the waves of darkness roll forward to engulf everything. Our next task is to analyse each of the sections in closer detail.

In addition to the sky and sea becoming indistinguishable, the first section mentions 'white fans' of breaking waves, and 'sonorous caves'. The waves are personified, rolling back 'sighing'.

In the second section we find powerful use of imagery and language. We find 'scattering', 'dissolution', 'broken', 'blackened', 'whitened', 'hollow' and 'rotten' in the space of these few lines. This creates a strong impression of loss, decay and destruction. 'Blackened' and 'whitened' also remove all colours from the scene. The imagery is equally negative. The sun is a 'broken vessel', a development of the idea in the previous symbolic interlude, where 'the hard stone of the day was cracked and light poured through its splinters' (p. 138). The 'cracked' sun has become 'broken', then, and where earlier 'red and gold shot through the waves' (p. 138), now

'Black and grey were shot into the garden'. The image is shocking both because it describes sunlight as 'black', which contradicts reason, and because of the contrast with the previous interlude. The next sentence repeats this idea with shadows which 'blackened', suggesting that darkness exists as a concrete physical thing, not merely an absence of light. A negative attitude is ascribed to natural creatures and objects, also. Woolf's leaves express their passive fatalism as they, in 'perfect composure . . . await dissolution'; and the worm 'sucked itself back into its narrow hole'. All the features of this section, then, emphasise destruction, nature's submission to the coming night; and the startling solidity of the dark.

The third section focuses on shapes and colours. The description is of objects becoming indistinct as the daylight fades, but Virginia Woolf again chooses words which convey movement and action by both the darkness and objects in the house: colours 'overflowed', objects are 'swollen' and things 'melted their brown masses'; darkness is 'shaking' like a curtain. The juxtaposition of 'huge' (enormous and solid) and 'obscurity' (unseeable, lightless) expresses the odd effect Woolf achieves by treating darkness, an absence of light, as solidly physical. At the end of this section, as in the first, a cave is mentioned.

The two sections we have just examined progressively build our impression that darkness has a substantial physical presence. The fourth section enhances this effect by the contrasting use of softer, less definite language to describe the land. 'The substance had gone from the solidity of the hills', it begins; and continues to 'the folded wings of the hills' (like feathers, or the insubstantiality of an insect's wing) and the vague 'some lonelier tree' that may not exist. So, as the darkness becomes substantial, the world it covers is deprived of its solidity. The effect is that the world is not merely disappearing from sight, but is actually ceasing to exist.

The author has prepared us for an image of darkness as substantial. At the start of the final paragraph she uses a simile to give darkness the solidity of 'waves of darkness in the air'. The land is compared to a 'sunken ship' and the darkness now has active verbs: it 'moved on', 'wash[ed] round the sides', 'washed down', 'eddying', 'engulfing', 'blotting out'; it 'rolled its waves', 'enveloping', and 'mounting', it 'blew' and 'met', and finally 'Them, too, it covered'. Darkness is described as waves of liquid, then, throughout this paragraph. The simile of the first sentence is exploited as often as possible to intensify our sense of night's tangible substance.

There is an obvious conclusion about nature to be drawn from study of this extract: it is inevitable that everything, both human and natural, will be obliterated by a 'darkness' symbolic of destruction and death. In this extract we also see an unequal struggle. On the one side, worms, birds, people, hills, streets, and so on – all the details of life on land – are victims. On the other side, much larger forces and much greater distances are invoked to convey Woolf's idea of 'darkness': the broken sun and the distant ocean. These forces are described as so great that they easily overwhelm the land-based nature in their path. So, we can conclude that all nature is inevitably overwhelmed by 'waves', the unavoidable cycles of death which 'rolled [their] waves' over everything. The struggle is ironic because it is ultimately between two aspects of nature itself, as we have found in our analysis of other extracts in this chapter.

A further conclusion is derived from our analysis of the language. We noticed that the darkness is portrayed as becoming increasingly solid as everyday objects cease to exist distinctly, being deprived of 'substance' and 'solidity'. It is reasonable to suppose that the author wants to convey the feeling of increasing age. She seems to suggest that, as we pass through the evening of our lives, things that were once important to us become less substantial; and we are more and more aware that we face a huge, indifferent natural force: death. To confirm this insight, we can look for related ideas elsewhere in the text. In Bernard's final section, where he reminisces as an old man, we could logically expect to find such confirmation. Turning to page 198, we find:

> My book, stuffed with phrases, has dropped to the floor. It lies under the table, to be swept up by the charwoman when she comes wearily at dawn looking for scraps of paper, old tram tickets, and here and there a note screwed into a ball and left with the litter to be swept up. What is the phrase for the moon? And the phrase for love? By what name are we to call death? I do not know . . . When the storm crosses the marsh and sweeps over me where I lie in the ditch unregarded I

need no words. Nothing neat. Nothing that comes down with all its
feet on the floor. None of those resonances and lovely echoes that
break and chime from nerve to nerve in our breasts, making wild
music, false phrases. I have done with phrases.

(*The Waves*, p. 198)

Here, Bernard discards his 'phrases' and his notebook, which have
been of great importance to him throughout his life. They seem less
meaningful now that he is old. Language has lost its attraction and
significance. By contrast, the massive power of nature, 'When the
storm crosses the marsh and sweeps over me' (also described on p.
159, when Bernard refers to the storm's 'confusion, the height, the
indifference and the fury'), is real and overwhelming to him.

On the next page, in the final paragraph of the novel, Bernard
clarifies this change of perception in old age: 'What enemy do we
now perceive advancing against us . . . ? It is death. Death is the
enemy' (*The Waves*, p.199). These references to the final section of
the book confirm our interpretation, then. In our extract Virginia
Woolf uses language and imagery to convey the solidity of death and
the lack of substance in anything else, which is perceived and
expressed by Bernard as an old man.

Our ideas have become clearer and firmer, then, by referring to
another part of the text for confirmation. In the same way, we
should relate this symbolic interlude to others in the series, hoping
to add precision and sureness to our conclusions about nature.

We interpret the waves as symbolic of death. They represent a
repetitive force, so they suggest that death comes again and again, at
intervals, inevitably. If we look back to the first symbolic description, we find that Virginia Woolf has evoked the perceptions of different stages of life throughout her novel. As the sun rises, 'The
surface of the sea slowly became transparent and lay rippling and
sparkling until the dark stripes were almost rubbed out' (*The Waves*,
p. 1). We have already found that the waves of death become solid
and obliterate everything else, in old age. Here, in childhood, the
hopeful 'sparkling' of new life almost obliterates the waves. In other
words, the child hardly perceives death, being dazzled by the excitement of new life. Next, as the children make ready to leave for

school, the waves can be heard in the distance falling 'with muffled thuds' (*The Waves*, p. 16): death is still not a part of the children's lives; but it is a constant 'muffled' background presence to them. We could follow the descriptions all through the novel in this way, using them to provide a key to the characters' attitudes to existence, at that point in their lives.

We already noticed that the image of the sun as a 'broken' stone developed the preceding image of the sun as 'cracked' and leaking its colour. It is rewarding to trace all the elements of these descriptions through the book, as in each case the development of the describer's perceptions, from interlude to interlude, provides a significant story which expresses some aspect of the six characters' lives.

Conclusions

Our analyses have highlighted how nature is presented as engaged in an eternal struggle. At first it appeared to be a fight between nature and 'civilisation'; but more and more we have come to realise that Woolf presents this struggle as being between different aspects of nature itself. In *Mrs Dalloway*, Clarissa's repression of her unconscious needs sets her in conflict against nature, and she expends her energy sustaining an artificial social persona, struggling against the vastness of nature as seen in the night sky. We can look at this from another angle, and say that she defends what she has made of her life, against negatives – the old lady's futile loneliness, and death. In *To the Lighthouse*, the emphasis is on the mindlessness of natural growth and destruction, set against some primitive human instinct which struggles to survive. In *The Waves*, there are clear battle-lines drawn between all things that struggle to live for a time, and those constant and huge powers (the ocean, death, a storm, the turning of the earth around the sun) that will always be victorious over the small, individual life.

The three presentations of nature's destructive force have elements in common. In *Mrs Dalloway* the sky was indifferent to her wishes. She found it 'ashen' and 'pale' with a shock, because it paid no heed to her dreams. In *To the Lighthouse* the forces attacking the house are described as threatening 'the depths of darkness' and 'the sands of oblivion' and as 'insensibility', a mindless state of unconsciousness. In *The Waves*, Bernard describes the storm as having 'indifference' and night brings 'one huge obscurity'. Bernard explains that words are no longer meaningful in the face of death, and remarks 'I need a howl; a cry' (*The Waves*, p. 198). All three novels, then, present this aspect of nature as dark, insensible, and without thoughts or words. We can therefore conclude that Woolf shows one side of nature as a principle of mindless negativity, associated with chaos and unconsciousness.

Individual creatures – whether human, bird, animal or plant – pursue an opposite principle. They use any means available to them to survive. Clarissa, for example, uses her vicarious experience of Septimus's suicide to stave off her own despair, fighting for the strength to return to her party. In *To the Lighthouse*, the cleaners' groaning and lurching is not admirable, nor is the something that 'leers': but there is an extreme struggle for survival. In *The Waves*, we find the worm that 'sucked itself back into its narrow hole' and a bird that is 'seeking some lonelier tree', all retreating from the enemy darkness, hiding and hoping to survive. This side of nature is shown pursuing its own life, controlling its environment (see, for example, the birds hunting at midday in *The Waves*, or look back at Mrs Ramsay's dinner-party in *To the Lighthouse*), creating deliberate form and striving to better its own lot. In the first two novels, this principle in nature is largely embodied in the characters; but in *The Waves*, the characters and other small creatures seem to fight together, having the common interest of the short-lived against the dark.

Nature, then, is presented in the form of two opposed principles that struggle eternally against each other. We have built up a certain amount of detail about them during our analyses. To simplify these two ideas, we could see them as the creative and destructive aspects of nature; or as the temporary and the constant in nature. They are engaged in a permanent struggle – who wins? The answer, as we might expect, is a paradox: both do.

We have found a great deal in Virginia Woolf's writing that emphasises the enormous power of destructive nature; and much of her writing is devoted to conveying the 'huge obscurity' of death. It is necessary to redress this balance, however – for there are passages that evoke something more optimistic. Woolf certainly emphasises death and the end for her characters, but the shape of her own idea leads into some guarded optimism. Here is part of the final page of *The Waves*:

> Again I see before me the usual street. The canopy of civilization is burnt out. The sky is dark as polished whalebone. But there is a kindling in the sky whether of lamplight or of dawn. There is a stir of some sort – sparrows on plane trees somewhere chirping. There is a sense of the break of day. I will not call it dawn. What is dawn in the city to an elderly man standing in the street looking up rather dizzily at the sky? Dawn is some sort of whitening of the sky; some sort of renewal. Another day; another Friday; another twentieth of March, January, or September. Another general awakening. The stars draw back and are extinguished. The bars deepen themselves between the waves. The film of mist thickens on the fields. A redness gathers on the roses, even on the pale rose that hangs by the bedroom window. A bird chirps. Cottagers light their early candles. Yes, this is the eternal renewal, the incessant rise and fall and fall and rise again.
>
> (*The Waves*, p. 199)

Bernard does not suffer from an illusion in this paragraph. Notice that he prosaically describes himself as 'an elderly man standing in the street looking up rather dizzily'; the weariness of life's routine is still present in 'another Friday; another twentieth' of this or that month; and Virginia Woolf's ambiguity has an amused irony about what he can truly perceive: 'whether of lamplight or of dawn'. However, the waves themselves have, conclusively, two movements: what goes down will come up again, and the end of the novel senses what Woolf calls the 'renewal' – presumably the cycle of birth and growth beginning, constantly, all over again.

In addition to this balanced hint of optimism, at least about life in general, we should notice that the end of *The Waves* conveys Bernard's romantic heroism in a tone of admiration: in the way that the final two sentences are written, we can almost hear the statement 'there is something marvellous about human courage, and something even more admirable when it knows how hopeless its own efforts are':

> It is death against whom I ride with my spear couched and my hair flying back like a young man's, like Percival's, when he galloped in India. I strike spurs into my horse. Against you I will fling myself, unvanquished and unyielding, O Death!
>
> (*The Waves*, p. 199)

There is still irony, because Bernard's posturing is consciously ridiculous; and the Percival character has been an ambiguous figure throughout the novel. As a bluff man of sport and action, without any subtlety of mind, he has hovered on the edge of being a figure of fun. None the less, the tone of this passage urges the reader's emotions to flow with Bernard's heroic defiance.

We will concentrate on the creative principle of nature in the next chapter, looking at the analysis of human endeavour provided in these three novels much more closely. For the present, we should remember that the creative principle is 'something not highly conscious, something that leers', not a high embattled civilisation, but Virginia Woolf's trenchant analysis of basic human motives and drives.

Methods of Analysis

In this chapter, we have made use of analytical techniques already applied in previous chapters. We have developed our technique, however, picking and choosing the method of approach that seems most likely to bring rewards, according to the nature of the extract we are working on. Focus on long sentences where they stand out, or on imagery, and the use of language, where it seems appropriate. This is natural – as your skill at analysis develops, your methods will become increasingly flexible. Two points about the approach demonstrated in this chapter are worth remembering, however.

1. With the symbolic 'interludes' from *To the Lighthouse* and *The*

Waves, we found it helpful to gain a precise understanding of the content before looking at other aspects of the extract. We worked in the following order.

- Using common sense, divide the extract into sections, or parts which seem to hang together, making the same point or sharing a single direction.
- Write down a short sentence which expresses the main statement of each section.
- Read your 'summary-sentences', and think about them to gain an understanding of the meaning and aim of the extract as a whole, or the shape of its argument.

This method helped us to realise the surprising paradox at the heart of our extract from *To the Lighthouse*, and showed us how the author's viewpoint moves, hovers, and then moves again in the extract from *The Waves*.

2. We have assumed that we can interpret nature in literature, using our sense of natural 'archetypes'. So, for example, we have assumed that night, winter and death all suggest each other, as do dawn, spring and birth. We have allowed our minds to make connections between natural things and abstract ideas, quite freely. Making use of nature in this way is part of a long literary tradition, and there seems no doubt that Virginia Woolf's use of nature in her novels provokes this kind of interpretation. For example, there is no doubt that both despair and death are symbolised by night, more or less, in all three novels; and there is strong evidence that the author intends her novels to be read interpretatively.

Suggested Work

Nature or natural things appear on most of the pages in these novels, often making a significant contribution to the meaning of the work. You may therefore choose almost any extract and examine it for yourself in the way we have done in this chapter, looking for the relevance of nature in particular. Here are three suggested extracts. You could begin your further study of nature by making a study of them.

1. In *Mrs Dalloway*, look at the intensity of Septimus's response to nature on page 18. Study from '"K . . . R" said the nursemaid' to 'the birth of a new religion'.

2. In *To the Lighthouse*, look at Chapter 10 of Part III, 'The Lighthouse', on pages 179–82. This chapter elaborates Cam's view of the island, and it is interesting to note how skilfully Woolf shows that the girl's perceptions of both the island, and her father, change during their voyage to the lighthouse.

3. In *The Waves*, the obvious place to start is with another of the symbolic interludes that appear in italics in the text. The one preceding our analysed example will provide rewarding study and many points of direct comparison: see pages 138–9, from '*The sun was sinking*' to '*gleam of pearl on the misty sand*'.

7

Life and Art

In the last chapter we established that two opposed principles struggle continuously in the world of Virginia Woolf's novels: a principle of chaos, a destructive force; and that of deliberate form or order, a creative force. We discovered that both of these principles are driven by a primitive form of energy. The destructive force is based on 'insensibility' and 'indifference': it is not conscious. It shows itself in vast elemental powers such as the sea, the sun and the waves. The creative force is also 'not highly conscious'. It originates in primitive drives for survival and procreation. Virginia Woolf seems to describe human beings and other creatures – animals, fish and birds – as sharing the 'creative' force, as a combative survival instinct.

We have met simple examples of the creative drive already. Mrs McNab 'rescued from the Pool of Time' the ordinary utensils of a house, 'now a basin, now a cupboard' (*To the Lighthouse*, p. 133). In *The Waves*, the birds built nests for their protection and the protection of their young; and in the final description, when waves of darkness roll over everything, the destruction of the birds' nests is also mentioned: 'Now and again a whitened and hollow straw was blown from an old nest and fell into the dark grasses among the rotten apples' (p. 157). Woolf associates the instinct to build and protect shown by Mrs McNab and the birds, with more sophisticated forms of human culture. For example, Mrs Ramsay imagines her dining-room, the well-cooked food and the cultured conversation of her guests as 'order and dry land' with common cause against 'that fluidity out there', the dark watery night (*To the Lighthouse*, p. 90). We know that she works hard to create this 'order'. Not only does she ensure that the food is served, she also labours to bring people into harmony. She manoeuvres Lily into charming Mr Tansley, for example; and she triumphs in the achievement of bringing Paul and Minta together. So, Woolf implies, the same simple instinct that prompts a bird to build its nest, is the motive that drives Mrs Ramsay when she builds harmony among her family and guests. She also battles against intrusions from the opposing force. We remember that she covers the boar's head, a sombre reminder of death, with her shawl. Woolf uses the progressive uncovering of this gruesome head as a measure of the destructive principle's victory over the house, in 'Time Passes'.

In this chapter, we focus on the principle we have called the 'creative' principle. We will build upon the analysis of nature in Chapter 6, so our study is not limited to three extracts. We begin by further exploring the origin of the creative principle in human nature; then we look at how it is displayed in the characters' lives. Finally we will consider 'Art' with a capital 'A', or 'vision', as Lily Briscoe calls it.

Woolf emphasises the direct connection between these different efforts of the creative principle. For example, Lily Briscoe thinks about the 'moment of friendship and liking' Mrs Ramsay created between herself and Charles Tansley as part of her effort to bring people together in harmony. Lily comments that this 'stayed in the mind almost like a work of art' (*To the Lighthouse*, p. 153) and compares it to her own work of art, her painting: 'Mrs Ramsay making of the moment something permanent (as in another sphere Lily herself tried to make of the moment something permanent)' (p. 154). We are clearly expected to treat creativity in life (Mrs Ramsay) and creative Art (Lily) as essentially the same impulse.

Origins in Human Nature

Clarissa Dalloway devotes her life to 'being Mrs Dalloway; not even Clarissa any more; this being Mrs Richard Dalloway' (*Mrs Dalloway*, p. 8). This effort makes her imitate Lady Bexborough (she wished

she had been 'dark', 'slow and stately; rather large; interested in politics like a man; with a country house; very dignified, very sincere'
like Lady Bexborough [p. 7]); and the Queen ('to blaze among candelabras . . . that night in Buckingham Palace. And Clarissa, too,
gave a party. She stiffened a little; so she would stand at the top of
her stairs' [p. 14]). Our analysis of the moment at her party when
she is caught between the pull of her social existence and the dark
sky outside the window (see Chapter 6) revealed that Clarissa feels
compelled to devote her life to 'being Mrs Dalloway': she feels
'forced to stand here in her evening dress', and describes her prepara-
tions and social activity in derogatory terms as 'schemed' and 'pilfered' (*Mrs Dalloway*, p. 164). We also know that she spends time
mending her dress; and Peter Walsh uses this as a metaphor for the
activity of her entire married life (see Chapter 5). Something
compels Clarissa to manufacture her social life and marriage, then.
What is her motive?

On page 9, Clarissa is revolted by the primitive, 'brutal monster'
she briefly senses in her own subconscious. Woolf gave a clear
answer to our present question then: 'the brute' made:

> all pleasure in beauty, in friendship, in being well, in being loved and
> making her home a delightful rock, quiver, and bend as if indeed
> there were a monster grubbing at the roots, as if the whole panoply of
> content were nothing but self love! this hatred!
>
> (*Mrs Dalloway*, p. 9)

The answer, then, is 'self love' which causes 'this hatred'. At the time,
she is thinking about why she hates Miss Kilman; but we can see the
same pattern in her relations with Peter Walsh and Richard
Dalloway. Clarissa felt fully happy only once in her life, on the
terrace at Bourton with Sally, when 'the radiance burnt through, the
revelation, the religious feeling!', and her happiness was destroyed by
Peter. Her reaction is described as 'It was like running one's face
against a granite wall in the darkness! It was shocking; it was horrible!' Clarissa does not take direct vengeance because, rationally,
'she had known all along that something would . . . embitter her
moment of happiness' and she denies that she feels horror 'for

herself' (p. 30). Yet the movements of her thoughts after she remembers that moment tell us that there is a connection between the hurt she experienced then, and the present efforts of 'the woman who was that very night to give a party; of Clarissa Dalloway; of herself'. Notice that she has to progress from 'the woman' to 'Clarissa Dalloway' before identifying 'herself' with this social façade, showing the effort that this costs her. Also, she avoids the 'icy claws' of her memory when she 'plunged into the very heart of the moment . . . of this June morning' and focuses on 'the glass, the dressing-table, and all the bottles'. Clarissa, then, uses her concentration on the dressing-table, a symbol of her artificial social existence, to banish negative memories and reassemble herself.

In the next paragraph her thoughts begin to become negative again. She reflects that she had 'tried to be the same always, never showing a sign of all the other sides of her – faults, jealousies, vanities, suspicions' and calls herself 'utterly base!' for resenting Lady Bruton. Immediately, this self-critical tendency is halted by the question: 'Now, where was her dress?' and she is soon 'plunging her hand' into the cupboard. It is obvious that she reacts against any glimpse of the selfish side of her own character, blotting it out. Instead, she fills her mind with 'Mrs Dalloway' her artificial social persona. She feels an urgent need to do this, emphasised by Woolf's repetition in 'plunged' and 'plunging' (p. 31).

Clarissa blots out her own selfishness by becoming 'Mrs Dalloway', then. It is reasonable to suggest that her initial decision to marry Richard was a form of vengeance against Peter for destroying her moment of happiness. Several episodes show that she knows how deeply and permanently she has hurt Peter. At the same time, her marriage saves her from the emotional demands of others and from her own raw feelings: 'in marriage a little licence, a little independence there must be between people living together day in day out in the same house', which Richard gave her but 'with Peter everything had to be shared', which was 'intolerable' (p. 5). We can see, then, that the determining moment of Clarissa's life, when she rejects Peter and accepts Richard, is motivated by revenge, and a self-protective reaction against emotional pain. In short, it is selfish. The energy that fuels her lifetime of devotion to being 'Mrs Dalloway' is the 'brutal monster' of her own primitive drives.

In *To the Lighthouse*, Mrs Ramsay provides a parallel example, confirming that primitive urges and sophistication are directly connected. We know that Mrs Ramsay devotes her energy to matchmaking. She takes credit for arranging the engagement of Paul and Minta, and she tries to induce Lily Briscoe to marry William Bankes. Yet Mrs Ramsay is aware that love is 'illusion' and bears within it 'the seeds of death' (*To the Lighthouse*, p. 93). Why, then, does she take every opportunity to promote marriage?

Virginia Woolf leaves us in no doubt that the engagement of the Rayleys is, at base, a primitive ritual. It is closely associated with eating and drinking and surrounded by references to ancient mythology, particularly the fertility myths of Bacchus. Mrs Ramsay thinks the *Boeuf en Daube,* its 'confusion of savoury brown and yellow meats, and its bay leaves and wine' a fitting dish to 'celebrate the occasion' like a 'festival' because 'these lovers, these people entering into illusion glittering eyed, must be danced round with mockery, decorated with garlands'. Lily senses the primitive power of Paul's love, conveyed in the violent words 'glowing, burning', the 'heat' of love, 'horror', 'cruelty', 'unscrupulosity' and 'scorched'. She 'flinched' at his love which leaves Minta 'exposed to those fangs'. The idea that this primitive fertility ritual, with its bestial overtones, is the result of Mrs Ramsay's selfish desire, is tellingly conveyed by Lily's insight. She felt something 'frightening' about Mrs Ramsay at that time because 'Always she got her own way in the end' and 'led her victims, Lily felt, to the altar'. The image of 'victims' is ambiguous: Paul's and Minta's wedding will take place at an altar, but the word 'victims' suggests a sacrifice. Mrs Ramsay's ambiguous motive is expressed in another metaphor also, where she 'held her hands over' their passion for two reasons: 'to warm them, to protect it' (all pp. 93–5). This shows Mrs Ramsay simultaneously nurturing the young couple's feelings, and using the heat of their passion to warm her own emotions. How are Mrs Ramsay's emotions 'warmed' by the passion between Paul and Minta, then?

Mrs Ramsay's emotions are 'warmed' by the glow of Paul's and Minta's passion: they inspire her to re-create feelings that she has not indulged since her own courting days: 'for a moment she felt what she had never expected to feel again – jealousy', and she can suddenly see her husband as 'a young man; a man very attractive to women . . . as she had first known him, gaunt but gallant; helping her out of a boat, she remembered' (p. 92). Put crudely, Mrs Ramsay feeds off the young couple's passions. Mrs Ramsay's devotion to the idea of marriage, then, is connected to a densely metaphorical diction filled with images of food, drink, savage beasts, primitive fertility rituals and sacrifices; and is driven by selfishness. It is an indirect, artificial way of reanimating her own dead passion for her husband.

In *The Waves*, Susan sees the servants kissing in the kitchen-garden. The language again emphasises elemental passion, and reminds us of the primitive sexuality of Greek myths, where Zeus takes the form of a bull to achieve his satisfaction: 'He was blind as a bull, and she swooned in anguish' (*The Waves*, p. 13). In the context of this elemental power, which Susan likens to a volcano ('I see a crack in the earth and hot steam hisses up' [p. 13]), she observes the other children. Bernard 'moulds his bread into pellets and calls them "people"' and 'Jinny spins her fingers on the table-cloth, as if they were dancing in the sunshine, pirouetting' (p. 14). In other words, both Bernard and Jinny begin to create fantasies about 'people' and courtship rituals ('dancing, . . . pirouetting').

In conclusion, Virginia Woolf shows sophisticated forms of 'civilisation' deriving from primitive human urges. Mrs Dalloway's society, the rituals of courtship and marriage, and the first creative fantasies of children have all been seen to arise as a response to what Clarissa calls 'the brutal monster' of 'self love'. The principle we call 'creative' is of primitive origin, then, and it manifests itself throughout the structures and manners we call 'society' or 'civilisation'. Virginia Woolf also explores some higher manifestations of this creative energy, however; and we look at these in the next section.

Learning, Reason and Poetry

We will focus on the character of Mr Ramsay. In *To the Lighthouse*, his ambition to be a great philosopher, and his struggle to analyse the world, embody the human pursuit of reason and understanding. He is depicted with a mixture of sympathy, irony and amusement. In Chapter 6 of Part I, 'The Window', Mr Ramsay meditates as he paces up and down in the garden of the house on Skye. He feels fortified after briefly conversing with his wife and son. Woolf writes that this 'consecrated his effort to arrive at a perfectly clear understanding of the problems which now engaged the energies of his splendid mind' (*To the Lighthouse*, p. 31). To 'consecrate' is to devote a task to something sacred. Mr Ramsay devotes his meditative achievements, in a religious manner, to his wife and son, then. Why? They are his family, after all, not a god. Elsewhere, we understand that his family causes a conflict for him. We learn that he might have attained the perfect understanding, and confronted 'human ignorance and human fate', 'But the father of eight children has no choice' (p. 41). It is reasonable to suppose that his effort is 'consecrated' by them as a compensation for this discomfort, because he is anxious about his own ability and his failure as a philosopher. Virginia Woolf describes his mind as 'splendid', but her similes for the way his reasoning works are tongue-in-cheek. 'If thought is like the keyboard of a piano, divided into so many notes, or like the alphabet is ranged in twenty-six letters all in order,' she writes, 'then his splendid mind had no sort of difficulty' (p. 31). Of course, 'thought' is not an organised, logical and limited thing, like a keyboard or an alphabet. The satire is emphasised by the absurdity of 'if'; and by the repetition of 'his splendid mind' three times within five lines, each iteration increasing the sarcasm of 'splendid'. Mr Ramsay is not merely a man who mistakenly attempts to reduce life to logic, however. He is also described as comically struggling with his logic. The following passage is one of the funniest in the novel, and the derisive irony forces us to realise that Mr Ramsay's intellectual struggles are pathetic. If 'thought' is like an alphabet, he reaches Q with ease:

> Very few people in the whole of England ever reach Q. Here, stopping for one moment by the stone urn which held the geraniums, he saw, but now far far away, like children picking up shells, divinely

innocent and occupied with little trifles at their feet and somehow entirely defenceless against a doom which he perceived, his wife and son, together, in the window. They needed his protection; he gave it them. But after Q? What comes next? After Q there are a number of letters the last of which is scarcely visible to mortal eyes, but glimmers red in the distance. Z is only reached once by one man in a generation. Still, if he could reach R it would be something. Here at least was Q. He dug his heels in at Q. Q he was sure of. Q he could demonstrate. If Q then is Q – R – Here he knocked his pipe out, with two or three resonant taps on the ram's horn which made the handle of the urn, and proceeded. 'Then R . . .' He braced himself. He clenched himself.

(To the Lighthouse, p. 31)

Physical details – his wife and son, his pipe, the urn full of geraniums – alternate with the abstract; but the abstract is in the absurdly childish form of learning an alphabet. Every so often, Mr Ramsay breaks off to compare himself against his scale of success and fame. In reaching R he equals 'very few . . . in England' and reaching Z is achieved by 'one in a generation'. If he could manage R, and reach S, that would 'be something'. His competitiveness and his aims are derisory, of course, because the whole activity is futile: it depends upon the premise 'if thought is like the keyboard of a piano', which thought is not.

Virginia Woolf adds to this portrait the image of a man in heroic confrontation against the forces of nature: 'It was his fate, his peculiarity, whether he wished it or not, to come out thus on a spit of land which the sea is slowly eating away, and there to stand.' He is heroic and admirable because 'he kept even in that desolation a vigilance which spared no phantom and luxuriated in no vision'; he is like 'a stake driven into the bed of a channel upon which the gulls perch and the waves beat' and he inspires 'reverence' and 'gratitude' in others because he has taken on himself the duty of 'marking the channel out there in the floods alone' (all pp. 40–1). This image, of a man heroically wrestling with nature's vastness, recurs in *To the Lighthouse*. The very nature he tries to understand continuously undermines him: 'the sea eating the ground we stand on'. He is treated with a combination of satire and respect; as Lily and William observe, 'he was venerable and laughable at one and the same time' (p. 42).

Mr Ramsay has heroic qualities. Qualities 'that would have saved a ship's company exposed on a broiling sea with six biscuits and a flask of water – endurance and justice, foresight, devotion, skill' (p. 31) and 'Qualities that in a desolate expedition across the icy solitudes of the Polar region would have made him the leader, the guide, the counsellor'. Finally, he has 'Feelings that would not have disgraced a leader who, now that the snow has begun to fall and the mountain-top is covered in mist, knows that he must lay himself down and die before morning comes . . . Yet he would not die lying down . . . he would die standing' (both p. 32). These are ironic descriptions of a hero, as the *Boy's Own Comic* vignette of a ship's crew with six biscuits and a flask of water reveals. Woolf's sentence-structure is deliberately classical, satirically echoing Milton's or Virgil's extended similes, in a 'mock-heroic' style. The amusement Virginia Woolf feels when contemplating fruitless male endurance is apparent in various places. Most concisely, and with withering effectiveness, when Lily combines ironic and colloquial diction to think: 'If you are *exalted* you must somehow *come a cropper*' (p. 42, my italics).

Mr Ramsay is a satirical figure, then: we are encouraged to laugh at the narrow-mindedness of his pathetic struggle with the alphabet, and we are firmly nudged towards seeing his heroism as a boy's adventure-fantasy, while he stares at the 'long wastes of the ages' in a hedge. However, his quest for understanding of the universe belongs to the great struggle we are analysing, that between the 'creative' and 'destructive' principles, and has its more serious moments. In 'Time Passes', the same heroic figure appears as 'any sleeper'. Typically he seeks the answers to life's questions on a beach, as Mr Ramsay is repeatedly imagined standing indomitable against the sea:

> fancying that he might find on the beach an answer to his doubts, a sharer of his solitude, throw off his bedclothes and go down by himself to walk on the sand, no image with semblance of serving and divine promptitude comes readily to hand bringing the night to order and making the world reflect the compass of the soul. The hand

dwindles in his hand; the voice bellows in his ear. Almost it would appear that it is useless in such confusion to ask the night those questions as to what, and why, and wherefore, which tempt the sleeper from his bed to seek an answer.

(*To the Lighthouse*, p. 122)

Notice that this picture of the intellectual hero has sympathetic touches. Life 'bellows', an incoherent and animal noise, in his ear; 'the hand dwindles in his hand' as any person who is the 'sharer of his solitude' inevitably dies; and the futility of his questions is gently treated: it is not obvious, but 'Almost it would appear that it is useless'. This more sympathetic treatment of the intellectual hero prepares us for the bald statement of Mrs Ramsay's death, in brackets, in the next paragraph.

In conclusion, then, Woolf presents intellectual endeavour as a grand, heroic enterprise which is part of the creative principle's struggle against chaos, or the 'dark'. It is misguided, because logic is not the appropriate weapon against nature's confusion. So it is in some ways 'laughable'. However, it can also be magnificent and evoke our sympathy. It is helpful to realise that Mr Ramsay is an emblematic figure. His portrait represents a whole area of human activity: education, learning, reason and logic all strive to bring the vastness of nature within an orderly compass. In this effort, they are doing the same thing as Mrs McNab does when she rescues a tea-set, or as Mrs Ramsay attempts when she organises a meal in her dining-room.

The human efforts we have discussed are attempts to reduce the world to orderliness. Mr and Mrs Ramsay try to impose their own idea of order (marriage, or logic) upon reality. Another way to put this is that they try to understand reality by means of their limited idea of order. In *The Waves*, the two characters Bernard and Neville also strive to understand life, and their own place and purpose within it. They focus their interest upon imaginative writing – Bernard wants to write a letter and imitates Byron, while Neville has written a poem. However, Woolf makes clear that their effort is produced by the same fundamental desire which drives Mrs Ramsay to create dinners and engagements, or Clarissa to create a brittle social persona. Here is the moment when Bernard becomes aware of failing in his effort to be an 'artist'. He tries to write a letter to a girl 'with whom he is passionately in love':

> Now, as a proof of my susceptibility to atmosphere, here, as I come into my room, and turn on the light, and see the sheet of paper, the table, my gown lying negligently over the back of the chair, I feel that I am that dashing yet reflective man, that bold and deleterious figure, who, lightly throwing off his cloak, seizes his pen and at once flings off the following letter . . . It is going to be a brilliant sketch which, she must think, was written without a pause, without an erasure . . . It is the speed, the hot, molten effect, the laval flow of sentence into sentence that I need. Who am I thinking of? Byron of course. I am, in some ways, like Byron. Perhaps a sip of Byron will help to put me in the vein. Let me read a page. No; this is dull; this is scrappy. This is rather formal . . .
>
> Yet it falls flat. It peters out. I cannot get up steam enough to carry me over the transition. My true self breaks off from my assumed.
>
> (*The Waves*, p. 50)

The first thing we notice is that Bernard focuses on his surroundings, his appearance and the effect of the letter. There is nothing about what he will write. In his mind, the important elements are 'the sheet of paper, the table, my gown lying negligently' and the image of 'that dashing yet reflective man' he wishes to become. Woolf chooses words which do not convey a convincing picture. For example, 'dashing' and 'reflective' do not go together; and the next pair of words couples 'bold' (a clear and positive description) with 'deleterious': a ridiculous word which describes no recognisable quality.

Bernard describes the quality he wants in his writing in metaphors about powerful natural forces ('molten', 'laval flow') and music ('beat', 'rhythm', 'on the very lilt of the stroke'). In other words, Bernard wants to create the effects of wordless things, in words. In the end, his attempt to do this 'falls flat'. His final image for his attempt ironically indicates a machine, in contrast to the volcanic natural forces he hoped to harness: in the end, he 'cannot get up steam'. The narrative details, choice of words, and use of imagery in this passage, then, reveal that Bernard is chasing an illusion; and that his effort is mechanically forced, not natural.

Here is Neville's realisation that he has failed to become a poet:

> Now begins to rise in me the familiar rhythm; words that have lain dormant now lift, now toss their crests, and fall and rise, and fall and rise again. I am a poet, yes. Surely I am a great poet. Boats and youth passing and distant trees, 'the falling fountains of the pendant trees', I see it all. I feel it all. I am inspired. My eyes fill with tears. Yet even as I feel this, I lash my frenzy higher and higher. It foams. It becomes artificial, insincere. Words and words and words, how they gallop – how they lash their long manes and tails, but for some fault in me I cannot give myself to their backs; I cannot fly with them, scattering women and string bags. There is some flaw in me – some fatal hesitancy, which, if I pass it over, turns to foam and falsity.
>
> (*The Waves*, pp. 52–3)

This description continues the image of music in Neville's idea of 'familiar rhythm' and words that 'fall and rise, and fall and rise again'. However, other metaphors for his poetic inspiration soon take over. These words 'toss their crests' and he 'lashes' his frenzy until it 'foams'; the words 'gallop': they 'lash their long manes and tails'. These metaphors conjure up the idea of horses, as well as 'crests' and 'foam' bringing the sea to mind. So Neville imagines a poet's inspiration as a combination of wild, galloping horses, and the waves themselves. In contrast, his failure is described as 'some fault', 'some flaw', 'a fatal hesitancy'. Neville distinguishes between himself and the wild, natural force of inspiration. Unlike poetry, 'I cannot give myself' and 'I cannot fly'. We again find that Woolf's description of creativity is couched in terms of an overwhelming and wild natural force.

This extract does not have the heavy satire we found in the description of Bernard. Neville is not absurd, whereas Bernard's Byronic posturing is. Neville's failure is subtly defined for us. He is watching punts on the river while he has these thoughts. Ironically, his mind is filled with wild sea-horses, while his eyes are occupied with a very tame subject, 'boats and youth passing and distant trees', and his words use 'falling fountains' – a metaphor of landscape gardening, not wild nature. In this way, Woolf hints that there is a fatal limitation in Neville's vision, as well as the 'hesitancy' of conscious thought, which prevents him from making a poem out of his inspiration. On the other hand, the author does not cast doubt on his inner vision. Neville says, in short, categoric sentences: 'I see it all. I feel it all. I am inspired', and this is so.

Bernard and Neville, then, try to express the world in the form of art. In Bernard's case the attempt is rather absurd, and Woolf's style indicates condescending amusement at the little engine that wanted to be a volcano but 'cannot get up steam'. In Neville's case the attempt is taken seriously. This reveals an important point: Virginia Woolf does describe a moment of inspired vision, when Neville can 'see it all' and 'feel it all'. Neville also senses the words that would capture his vision, but his 'hesitancy' prevents him from writing the poem. In Neville's case, then, we are in the presence of a real vision, and the means to turn it into art. The fact that Neville fails does not alter the underlying optimism of this passage, then. Virginia Woolf asserts that it is possible to transform a vision of life into art.

We have come a long way, following the 'creative' force. We have studied such human efforts as Clarissa's artificial social life, Mrs Ramsay's manipulation of the people around her, Mr Ramsay's doomed attempt to reduce infinity to logic, and Bernard's posturing pretension of art. Finally, the example of Neville reveals to us that there is a real artistic 'vision' of life – that humanity can find a vision that will express the 'fluidity out there', the chaos of nature and life-experience. At the same time, Virginia Woolf stresses the difficulty of the artist's struggle. Only a 'hesitancy' causes Neville's failure, but it is enough to prevent him from being a poet.

Before we move on to examine Lily Briscoe's successful painting, in *To the Lighthouse*, it is worth understanding Bernard's and Neville's motives, and the point Virginia Woolf adds in this part of *The Waves*, about the artist's need to remain solitary.

Bernard's motive is made clear when he focuses on the effect of his letter, 'a brilliant sketch which, she must think, was written without a pause'. Later, he comments: 'I want her to say as she brushes her hair or puts out the candle. . . '. In fact, Bernard has a fully developed fantasy about the girl reading his letter. He even imagines what she will be doing after she has read it. In his fantasy, the letter impresses her. This coincides with Freud's comments about art. In Freud's view, the artist has a powerful but frustrated desire. This gives rise to 'wish-fulfilment fantasies' which the artist has the ability to transform into beauty. According to Freud, the artist's desires are the same as any other person's: 'money, power, and the love of women'. We can see that Bernard's letter has all the elements Freud mentions, except for that final ability to make a thing of beauty.

Neville's motive is also love. He gives his poem to Bernard, and in his thoughts asks: 'whether I am doomed always to cause repulsion in those I love?' He is precise and orderly, but 'I would rather be loved. . . . The desire which is loaded behind my lips, cold as lead, fell as a bullet, the thing I aim at shop-girls, women, the pretence, the vulgarity of life (because I love it) shoots at you as I throw – catch it – my poem' (*The Waves*, pp. 56–7). The image of a loaded gun, where the bullet is 'behind my lips', expresses his frustration, since he has not spoken his desire. The bullet – his unspoken desire – then becomes the poem. At the same time, Woolf repeats the word 'love', like a recurrent motif expressing Neville's desire. Neville's motive – as we would expect – is more complex and less adolescent than Bernard's; but it shares the same essential characteristics of frustration and desire.

Both Bernard and Neville comment on their relation to other people. Bernard admits 'I need the stimulus of other people', unlike 'the real novelist' who could 'go on, indefinitely, imagining' (p. 51). When he is with Neville, Bernard is inspired to talk, and his 'flow of language, unexpected and spontaneous as it is, delights me'. A natural spring is evoked as 'more and more bubbles into my mind as I talk'. Bernard concludes: 'This, I say to myself, is what I need: why, I ask, can I not finish the letter that I am writing?' (all p. 54). Bernard, then, contrasts the solitary pursuit of an artist to the satisfaction he gains in the society of others. From Neville's point of view, on the other hand, meeting Bernard is expressed in negative terms. Virginia Woolf lists several words for diminishing, beginning with Neville's observation that 'Something now leaves me; something goes from me to meet that figure who is coming', and leading to the reflection 'how painful to be recalled, to be mitigated, to have one's self adulterated; mixed up, become part of another' (p. 53). The clear conclusion we draw from both of these views is that the artist is in a problematic relation to other people: he – or she – cannot afford to become vitally related to others, yet they are a necessary audience. This conclusion develops Mr Ramsay's wry comment about his failure to master 'R' or to reach 'Z': 'But the father of eight children has no choice' (*To the Lighthouse*, p. 41), where he acknowledges that his family disturbs his concentration.

Art: Lily Briscoe's Painting

At the beginning of Part III of *To the Lighthouse*, Lily suddenly remembers the painting she was working on ten years before, which was never finished; and decides to paint it that morning. She remembers a moment that occurred during dinner, in Part I, 'The Window'. Lily felt pressurised by Mrs Ramsay to pity William Bankes. Suddenly she remembered that she had her 'work', and it was 'as if she had found a treasure' (p. 79). At the same moment she had a vision of how to finish her painting. She placed a salt-cellar on a flower in the pattern of the tablecloth, to remind herself of this inspiration. Now, ten years later, Lily needs to escape from Mr Ramsay's demand for sympathy: 'to escape his demand on her, to put aside a moment longer that imperious need' (p. 140), and the memory of 'a little sprig or leaf pattern on the table-cloth, which she had looked at in a moment of revelation' (p. 141) comes back to her. On both of these occasions, then, Lily finds that her 'art' is a refuge from the demand to respond to a man.

At the same time, Lily knows the elements that will make up her picture: 'Going to the Lighthouse. But what does one send to the Lighthouse? Perished. Alone. The grey-green light on the wall opposite. The empty places. Such were some of the parts, but how bring them together?' (p. 141). Lily struggles in her mind to bring these elements together for the remainder of the novel, and the final sentence tells us that she has accomplished her task: 'Yes, she thought, laying down her brush in extreme fatigue, I have had my vision' (p.

198). In this broad sense, then, all of these final fifty-odd pages are about creative art: the making of Lily Briscoe's painting.

We have looked at various forms of human endeavour, and some of these are echoed in the process Lily undergoes as she makes her painting. First, she must be isolated from others: whenever Mr Ramsay approaches, 'she could do nothing' because 'ruin approached, chaos approached' (p. 141). When the Ramsays are gone, she finds herself 'sighing with relief' (p. 149). This reminds us of both Bernard's inability to be natural when he is alone, and Neville's feeling of being diminished when he is with another person. In Lily's case, however, there is a difference. Mr Ramsay demands her sympathy and she is unable to give it. Then, just as she feels able to offer sympathy, James and Cam arrive and the party sets off for the lighthouse. Lily is left feeling frustrated: 'Her feeling had come too late; there it was ready; but he no longer needed it' (p. 147). The result of this awkward encounter is that Lily feels 'curiously divided, as if one part of her were drawn out there . . . [while] the other had fixed itself doggedly, solidly, here on the lawn'. Woolf emphasises the contrast between 'out there' and the plain reality of 'here on the lawn', by describing the day as 'hazy' so that 'the Lighthouse looked this morning at an immense distance' (all p. 149). This division of Lily's concentration, between hazy distance and the solid world close at hand, continues throughout her creative effort. Eventually, the lighthouse 'had become almost invisible, had melted away into a blue haze' (p. 197). The strain of maintaining this dual concentration over the ever-widening distance between herself on the lawn, and Mr Ramsay travelling to the lighthouse, exhausts Lily: it 'had stretched her body and mind to the utmost' (p. 197). Notice that this division, which leads her to focus herself simultaneously on two different objects, begins with the ambivalence of her relationship to Mr Ramsay: she both defends herself against Mr Ramsay's encroaching demands, and longs to express the sympathy he eventually arouses in her.

Secondly, Lily is engaged in a search for something which she sees as 'truth'. Virginia Woolf uses imagery which reminds us of Mr Ramsay standing above the sea, or walking the beach and searching the stars for an answer to the riddles of life (see above), to describe this search for truth. Lily begins from a high place overlooking the sea: 'As the waves shape themselves symmetrically from the cliff top, but to the swimmer among them are divided by steep gulfs, and foaming crests' (p. 150), and we are reminded of the heroic philosopher-figure again as we read that she was 'hesitating on some windy pinnacle and exposed without protection to all the blasts of doubt' (p. 151). Later, she describes painting as walking out and out until 'at last one seemed to be on a narrow plank, perfectly alone, over the sea' (pp. 163–4). Lily also shares the unwavering determination of the philosopher. She bewails the weakness of the 'human apparatus', but 'heroically, one must force it on' (p. 184); and when approaching the final crisis of her vision, she thinks, 'One must keep on looking without for a second relaxing the intensity of emotion, the determination not to be put off, not to be bamboozled' (p. 191). These qualities make Lily's effort comparable to Mr Ramsay's attempts, when he imagines life to be limited like a keyboard, or an alphabet, and struggles heroically with the letter 'R'.

There is a decisive difference, however. Mr Ramsay had a limited system in his mind (a keyboard or an alphabet), and tried to force life to fit it. Lily, on the contrary, has no limited 'system' and determinedly commits herself to an exploration that she knows is endless, and is likely to overwhelm her. This takes courage, but 'Still the risk must be run; the mark made' (p. 150). Virginia Woolf uses the image of the sea to portray the idea that, when she begins to paint, Lily dives into a sea of life, and compares the rhythm of her painting to the rhythm of waves: 'she attained a dancing rhythmical movement . . . Down in the hollow of one wave she saw the next wave towering higher and higher' (p. 151). This natural rhythm is important, as it induces a state of mind similar to the one we have met before in Mrs Ramsay, when the repetitive action of knitting and the rhythmic stroke of the Lighthouse put her into a semi-conscious trance. Lily enters a state where she loses her awareness of the solid world around her. She is 'drawn out of gossip, out of living, out of community with people' (p. 151), and 'Certainly she was losing consciousness of outer things.' In this state, Mrs Ramsay's mental defences relaxed, and her mind threw up a surprising, unwelcome thought. The same effect occurs within Lily: 'her mind kept throwing up from its depths, scenes, and names, and sayings, and memories and ideas' (both p. 152). Virginia Woolf insistently compares Lily's creative effort with a natural and fertile process – with the sea, and with other positive, fertile natural images. It is, for example, 'as if some juice necessary for the lubrication of her faculties were spontaneously squirted', and the ideas come from her mind's depths 'like a fountain spurting' (both p. 152). When her memories perplex her, the author says that she has 'come to the surface, . . . half out of the picture' (p. 169). This insistence on Lily progressively committing herself to being submerged is densely woven into the language Woolf uses throughout these chapters, so, for example, an idea 'sunk back again', the 'whole world seemed to have dissolved' into a 'pool' of thought or a 'deep basin'; and eventually the metaphor of her, like the philosopher-figure, standing above an encroaching sea, is developed to convey the vital difference. Where Mr Ramsay's utmost effort is to 'find some crag of rock' and 'die standing', his eyes trying to 'pierce' the darkness, Lily does not hopelessly oppose a hostile nature. Instead, she is said to 'step off her strip of board into the waters of annihilation' (p. 172). Committing herself to nature and life, instead of fighting it, puts Lily eventually 'up to the lips in some substance, to move and float and sink in it, yes, for these waters were unfathomably deep' (p. 183).

This difference is vital, as it leads Lily to her 'vision'. There are several images for the truth she manages to discover about life. Woolf begins by presenting a paradox: 'In the midst of chaos there was shape; this eternal passing and flowing . . . was struck into stability' (p. 154). Then, following a list of apparently unrelated details such as 'a rook; a red-hot poker', there is 'some common feeling which held the whole together' which is clarified for Lily as a 'feeling of completeness' she calls 'love'. This feeling, which is also called love, brings a 'wholeness' and makes of 'some scene' 'one of those globed compacted things over which thought lingers, and love plays' (all p. 183). These descriptions of what Lily finds are attempts to describe her imagination when her artistic faculty is fully aroused. It is not useful to analyse abstract words like 'wholeness' or 'completeness' too closely, but the 'shape' found in 'chaos' adds a final distinction between Lily's art and Mr Ramsay's logic: he tries to impose 'shape' but all he sees is chaos. Lily looks at 'chaos' and 'shape' is revealed within it. The vital difference between them is clearly that between his rigid, systematised approach to the problem; and Lily's open, receptive approach.

We have noticed the importance of rhythms in this process, several times. Mrs Ramsay's knitting and the rhythm of the Lighthouse-beam, and Lily's 'rhythmical' painting, both induced a receptive, semi-conscious state. There is also rhythm and repetition in nature itself, and Woolf's metaphors suggest that rhythmic repetition is the key to perceiving 'shape' in life's 'chaos'. In the following quotation, Lily muses about the past and the Ramsays, thinking about many events spanning many years. Notice that Woolf underlines how far Lily's perception travels, by beginning with 'rough and tumble' and ending with the metaphor of a bell, stressing resonance and harmony:

> For in the rough and tumble of daily life, with all those children about, all those visitors, one had constantly a sense of repetition – of one thing falling where another had fallen, and so setting up an echo which chimed in the air and made it full of vibrations.
>
> (*To the Lighthouse*, p. 189)

To understand life, or achieve a 'vision', then, a sympathetic 'vibration' of rhythmical repetition must occur in the individual, in harmony with the rhythm that makes the 'shape' in life's chaos. To do this, self-consciousness (such as Mr Ramsay's dreams of heroism and his suffering poses; or his anxiety about fame) must be abandoned. Lily loses consciousness of both the world around her and herself, and steps into 'the waters of annihilation' (p. 172). Virginia Woolf repeatedly underlines the openness and acceptance of Lily's creative effort: she tells us plainly that 'one got nothing by soliciting urgently. One got only a glare in the eye' and Lily decides to 'Let it come, she thought, if it will come' (p. 184). We are left in no doubt about Mr Ramsay's mistake.

We have assembled and clarified the elements of an 'artistic' experience in this discussion so far. There is one further element for us to consider. We already commented that Lily's concentration is 'curiously divided' between the present reality and the distant Lighthouse. During the descriptions of Lily painting, Virginia Woolf uses this idea of balance between opposites as a recurrent motif. Lily is repeatedly conveyed as between opposing forces: she is 'half unwilling, half reluctant', and the narrative constantly jumps between her engrossed thoughts and her movements. For example, between her memory of Mrs Ramsay on a beach, and her medita-tions about painting, comes this single sentence: 'Lily stepped back to get her canvas – so – into perspective' (p. 163). So there is a repet-itive shifting between subjective and objective narration. Lily's view-point also continually shifts between extremes – from examining tiny reality such as the plantain she digs with her brush, to searching for distance out over the bay and the hazy blue of the horizon.

We have already noticed that the effort to concentrate simultane-ously on extreme opposites exhausts Lily. She describes it as trying to 'achieve that razor edge of balance between two opposite forces; Mr Ramsay and the picture; which was necessary' (p. 184). Later, as Lily approaches success in her struggle to 'see' Mrs Ramsay at the empty centre of her picture, she insists that the duality she seeks is to live and perceive in two opposite ways at the same time. She wants 'to be on a level with ordinary experience, to feel simply that's a chair, that's a table, and yet at the same time, It's a miracle, it's an ecstasy'. When Lily finally succeeds in combining these two perceptions, one of them comes in the form of shock and grief at Mrs Ramsay's death. Pain is described as 'the old horror' and personified: 'Her heart leapt at her and seized her and tortured her' (both p. 192). The other – being on a level with ordinary experience – comes because Lily 'refrained', so that the extreme of horror also 'became part of ordinary experience, was on a level with the chair, with the table' (p. 192). This unlikely combination of extreme emotion and utter calm brings success in her struggle for 'vision': the moment when she sees Mrs Ramsay.

We can now summarise the elements that contribute to Lily's artistic success. First, she is torn between opposites (a need to be alone, yet a desire to express her sympathy to Mr Ramsay), and she manages to hold extreme opposites together in one moment (her paroxysm of grief and utter calm; distant romance and close detail;

the canvas in front of her, and Mr Ramsay going to the edge of imagination where the Lighthouse 'had become almost invisible'). Second, she enters into a rhythmic, repetitive state in which she is open to her unconscious ideas and memories, and sensitive to the rhythmic repetition that is the 'shape' in the 'chaos' of the world. Third, she is without a preconceived system for understanding the world. Instead, she loses self-consciousness, giving herself to life or stepping into the 'waters of annihilation'.

Much passes through Lily's mind while she is painting. We read her memories of Mrs Ramsay, Mr Tansley, William Bankes and Mr Carmichael, the Rayleys, and Mr Ramsay. There is not enough space in this chapter to study these in any useful detail. However, her comparison of herself with Mrs Ramsay is relevant. Lily regards Mrs Ramsay's knack of bringing people together (which gave her a few minutes of friendship with the odious Charles Tansley) as 'like a work of art' because it remains with her as a 'complete' memory. This memory is a 'little daily miracle' like 'matches struck unexpect- edly in the dark', but not 'the great revelation' about 'the meaning of life' that she seeks. Mrs Ramsay created the moment Lily remem- bers, and she compares their vocations:

> Mrs Ramsay making of the moment something permanent (as in another sphere Lily herself tried to make of the moment something permanent) – this was of the nature of a revelation.
>
> (all quotations from *To the Lighthouse*, pp. 153–4)

We are provoked into comparing the two activities – painting, and bringing people together. We have already looked at Mrs Ramsay's matchmaking of Paul and Minta, finding that her need to create harmony between people comes from her own fears and inade- quacy. Now we should turn our attention from analysing *how* Lily paints her picture, and ask *why* she paints it.

We have found impressive qualities in Lily Briscoe. We under- stand the difficulty and pain of her struggle to reach 'vision', and we appreciate the courage and determination she shows. We may also admire her openness, her willingness to be annihilated by the experi- ence. Remember, however, that Virginia Woolf presents all human endeavours as beginning with something 'not highly conscious' that 'leered' and 'lurched' (see Chapter 6). Lily Briscoe's creative impulse is likely, then, to be of primitive origin, if the author remains consistent.

Looking for an explanation in Chapters 1 and 2 of 'The Lighthouse', we find our expectation to be justified. Lily begins by wishing to escape Mr Ramsay's need. She 'pretended to drink out of her empty coffee-cup so as to escape him', but she is unable to stop herself from hearing his suffering in the words 'perished' and 'alone' (p. 140). We already remarked that the 'revelation' in the tablecloth comes to her aid twice in the book. This time, as last time, it springs into her mind when she feels pressured to sympathise with a man. Lily is suddenly spurred on to begin painting. Virginia Woolf wryly implies that painting is a form of escape, an alternative to facing Mr Ramsay's demanding grief: 'She got up quickly, before Mr Ramsay turned' (p. 141).

The subsequent scene between them, on the lawn, is written with an edge of amusement in the author's tone. We are clearly meant to understand how basic and predictable the two characters' behaviour is. Mr Ramsay's childish, self-centred demand is apparent, for example, when he thinks 'She is a stock, she is a stone'; and Woolf's descriptions of him convey incredulity: she can hardly believe that he overacts so grossly: 'he had assumed a pose of extreme decrepitude; he even tottered a little as he stood there' (both p. 145). We quickly realise that Mr Ramsay is playing a gender-game, acting out his misery in order to gain a feminine response: he expects to be mothered, 'for after all . . . what woman could resist him?' (p. 146), and this was a time when he needed to 'approach any woman, to force them, he did not care how, his need was so great, to give him what he wanted: sympathy' (p. 144). Virginia Woolf must be laughing at Mr Ramsay's expense as she describes his most powerful weapon: he heaves a sigh – a 'primeval gust' – so that 'there issued from him such a groan that any other woman in the whole world would have done something, said something' (pp. 144-5). 'Gust' is hilariously bathetic after 'primeval'; and the classical construction 'there issued from him' is also obviously tongue-in-cheek. There is abundant additional evidence in these pages to support our clear conclusion: Mr Ramsay is described here as a typical and rather childish man, with primitive, attention-seeking needs. Lily even expects a tantrum from him when she does not give him what he wants. His behaviour is absurd, then, and we are encouraged to laugh at him. What of Lily herself?

Gender-role issues dominate this passage. Lily is conscious of his need and bitter about her own inadequacy as a woman: 'myself . . . who am not a woman, but a peevish, ill-tempered, dried-up old maid presumably' (p. 145); and she feels unhappy at being unable to respond to him in a normal feminine way: 'No; she could not do it. She ought to have . . .', and 'But she remained stuck' (both p. 144) convey how much she wishes that she could play the gender-game Mr Ramsay demands. We should notice, then, that Lily agrees with the man's assessment of her when he cries out the old, self-centred male insult *'Frigid!'*, saying 'She is a stock, she is a stone', in his ego-centric amazement. She castigates herself in the same way, thinking that she is a 'dried-up old maid'. On the other hand, Lily can see Mr Ramsay's behaviour clearly. It 'nauseated her' and was 'horrible' and 'indecent' (p. 145).

Woolf's joke develops further when Mr Ramsay adopts a different cliché of male behaviour. He talks about boots, knowledgeably, posing as an expert; and he adopts a courtly manner, stooping to tie and untie her shoe for her. Amusingly, this approach does spark a conventional feminine response in Lily. 'Her heart warmed to him' and 'the blood rushed to her face . . . she felt her eyes swell and tingle with tears'. Now, at last, she 'wished to' and 'could have' given him her sympathy (all p. 147).

Virginia Woolf places other primitive responses from Lily around this satirical portrait of gender-play. She is angry with Mrs Ramsay for dying and leaving Mr Ramsay alone – this, thinks Lily, is unfair and it 'was all Mrs Ramsay's fault' (p. 143). The logic of her feelings is clear, and ironic. Mr Ramsay wants somebody to feel sorry for him. Lily feels that this ought to be his wife's job, so his wife should not have died – it was irresponsible of her to leave him alone like that! Later, she is annoyed at Cam and James when they arrive: she is angry because they will not give their father the sympathy she now desires to give him.

The obvious conclusion is insistently underlined throughout these pages: Lily is left frustrated, needing to channel her aroused sexual feelings, both fears and desires, which are 'stuck' and cannot find expression. The origin of Lily's desire to paint is just this: that her sexual energy, her femininity, has no other outlet. Here is an extract from Freud's *Introductory Lectures on Psychoanalysis*. If we read this and compare Freud's theory with Lily's character, the parallel is clear and close:

> An artist is once more in rudiments an introvert, not far removed from neurosis. He is oppressed by excessively powerful instinctual needs. He desires to win honour, power, wealth, fame and the love of women; but he lacks the means for achieving these satisfactions. Consequently, like any other unsatisfied man, he turns away from reality and transfers all his interest, and his libido too, to the wishful constructions of his life of phantasy.
>
> (Sigmund Freud, *The Complete Introductory Lectures on Psychoanalysis*, trans. and ed. James Strachey, London, 1971, p. 376)

Simply substitute 'Lily' for 'An artist' and change the sex of each pronoun, and the description fits her character. This is confirmed by a motif of quite explicitly sexual imagery associated with Lily's painting (see, for example, how her 'juice' is 'spontaneously squirted' and her ideas are like a 'fountain spurting' [p. 152]); and by the erotic description of Paul Rayley (see p. 167) in metaphors of passionate red and fire. She becomes aroused by thinking about Paul Rayley, and we notice that this again provokes her memory of the moment when she 'escaped by the skin of her teeth' (p. 167) by looking at the tablecloth. Her later memories of Mr Ramsay's courtly behaviour (see pp. 188-9) remind us of both the memory of courtship Mrs Ramsay revives in herself (see 'helping her out of a boat, she remembered', p. 92), and his courtly behaviour in stooping to tie Lily's shoes. Virginia Woolf hammers home the fact that the painting is Lily's alternative to an aroused, feminine response to Mr Ramsay. In the final chapter we read that: 'Whatever she had wanted to give him, when he left her that morning, she had given him at last' (p. 197). 'Stuck' and sublimated gender urges, then, compel Lily's 'art'; and the finished painting is her feminine response to Mr Ramsay.

This insight implies a wicked ironic joke. Remember that Lily was angry with Mrs Ramsay for being dead. By painting her picture, Lily brings Mrs Ramsay back from the dead and places her in the empty middle of the painting ('she drew a line there, in the centre. It was done; it was finished' [p. 198]). In other words, her gift for Mr Ramsay is not her own feminine sympathy, which she is still unable to give. She struggles and strains to give his wife back to him instead. After all, it is the wife's job to sympathise with the man!

These sexual frustrations and motives are Lily's 'something not highly conscious' that 'leered' and made her become an artist. Virginia Woolf suggests that such a primitive instinct is the energy that fuels all human effort, from Mrs McNab's rough battles against mildew and weeds, to Lily's sophisticated artistic 'revelation'. However, the novel does not present this as merely one character's hidden desire. There are numerous references to fertility and nature-mythology in the final section of the book. These connect the sexual origin of Lily's effort to a grander and more universal idea than one person's shame. Mr Carmichael is repeatedly likened to a nature-god or a sea-monster. Eventually, on the final page, we find him 'surging up . . . looking like an old pagan God, shaggy, with weeds in his hair and the trident . . . in his hand' (pp. 197–8). Through the comparison of Mr Carmichael to Neptune, then, Lily's private problem becomes connected with universal experiences that exist throughout history and are expressed in myth. Woolf additionally uses the God-metaphor for Mr Carmichael, to suggest the sadness and sympathy for humanity that fills her own ambivalent descriptions of Lily and the other characters:

> He stood there spreading his hands over all the weakness and suffering of mankind; she thought he was surveying, tolerantly, compassionately, their final destiny. Now he has crowned the occasion, she thought, when his hand slowly fell, as if she had seen him let fall from his great height a wreath of violets and asphodels which, fluttering slowly, lay at length upon the earth.
>
> (*To the Lighthouse*, p. 198)

In the same way, the author uses an allusion to Arthurian legend – referring to the Lady of the Lake and the finding of the sword

Excalibur – to relate Lily's question about life ('What does it mean? How do you explain it all?' [p. 170]) to a universal but primitive idea. 'A hand would be shoved up, a blade would be flashed' (p. 170) reminds us of the legend in which a goddess gives to a male hero the phallic symbol that will make him invulnerable.

Art and the Structure of Virginia Woolf's Novels

Whenever artists discuss art, they are talking about themselves; and Virginia Woolf is no exception to this rule. In the final part of this chapter, then, we can briefly consider what we learn about Woolf's approach to her novels, from the above analysis of Lily Briscoe.

Lily strives to answer the question 'What does it mean? How do you explain it all?' (p. 170) by means of her painting. So many of Virginia Woolf's characters in all three of the novels pose the same fundamental question about the meaning of life, that we can take this as an expression of Woolf's own motive: writing novels is her means of exploration, searching for an answer to the age-old question: what is the meaning of life?

In Lily Briscoe's struggles, this huge question seems to divide into two subsidiary problems. First, she finds herself in life's 'chaos' and searches for a 'shape' within it. There are several terms and images for this 'shape': we have met 'wholeness' and 'completeness', and we have come across both a 'globed compacted thing', and the bell-image of 'a sense of repetition – of one thing falling where another had fallen, and so setting up an echo which chimed in the air and made it full of vibrations'. Notice that the vision of 'shape' Virginia Woolf tries to create is always found in 'chaos': in 'rough and tumble', things 'all gone now and separate', or the list of unrelated details given on page 183 where she mentions 'some common feeling' called 'love' which 'held the whole together'.

Compare these ideas to the three novels we are studying. They, like life, seem like 'chaos' at first. There is hardly any plot: *Mrs Dalloway* is a day in the life of a middle-aged political wife who gives a party, interwoven with the last day and suicide of a traumatised ex-soldier. The two main characters never meet, however, and nothing significant happens to one of them. *To the Lighthouse* narrates two days, separated by a ten-year gap. Again, there are hardly any physical events, only mental ones, except during the 'gap' when marriages, a war, and deaths take place. In *The Waves*, the normal physical world of a novel's plot recedes into the background. We are still not sure who Neville loved, and we know nothing of Bernard's wife and children, even at the end of the novel. All three novels, then, deliberately lack the conventional 'shape' of a novelist's 'plot'. Additionally, the narrative in all three texts hops and changes between different characters' thoughts, between different places and times, without warning and with no explicit purpose. Woolf's intention is clearly to present us with superficially 'chaotic' novels.

Secondly, Lily faces the problem of death. Her struggle is to re-create Mrs Ramsay, to bring her back from the dead. This is expressed as 'a centre of complete emptiness' because '"you" and "I" and "she" pass and vanish; nothing stays; all changes', which provokes Lily to pose the age-old question, 'What did it mean?' (pp. 170–1). Woolf also conveys the pain of bereavement as an emotional need, 'to want and want and not to have' (p. 192).

The artist's solution to this problem is to 'make of the moment something permanent' by finding a form in which all the different elements of 'chaos' are held together or 'chime' due to a 'common feeling'. To Lily, death is 'some obstacle in her design' which her 'vision' is ultimately able to overcome.

These ideas also provide fruitful points of comparison with the structure of the novels. For example, in *Mrs Dalloway* Clarissa might have committed suicide; Septimus did commit suicide; and pure chance (he consulted Sir William Bradshaw; Sir William Bradshaw went to her party) allows these two unrelated facts to be 'held together' so that they 'chime'. We examined this 'chiming' relationship between Septimus's and Clarissa's lives in Chapter 6. In *To the Lighthouse*, the prospect of visiting the Lighthouse occurs on two days separated by ten years. When the three remaining Ramsays finally go there, their journey gives 'completeness' to such widely different and apparently unrelated elements as James's childhood fantasies and Lily's relationship with Mrs Ramsay. In *The Waves*, the progress of symbolic passages of description help to make the novel a 'globed, compacted thing' within the cycle of a single day from sunrise to sunset – yet it contains countless experiences and events which seem to be held together only by chance. In these ways, then, Virginia Woolf has structured her novels to imitate the effect Lily describes when she finds 'shape', or when the numberless chaotic details of life 'chime' and fill the air with 'vibrations'.

One subtle example will underline how Virginia Woolf has laboured to create the sense of a 'common feeling', the effect of a 'chime', in the apparent shapelessness of her novels. When Mrs Ramsay revives her jealousy of her husband, she remembers how 'gallant' he was during their courtship. In six words, Virginia Woolf mentions one memory ('helping her out of a boat') in passing (see p. 92). More than a hundred pages later, Lily remembers Mr Ramsay raising his wife from her chair, and her thoughts continue:

> It seemed somehow as if he had done it before; as if he had once bent in the same way and raised her from a boat which, lying a few inches off some island, had required that the ladies should thus be helped on shore by the gentlemen. An old-fashioned scene that was, which required, very nearly, crinolines and peg-top trousers.
>
> (*To The Lighthouse*, p. 188)

Lily imagines and elaborates in her mind, basing her fantasy upon the slightest actual memory. She creates a scene complete with period costumes, and goes on to imagine that it must have been at that moment that Mrs Ramsay agreed to marry him. Only six words, more than a hundred pages away, reveal to us that Lily's fantasy is ironically true. This is a perfect example of the subtle attention to detail in Virginia Woolf's writing, and shows how densely the 'chime' effect is worked into the novels, so that words, chance events and passing references revive each other in our minds as we read, and the book gives 'a sense of repetition' until its air is full of 'vibrations'.

Finally, notice that Lily indulges her imagination in this way more than once. She allows memories of various people to fill her mind while she is painting, but she also allows herself to create imaginary scenes involving these people. For example, Lily heard Paul Rayley say that he 'went to coffee-houses and played chess' (p. 165). On this basis, she imagines a dramatic quarrel between the Rayleys, 'on the staircase at dawn'. It does not matter whether the quarrel actually happened, or only exists in Lily's imagination. Because of the way Lily's creative mind works, imagination is a sensitive extension and elaboration of actual life: she notices a small detail, and can build a story, an accurate fantasy, upon that tiny piece of evidence.

In this manner of imagining, Lily seems to be a direct representative of her author, and her fantasies reveal the creative process in Virginia Woolf which is responsible for making her novels. External reality, physical 'plot' or 'fact', are uncertain and not important. It is the internal reality that Virginia Woolf is excited by, and she concentrates her energy on conveying this internal form of truth faithfully. As Lily expresses it, what she wished to get hold of was 'that very jar on the nerves, the thing itself before it has been made anything' (p. 184).

It is appropriate to the odd 'globed, compacted' structure of these novels that we end this seventh chapter with a point that, in slightly different terms, we first noticed in Chapter 1. Then, we realised that narrative events and dialogue were of secondary importance, because of 'Virginia Woolf's effort to create and express mental experience at a pre-rational level' (see Chapter 1). The particular features of her novels we have analysed throughout have this in common: they all contribute to Woolf's expression of her 'vision', an internal reality that is not apparent on the confusing and detailed surface of a character's life, but is a hidden 'shape' deep within the world's 'chaos'.

One final irony, and we are done. Virginia Woolf depicts Lily as a frustrated, 'dried-up old maid presumably', who diverts her sexual energy into her art. It is tempting to speculate that Virginia Woolf felt herself to be sexually inadequate, and ascribed her own compulsion to write novels to the same cause. It is better to resist this temptation, and to focus strictly on the novels themselves. After all, we should never forget that Mr Ramsay is absurd and his childish male behaviour is intolerable. Woolf clearly shows that there is no reason why any woman *ought* to respond to such male demands.

PART 2

THE CONTEXT AND THE CRITICS

8

Virginia Woolf's Life and Work

There is an enormous amount of information about Virginia Woolf's life. She herself wrote voluminously and almost continuously, so there are five volumes of her diaries, six volumes of her letters, her reading notebooks (more than sixty of these survive, which have been edited and published since her death), and the unfinished autobiographical sketch published in 1976 as *Moments of Being*. Additionally, she belonged to the 'Bloomsbury Group' of artists and intellectuals, many of whom became famous during their lives. Several of them wrote autobiographies and memoirs in which they describe Virginia Woolf; and her nephew Quentin Bell has collected a vast amount of hearsay and reminiscence from friends and relatives, in his landmark biography of his aunt Virginia (first published by the Hogarth Press in 1972). There are very few authors about whom we know so much. There is now a large and thriving academic industry devoted to considering, analysing and interpreting her life in terms of her writings and her writings in terms of her life. This industry has grown so pervasive that it is quite difficult for a present-day student to consider the novels as free-standing works of literature, without reference to some personal oddity, or the psychoanalysis, of Virginia Woolf herself.

Part 1 of this book has tried to steer clear of her life, however: our whole effort in those seven chapters has been to analyse the novels themselves. We have become involved in some 'psychoanalysis', but only about the characters, never about the author herself. Remember that our task as students of literature is to understand and assess the significance of the completed work; never to see the work as a by-product of some neurosis or trauma in the author's life. If you do become interested in Virginia Woolf's life, one section of *Further Reading*, at the end of this book, lists her autobiographical writings and one or two other titles, which will get you started. Our purpose in this chapter is merely to give outline information about her life, and the development of her writing. We will only attempt to draw the broadest conclusions from this information.

Virginia Woolf's Life

Virginia Woolf was born Adeline Virginia Stephen, in 1882. She had a sister and two brothers, two step-brothers and two step-sisters. Her father, Leslie Stephen, was an academic who had hoped to be a philosopher, but his life's work was in the history of philosophy, and a vast project called the *Dictionary of National Biography*, and he was not remembered as an original thinker. Her mother, Julia Stephen, believed in a traditional, subservient role for women, and was dedicated to ideals of service and duty. Julia died when Virginia was thirteen. Leslie died when she was twenty-two. By the time she was twenty-three, Virginia was living in Bloomsbury in apartments shared with her sister and brothers, and setting about her own career as a writer.

Virginia Stephen had a sporadic, unsystematic education. Her mother thought that she should know how to manage a household, and should leave intellectual pursuits to the men. Her father encouraged her to read and taught her a great deal, although there was no question of her going to university as her brothers did. After her mother's death, Virginia was ill, and her lessons were interrupted for two years on the advice of a doctor who thought that her head was using up all her nourishment, and that was why she had become thin and frail (we now think of her illness as anorexia). Instead of following his advice and emptying her head, Virginia read widely and precociously during those two years.

Virginia's childhood and youth exposed her to an unremitting series of emotional shocks. One of her half-sisters, Laura, was mentally retarded, and was sent away to a home after years of the family treating her as an idiot. A well-known cousin called Jem, who often stayed at the house, became deranged following a head injury. He was eventually forcibly restrained and locked up in an asylum. Virginia was sexually abused by her half-brothers, Gerald and George Duckworth. The abuse began before she was six years old, and continued for a number of years. Her mother's death brought on Virginia's first experience of what we call a 'breakdown', which also led to her becoming anorectic. Just as she was recovering, Virginia's half-sister Stella married, moved out, and died a few months later (when Virginia was fifteen). Leslie Stephen's death seven years later followed a lengthy illness during which Virginia nursed him, and only two years after that (in 1906) her favourite brother, Thoby, caught typhoid fever on a trip abroad, and died. In summary, Virginia Woolf's childhood was a series of emotional shocks and bereavements; at the same time she had considerable contact with actual and incipient madness, and suffered the indelible personal damage of long-term sexual abuse.

Following her father's death Virginia suffered another breakdown, and stayed for periods of time with her friend Violet Dickinson and her aunt Caroline Stephen, both strong and independent women whose influence encouraged Virginia's determination to reject the traditional role of a woman, and to live independently, earning her living as a writer. By December 1904, Virginia had published a review and an essay in the women's supplement of the *Guardian*, and was launched into journalism.

Between 1904 and 1909, Virginia built up her career as a journalist, travelled extensively throughout Europe, and lived in Bloomsbury. Her sister Vanessa married Clive Bell in 1907, but Virginia continued to live with her surviving brother Adrian. The early 'Bloomsbury Group' began to coalesce during this time. They were a collection of artists and intellectuals devoted to ideals of art and philosophy, but they did not yet include many of the people who would make the 'group' famous during the two succeeding decades, although the Bells and the Stracheys were already involved, as well as Virginia and her artist sister Vanessa.

In 1909 Caroline Stephen died, leaving Virginia a legacy which brought in £400 a year. This enabled her to give up some of her journalism work, and to concentrate more of her energy on her favourite project of writing novels. However, the next few years were difficult for her. Virginia suffered several mental breakdowns and often had suicidal feelings. She attempted suicide in 1913, and probably on another occasion before then.

In 1912 Virginia married Leonard Woolf. The next two and a half years were very turbulent due to Virginia's illnesses and her suicide attempt, and the couple had to face her frigidity and a final decision that they would not attempt to have children because of her health. In addition, they were struggling financially. Leonard had given up his job in the colonial Civil Service in order to marry; and he had to establish himself as a journalist while working for a small income. Virginia's earnings were almost nothing at this time, and much of her legacy was whittled away in doctors' and nurses' fees: it was very expensive to be mad. In the middle of this, in 1915, Virginia's first novel *The Voyage Out* was published. By 1916 the marriage had reached a stable and affectionate partnership, and from then onwards Leonard Woolf figures as a loving and supportive husband until Virginia's death in 1941.

In 1917 Leonard and Virginia bought a second-hand printing-press and set it up in the basement of their home, 'Hogarth House', in Richmond. They learned printing and began to publish as the Hogarth Press. This venture began gradually, but became a profitable business during the twenties and thirties. More importantly, it set Virginia free from publishers' readers, enabling her to write what she wanted, and in the way she wanted. The 'Bloomsbury Group' had grown and become much more important as an influential and talented group of young artists, including such people as T. S. Eliot, E. M. Forster, Maynard Keynes, Leonard Woolf, Lytton Strachey, Clive Bell, and the painters Roger Fry, Duncan Grant and Vanessa (Stephens) Bell. Throughout the 1920s the Woolfs' prosperity steadily increased, and Virginia's career as journalist and novelist gained her steadily increasing respect and success. We should never think of Virginia's personal life as quiet, however. Although this was, by and large, a stable decade in her life, she had a lesbian affair with Vita Sackville-West in 1925, which gave rise to a long and intensely passionate correspondence; and in 1926 she suffered another break-down, becoming very depressed and feeling suicidal again.

The 1930s was a different decade for Virginia Woolf. She con-tinued to write and publish novels; she was established as an impor-tant journalist and speaker; and the Woolfs were financially well-off. On the other hand, Lytton Strachey died in 1932 and Roger Fry in 1934. These were shocks which reminded Virginia that the 'Bloomsbury Group' had never been a permanent thing. In addition, the political situation demanded attention with the rise of fascism in Germany and Italy, and the fight against fascism in the Spanish Civil War of 1936–37. Several of Virginia's friends took part in the Spanish war, and her nephew Julian Bell was killed in Spain. Virginia Woolf's greatest successes had been in the twenties, and now her energies seemed to be uncomfortably divided between writing novels on the one side, and the political activities of writing, speaking, joining groups and going to meetings, in which her conscience told her she ought to be involved. She also wrote a fully researched biog-raphy of Roger Fry, which took some of her attention for several years and was published in 1940.

In March 1941 the Woolfs were staying in their country home at Rodmell in Sussex. Leonard became concerned about Virginia's health as she seemed to be heading for another breakdown, and he persuaded her to consult a friend who was also a doctor. On the morning after this consultation, Virginia wrote letters to her sister Vanessa Bell, and to Leonard, saying that she knew her madness was coming on and that she would not recover this time. She also said that she knew she would not be able to write again. Then she went out and drowned herself.

Clearly, even this rather detached account of her life displays several lures which tempt us to speculate about the novels. The early sexual abuse, for example, seems to command us to reread Clarissa Dalloway's and Lily Briscoe's attitudes to sex and men. The lesbian affair clamours for our attention, in relation to Clarissa's friendship with Sally Seton. The characters of Mr and Mrs Stephen, Virginia's parents, cry out to be compared to Mr and Mrs Ramsay in *To The Lighthouse*; and the repeated tale of nervous breakdowns, culminating in suicide, compels us to return to numerous passages from all three of the novels we are studying. However, it would be wrong to diminish the novels. Like most writers, Virginia Woolf used material that originated in her own experience; but the study of neurosis is not the study of literature, and her life must not explain away her novels – they remain complete and significant works of literature in their own right.

Virginia Woolf's Writings

Virginia Woolf wrote almost continuously, even as a child; and she continued to do so throughout her life. There were small gaps when she did not write – by far the longest was the two years after her mother's death – which usually coincided with some external crisis; but her determined vocation of writing was otherwise exercised every day. We will summarise her work, dividing her productive life broadly into three periods. The first period is from her first journalism until the publication of the first novel *The Voyage Out* (roughly between 1904 and 1915). The second period includes the success of the Hogarth Press, and the publication of her most successful novels, culminating in *The Waves* (1931). The third period is the final ten years of her life.

Virginia Woolf was writing during her childhood: the Stephens children produced a magazine for their parents, called *Hyde Park Gate News*, until their mother's death; and Virginia continued to write stories, essays and other incidental pieces. However, the first period of her writing career begins with the publication of a review and an essay in the women's supplement of the *Guardian* in December 1904. From then until 1909 her output increased steadily, averaging more than thirty published essays each year. She wrote reviews, articles and essays; and gradually stopped sending her work to the *Guardian*. By 1906 she had established herself as an author for the more prestigious (and higher-paying) *Times Literary Supplement* (*TLS*) and *Cornhill* magazines; and from 1909, when her legacy from Caroline Stephen enabled her to cut down her journalistic work, her journalism was published exclusively in the *TLS* for about ten years. In this period of her life, Virginia Woolf learned the business of writing articles and reviews to order. At the same time she experimented with several short stories which were not published, and she began the novel which was eventually published by Duckworth's in 1908 as *The Voyage Out*.

We have taken the first period as ending in 1915, but it may be that the legacy that enabled her to drop journalism and concentrate on fiction was in some way a double-edged gift. She published only two or three articles a year after 1909, none at all in 1914 and 1915, and went through personal crisis after personal crisis; while her novel went through draft after draft, taking more than six years to write. *The Voyage Out* is the story of a girl's struggle to become a woman without surrendering her 'independent self'. The outcome is pessimistic, as the heroine dies without having achieved her quest for maturity. Virginia Woolf revised the novel for a new edition in 1920, making considerable cuts and rewriting in order to even up what she considered bad passages, and to tighten the conceptual structure. This revised version is the one you can buy today.

The second period of Woolf's career begins in 1916 with a resumption of writing essays and other pieces for the *TLS*. During this time in her life her output of short pieces for the *TLS*, and later for the *New Statesman* and *Nation* magazines, was steady. At the same time, beginning in 1917 with a booklet containing two short stories – one by each of them – she and Leonard ran the Hogarth Press which published a variety of novels and other works by Virginia. The three novels studied in this book all belong to this period. *Mrs Dalloway* was published in 1925, *To the Lighthouse* in 1927, and *The Waves* in 1931. Brief details of her other works during this period are as follows.

Night and Day (1919) is a novel about class conflicts in England before the First World War. It was regarded as a disappointing second novel, and is not widely read today.

Monday or Tuesday (1921) is a collection of eight stories and other pieces. This was well reviewed, and enhanced Virginia Woolf's reputation, particularly as the stories tried to capture the process of characters thinking. Reviewers noticed that her approach to writing was both 'new' and had 'beauty'.

Jacob's Room (1922) is the first novel Virginia Woolf wrote in a 'modernist' form, and is her 'anti-war' novel. It tells the life of its eponymous hero until his death in the Great War; but there is hardly any conventional 'plot' so the episodes seem bluntly disconnected, and his death is not a conclusion, it is merely a sudden interruption, emphasising how incomplete his life was. This novel established her reputation for experimental and 'difficult' fiction, and reviewers divided between approving and deriding her achievement. Arnold Bennett's scathing comments on *Jacob's Room* revived the simmering hostility Virginia had felt towards him since he wrote about the inferiority of women, in 1920. She wrote a series of articles arguing that the older 'Edwardian' novelists (Bennett, Galsworthy, Wells) had brought the novel to a dead-end, and it was the job of new writers such as herself to smash their sterile conventions and create something new. The articles appear in several places and versions, all called *Mr Bennett and Mrs Brown* (1923, 1924).

Mrs Dalloway (1925) was the next novel, and in the same year the first series of *The Common Reader* was published. This was a book of criticism, largely based upon essays which had already been published, but revised, drawn together and with new material added. Both of these books were well received, and sold well.

To the Lighthouse (1927) was successful. Several reviewers hailed it as a great novel. It marked Virginia Woolf's arrival as a recognised and significant author; and sales, although not on the scale of a 'popular' novel, were much better than for any of her previous books and brought real financial comfort to the Woolfs.

Orlando (1928) is a novel about a character who seems to go through reincarnations between his (or her) childhood in Elizabethan times, and the twentieth century. Orlando's transformations also change the character's sex, so that experiences are narrated from both male and female points of view. This novel is light-hearted, full of period-parody and exuberant writing. It was very successful, selling even more copies than *To The Lighthouse*.

A Room of One's Own (1929) has a fictional element, the imaginary lecturer who supposedly wrote it; but it is a polemical work: a serious essay on the predicament of a woman who wants to be a writer.

The Waves (1931) was a critical success, and considering the difficulty of the novel, Virginia Woolf was surprised that it sold very well – more than 10,000 copies in Britain in the first six months.

The final period we describe follows the highest point of Virginia Woolf's success as a novelist with *The Waves*. In the final decade of her life, her career as a published writer seemed to move in two different directions. She wrote literary criticism, biography and polemic. There were debates and controversies over these books, and she herself disliked writing her formal biography *Roger Fry* (1940), feeling that biography was always a suspect form; but she was satisfied that these works successfully achieved her aims in writing them. In 1932 she published another collection of literary essays called *The Common Reader: Second Series*; and in 1938 her long pacifist and feminist essay *Three Guineas* came out. This is an attempt to ask what women can do to help prevent war. Woolf argued that men are victims in a cultural system that forces them to become immature despots, so women should work against the dominant culture in order to emancipate men. Men will then be able to become mature in a way that she thought impossible for them within society as it was. This polemical work attracted hostility from several of her contemporaries, but Virginia Woolf took their diatribes calmly.

The novels of this decade, on the other hand, were unsatisfying. *Flush* (1933) is a slight and comic piece about a dog. *The Years* (1937) was her next serious novel. Its form had passed through several transformations during the several years it took to complete. It is a novel about a family, following their lives over several decades, and was conceived on the grand scale. Woolf seems to have abandoned her fascinating depiction of intimate levels of thought, and *The Years* contains much description of external things, instead. Its reception was mixed – some reviews were in favour, while others were disappointed – but Virginia Woolf herself was never happy with the book because it had not turned out as she originally intended, and was 'an odious rice-pudding of a book'[1]

---

[1] *The Diary of Virginia Woolf*, ed. Anne Olivier Bell, Hogarth Press, London, 1977–84, Vol. 5, 2 April 1937.

Between the Acts (1941) was left as a complete manuscript, but unrevised, when Virginia Woolf committed suicide. It is commonly regarded as one of her most successful novels, and centres on the theme of a writer and the community her literature creates or invokes, developing the theme of an unending conflict between the tendency of things to fragment and disperse, and to unite or come together. This novel did not receive a great deal of praise when it was published, but its reputation has grown since then. In any event, Virginia Woolf was already dead before the reviewers read *Between the Acts*. As far as she was concerned, she produced no satisfying serious fiction in the last ten years of her life.

The Development of Themes in Virginia Woolf's Work

In Part 1 of this book, the extracts we analysed led us to discuss a fundamental conflict at work in all three novels. We called this a conflict between two forces: one a destructive force which fragments and disperses things, and whose end is chaos. The other is a creative force, found in humanity and among animals, based upon instincts for survival and self-protection. This force tends to pull and hold things together, to build and to create unity.

We noticed that in *Mrs Dalloway* and much of *To the Lighthouse*, these forces are identified with specific elements in the novels. For example, Clarissa's 'creative' energy maintains her social façade, while her subconscious is destructive and chaotic. For most of *To the Lighthouse*, the sea and nature appear chaotic, while Mrs Ramsay's 'creative' energy is spent maintaining her orderly view of 'civilisation'. In Part III of *To the Lighthouse*, however, Lily's painting broadens the idea. Here, and in *The Waves*, these forces are portrayed in a more emblematic and universal manner. They are no longer tied to specific parts of the narrative, but pervade everything. So, while *Mrs Dalloway* explores this basic conflict, Lily Briscoe's character proposes a solution to it. The new truth expressed in *To the Lighthouse*, and further elaborated in *The Waves*, is in the form of a paradox: plunge into the seeming chaos, suffer the danger of destruction, and 'shape' can be discovered within the 'chaos'. Clearly,

Virginia Woolf's exploration of this theme, and her ideas, moved forward between 1925 and 1931.

We also looked at Woolf's critique of society, in Chapter 4. The development we notice between *Mrs Dalloway* and *The Waves* seems to move from the specific to the general, in the same way. For example, the targets of social satire in *Mrs Dalloway* are specific hypocrisies such as the Empire, nationalism, and macho ideals of courage (see Septimus) or the dullness of Conservative politicians (Richard Dalloway). In *The Waves*, by contrast, material life is presented as myriad trivial objects and details, all superficial. Virginia Woolf conveys a more emblematic and analytical critique of society in the later novel: she seems more interested in an underlying truth, less concerned to hit a particular target. The social theme of *To the Lighthouse*, with its dysfunctional family and the academically ambitious Mr Tansley, presents a middle stage in this development.

A large part of Virginia Woolf's analysis of society is, of course, her critique of the politics of gender. We have studied how her awareness of male exploitation and 'feminine' roles is woven into the narrative and characters of all three novels. However, the development of Bernard in the final section of *The Waves* suggests that Woolf was moving towards a more universal perception. Bernard is developed to express the points of view of all six characters – three male and three female – in his retrospective memoir at the end. This suggests a vision which can pass beyond the social restrictions of male and female roles, a view that is not specific either to a man or to a woman. Woolf's novel *Orlando* is another essay on this theme.

Finally, Virginia Woolf portrays art, closely associated with ancient and primitive human expressions in natural mythology, as the means of vision (see Chapter 7) which will reveal life's 'shape' within 'chaos'. This is clear from both *To the Lighthouse* and *The Waves*.

Looking at Virginia Woolf's other literary output, this development of her themes is underlined. It is worth noticing that her unsatisfying but ambitious novel *The Years* aimed at a more emblematic and panoramic vision of human life in the form of a dynasty; while the final novel *Between the Acts* has a writer, Miss La Trobe, as its protagonist, and further explores the destructive (dispersing) and creative (uniting) forces in life, art and nature. Virginia Woolf's final feminist work, *Three Guineas*, also confirms her development from a focus upon specific things and towards the analysis of underlying truths. Her argument calls for women – and subsequently men – to pass beyond the socially engineered restrictions of sexual politics, and to be liberated into a mature existence as free, independent humans, without reference to gender.

9

Virginia Woolf's Contribution to the Development of the Novel

During the nineteenth century, the novel form established itself as a major means of literary expression. A variety of different kinds of novel appeared, ranging from the grand panorama of life in a country town we find in George Eliot's *Middlemarch*, to novels pursuing social injustice such as Dickens's *Hard Times* or life-stories like his *David Copperfield* and Hardy's *Tess of the D'Urbervilles*; thrillers such as Wilkie Collins's *The Woman in White*, and continuations of the gothic tradition such as Emily Brontë's romantic masterpiece *Wuthering Heights*. It was not difficult to analyse the history of the novel, and to see that the autobiographical novel had developed from early examples such as Defoe's *Robinson Crusoe*; or that *Wuthering Heights*, with its emphasis on dreams and visions, and its tragic intensity of emotion, inherited the gothic–romantic tradition from Mary Shelley's *Frankenstein* and Mrs Radcliffe's *Udolpho*. It was also clear that the novel had responded to the cultural shocks of rationalism in the second half of the century. Hardy's novels, for example, confront the rationalist's experience of atheism, after Darwin. Dickens in England, and even more Émile Zola in France, had written damning indictments of industrial exploitation, using the novel form to campaign for social justice and reform. At the end of the nineteenth century, then, it was relatively easy to see what novels had achieved; but much more difficult to imagine how novels might develop in the future.

Virginia Woolf's Approach to the Novel

Virginia Woolf intended to continue in the tradition of the great novelists. In *Mr Bennett and Mrs Brown* she mentions Tolstoy, Thackeray, Sterne, Hardy, Austen, Charlotte Brontë and Flaubert, saying that the essential genius of these writers was in creating 'some character who has seemed to you so real (I do not by that mean so lifelike) that it has the power to make you think not merely of itself, but of all sorts of things through its eyes'.[1] She then tells a story in which she observed the behaviour of a 'Mrs Brown' on a train journey, and dramatically imagined the stranger's character and circumstances. In her conclusion, Woolf clearly commits herself to pursuing character as the essential element of novels: 'Your part is to insist that writers shall come down off their plinths and pedestals, and describe beautifully if possible, truthfully at any rate, our Mrs Brown. You should insist that she is an old lady of unlimited capacity and infinite variety; capable of appearing in any place; wearing any dress; saying anything and doing heaven knows what.' Writers must focus on her, the character, because she has 'an overwhelming fascination' and is 'the spirit we live by, life itself' (both *Mr Bennett and Mrs Brown*, p. 87).

Clearly, then, Virginia Woolf intended to continue the work of great novelists of the past by focusing on character. On the other hand, she recognised that the novel form needed to change, because the conservative writers of her own youth had lost their way. She was particularly critical of Arnold Bennett, John Galsworthy and H. G. Wells, accusing them of giving all the details of life *except* character, in their books. In the essay already quoted, Woolf imagines these three in the same railway carriage, observing Mrs Brown. Mr Wells,

---

[1] From *A Woman's Essays: Selected Essays, Vol. 1*, ed. Rachel Bowlby, Penguin, London, 1992, p. 76.

she wrote, 'would instantly project upon the window-pane a vision of a better, breezier, jollier, happier, more adventurous and gallant world' but would not 'waste a thought upon [Mrs Brown] as she is' (*Mr Bennett and Mrs Brown*, p. 77). Mr Galsworthy would notice a passing factory outside the carriage-window, and 'Burning with indignation, stuffed with information, arraigning civilization, Mr Galsworthy would only see in Mrs Brown a pot broken on the wheel and thrown into the corner.' Mr Bennett would 'keep his eyes in the carriage' but he would only see the material details, 'how Mrs Brown wore a brooch which had cost three-and-ten-three at Whitworth's bazaar; and had mended both gloves', not the old lady's character at all (*Mr Bennett and Mrs Brown*, p. 78).

The novel had been taken into a dead-end, then: the real life of characters, which is the raw material of literature, was being ignored by the writers of Woolf's youth. The novel form needed to evolve, or be reborn. What was to be done about it?

Virginia Woolf understood that new writers, such as D. H. Lawrence, E. M. Forster and James Joyce, were doing this work. Their novels were new, and different from anything that had gone before. At the same time, she did not think that they had found the future form yet. Their work was necessary, but experimental, pulling down the dead conventions but not yet putting anything in their place. 'And so the smashing and the crashing began. Thus it is that we hear all round us, in poems and novels and biographies, even in newspaper articles and essays, the sound of breaking and falling, crashing and destruction' (*Mr Bennett and Mrs Brown*, p. 84).

Virginia Woolf was looking for a better way of creating her characters' inner experiences, their private and hidden mental and emotional experiences, then. She read *Ulysses*, in which James Joyce pioneered the style of narrative that tries to represent an apparently irrational and disconnected flow of thoughts and perceptions in the mind. This style was commonly referred to as 'stream-of-consciousness writing' and was a novelist's way of responding to the new insights of psychology. Virginia Woolf found in *Ulysses* a style which in its 'restless scintillations, in its irrelevance, its flashes of deep significance succeeded by incoherent inanities, seems to be life itself'.[2] Yet she was dissatisfied with Joyce because she thought his aim was to record every thought, and she was searching for a more shapely vision of the character's mind: she wanted her novels to have a new kind of form or 'shape', not merely the infinite mess she saw in Joyce's 'stream of consciousness'. Her image for the hidden processes of thought was of a chain sunk into the sea-bed: 'the links between one thought and another are submerged. The chain is sunk out of sight and only the leading points emerge to mark the course'.[3] She admired Dostoevsky's ability to see the whole length of the chain – the whole train of thought – and to illuminate that in his novels, as well as his ability to suggest an 'underworld' where 'desires and impulses are moving blindly'.

On the other hand, Woolf was suspicious of psychological theory: she wished to write about life itself in its rich complexity; and she knew that Freudian theory could become merely a simplification of reality. Reviewing a Freudian novel in 1920, she wrote: 'we do not wish to debar Mr Beresford from making use of any key that seems to him to fit the human mind. Our complaint is rather that . . . the new key is a patent key that opens every door. It simplifies'.[4] To sum up, Virginia Woolf was searching for a new way to convey character in writing. She was interested in re-creating the actual processes of the mind, but she wanted to convey a complete shape – the whole chain of ideas – not just the confusing mess of 'consciousness'; yet she wanted to convey life itself, and was wary of writing from any limited or fixed theory that would simplify and distance us from actual experience.

Virginia Woolf succeeded in these aims. We have found how tightly structured her novels are in terms of passing thoughts, echoes and contrasts, and in the use of metaphors. She managed to achieve that abstract quality called 'shape'. She also found a method of entering and revealing her characters' inner consciousness, although from the way she writes about this it seems that she hit upon her

---

[2] 'Modern Novels', in *The Essays of Virginia Woolf*, ed. Andrew McNellie, Hogarth Press, London, 1986–88, Vol. 3, p. 34.
[3] 'More Dostoevsky', in *ibid.*, Vol. 2, p. 83.
[4] 'Freudian Fiction', in *A Woman's Essays*, Vol. 1, p. 23.

particular technique almost by accident. Her diary note while she was writing *Mrs Dalloway* sounds full of glee, as if she had found a new toy: 'I should say a good deal about [*Mrs Dalloway*], & my discovery; how I dig out beautiful caves behind my characters; I think that gives exactly what I want; humanity, humour, depth. The idea is that the caves shall connect, & each comes to daylight at the present moment'.[5] She called this her 'tunnelling process' and used it to 'tell the past by instalments'.[6] Two points are worth noting here. First, that she wanted the 'caves' in her characters to 'connect': in other words, she was building unity, not disconnected bits and pieces of her character's mind. In her other image, this is the equivalent to exposing the whole length of submerged chain, all linked together. Second, she used the method to bring memories of the past into her character's present moment. The effect in her novels, then, is of a fully developed personality who grows a more and more detailed past experience as the novel progresses, as memories are dredged 'by instalments', as the present brings them back from their darkness. This method again enhances the coherence of the whole novel. Mrs Dalloway is the narrative of a single day – yet by this means Virginia Woolf overcomes the problem of explanation: her character's past can be included in the one day, without the need for clumsy flashbacks or any 'structure' of chronological connections, because the memories come to Clarissa and the other characters as fragments of the past. The result is a feeling of intensity, and the fullness of characterisation, without elaboration of plot or extension of the tight time-scheme of the novel.

Virginia Woolf was also very aware that she was a woman and a novelist. She wrote about this and developed ideas about how women had been able to express femininity within the 'patriarchal' tradition of the novel, in the past. In particular, Woolf was highly conscious that what she calls the 'scaffolding' of a traditional novel – the plot, or a narrative structure that is linear in time and depends

---

[5] *The Diary of Virginia Woolf,* ed. Anne Olivier Bell, Hogarth Press, London, 1977–84, Vol. 2, 30 August 1923.
[6] *ibid.*, 15 October 1923.

on external 'events' – reflects a male view of what is important in the world:

> there rises for consideration the very difficult question of the difference between the man's and the woman's view of what constitutes the importance of any subject. From this spring not only marked differences of plot and incident, but infinite differences in selection, method and style.[7]

Woolf adds detail to this perception in *A Room of One's Own*. She points out that 'the values of women differ very often from the values which have been made by the other sex . . . yet it is the masculine values that prevail'. The majority of critics make masculine assumptions when they assess a new novel:

> This is an important book, the critic assumes, because it deals with war. This is an insignificant book because it deals with the feelings of women in a drawing-room. A scene in a battlefield is more important than a scene in a shop.[8]

She criticised the 'patriarchal' establishment of Bennett, Galsworthy and Wells for their failure to create true character in their works; but at the same time she attacked the wider tradition as being a product of the masculine domination of culture.

Woolf's structural and narrative innovations all contributed to breaking down this male domination, and were deliberately intended to do so. Her feminism is thus another reason why we find so little 'scaffolding' in her novels; and why the external events she narrates are often mere accidental moments in external life, rather than events that a man would consider important. Notice, for example, that the visit to the lighthouse does not happen – it is not an event – in Part I of *To the Lighthouse*. The 'event' which provides

---

[7] 'Women Novelists', in *Women and Writing*, ed. Michèle Barrett, Women's Press, London, 1979, p. 71.
[8] *A Room of One's Own*, Harcourt, Brace and World, Harbinger Book, New York, 1929, 1957, pp. 76–7.

energy to the start of the novel is Mr Ramsay's adverse comment about the weather. This is a crucial event, of supreme importance in the lives of Mrs Ramsay and James; but it is not a war, a crime, or a dangerous adventure.

Woolf concluded that the woman writer of fiction, in the nineteenth century, was bound to produce a distorted view of experience. Whether she was docile and diffident, or angry, made no difference: 'She had altered her values in deference to the opinions of others'.[9] It is clear, then, that Virginia Woolf saw the task of a modern woman novelist as subversive: she had to undermine the dominance of male values in traditional fiction, subversively writing fiction in a new, different way, which would express a woman's values. She had no intention of altering these values 'in deference' to a patriarchal establishment.

Virginia Woolf's Contribution to the Novel

Virginia Woolf's work, regenerating the novel form, fits into the first decades of the twentieth century. Although she was always somewhat aloof, a critical 'outsider', she belonged to the 'Bloomsbury Group' and the writers who were called – and called themselves – 'modernist'. The contribution these artists made to the development of painting was considerable. They were responsible for introducing post-impressionism to Britain, in the exhibition of 1912; and the work of Roger Fry, Vanessa Bell and Duncan Grant was, for painting, like the 'smashing and the crashing' that Virginia heard in modernist literature. A complacent artistic establishment dominated the end of the Victorian era, still reproducing representational realism in the manner of the 'old masters'. Post-impressionism swept away all this: the representation of outside reality was not important, painting could do without it. Emotion or the soul of expression was all-important, conveyed by shape, pattern, colour, composition – without reference to whether the painting copied what the eye saw in external 'reality'.

---

[9] *ibid.*

Virginia Woolf performed a similar task for the novel. She swept away what she called the 'scaffolding' of novels – all the descriptive and reality-imitating details that made the novels of Dickens, for example, convincing copies of life in his time. She also dispensed with conventional beginnings and ends, and the traditional structure of events in time, which we call 'plot'. Virginia Woolf's structural experiments were also being tried by other authors. For example, *Mrs Dalloway* tells about one day's experiences for two characters whose lives are not connected with each other, except by the slightest coincidence at the end. This is substantially the same structure as Joyce's *Ulysses*. Also, there is no climactic 'event' which brings the plot to an end: Virginia Woolf's novels simply stop while life goes on. This was also true of Lawrence's *Sons and Lovers* or *The Rainbow*. On the other hand, no other author succeeded in taking the 'deconstruction' of the novel form as far as she did with *The Waves*. In this novel we are told hardly anything about events – or even the important relationships of marriage and parenthood – in the characters' lives. Bernard works, he is married, has children and a home, but the reader knows nothing whatsoever about that part of Bernard. We only meet his inner consciousness, not any framework of his external life. The structure of *The Waves* has nothing to do with plot, then: its shape is expressed by means of symbolic metaphor, in the series of 'interludes' printed in italics, which, when put together, describe the progress of a single day from dawn to dusk.

In this sense, then, Virginia Woolf took part in the 'smashing and the crashing' which took the entire idea of a 'novel' back to the drawing-board in the first decades of the twentieth century. She did without the conventional tools that had been thought necessary to the novel form up to that time. But she did a great deal more than this as well, for she found new forms for the novel, and made them work successfully. There are two particular achievements that survive as significant advances.

First, she succeeded in incorporating 'the dark region of psychology' in her fiction, through her 'tunnelling' technique. Eighty years later, James Joyce's *Ulysses* is an established classic, and decades of literary analysis has shown that his 'stream-of-consciousness' method is not the passive recording of disconnected detail that

Virginia Woolf thought it to be: it is constructed, and throws up moments of illumination. On the other hand it is still a huge, forbiddingly inaccessible novel, which seems discouragingly formless on the surface, and it is more often read in universities than anywhere else. Virginia Woolf's *Mrs Dalloway* and *To the Lighthouse*, on the other hand, succeed in illuminating experience in a more manageable compass. We can see the peaks and troughs in the submerged landscape of her character's mind, as the book illuminates them for us.

Second, Virginia Woolf developed and extended the use of symbol and metaphor in prose fiction, borrowing from the use of these devices in poetry. In *To the Lighthouse* and *The Waves*, in particular, symbols and metaphors are used to substitute for the old conventions of plot, exposition, denouement, setting and descriptive detail. These achievements show that she was not only a destroyer of tired old writing methods; she also left vital gifts behind which have been incorporated into the repertoire of the contemporary novelist. Even those who are not renowned for experiments with form, often show a debt.

If we think about William Golding's novels, for example, Woolf's legacy is clear. One of his most experimental novels, *Pincher Martin*, retells Martin's life in the form of memories, all of which occur between the moment when Martin lands in the water, and the moment when he drowns: the whole novel takes place at the moment before death, and its length is a protracted exercise of the technique Virginia Woolf called 'tunnelling'. More surprisingly, we should notice the ease with which Golding and other modern novelists slip into metaphor and out again when describing mental experience. Readers of *Lord of the Flies* will remember the 'flap' in Ralph's mind. A writer can now move confidently from narrative straight into metaphor, using this facility as a technique the reader will accept and follow. It would be an exaggeration to say that Virginia Woolf was solely responsible for this – I would mention D. H. Lawrence as another important contributor in this respect. However, we should recognise that she played a major part in the process of reinventing and modernising the novel form.

The 'New' Subject-matter: Psychology and Feminism

Virginia Woolf must have absorbed many of the new ideas of psychology from her Bloomsbury friends, before 1920. Her short review, 'Freudian Fiction', quoted earlier in this chapter, shows a working acquaintance with the main principles of psychoanalysis. Lytton Strachey's brother James translated Freud's works into English for the first time, and they were first published in Britain by Virginia and Leonard Woolf's Hogarth Press in 1924. So, although she did not read Freud for herself until the late 1930s, the obviously psychoanalytic interest and features of Virginia Woolf's novels can be accepted as part of the artistic community's response to new psychological theories at that time. This new subject-matter was revolutionary, and was shocking to many. We must remember that the traditional structure, for human activity, of motive–decision–action–result, was wiped out by Freud's theory of the unconscious. Speeches, conscious intentions, public behaviour and manners were suddenly seen as curiously irrelevant. Dark impulses and hidden instincts took their place. It is clear that there was a radical change of emphasis from the description of external reality, to an attempt at description of the inside. So, the new subject-matter of psychology was an inseparable part of the need to smash the conventions of the novel, and the need to find new techniques and forms.

Virginia Woolf's journalistic and polemical writings show that she made a significant contribution to the development of feminist thought. The study and assessment of her feminist views is not the subject of this book; except as far as the exploration of feminist insight and experience is a constant subject in her novels. At the time when she was arguing against Arnold Bennett, Woolf had been particularly offended by the argument in his *Our Women* (1920) that 'intellectually and creatively man is the superior of woman'. She expressed her hostility in essays, articles and letters to newspapers. We know that she saw Bennett, Galsworthy and Wells as inferior writers whose conventions were 'ruin' and whose 'tools [were] death', but it is also clear that she saw them as tyrannical patriarchs, examples of males who assume arrogant authority to oppress women. This view also extended to their books: the conventional novel was a patriarchal product, with its emphasis on material details and the dull mechanism of plot. It is just like men to be impressed by show and action – by what 'happens' – and to ignore or be blind to what 'is'. So, her consciousness of being a woman and a writer also urged Virginia Woolf to cast down the conventions the patriarchs had built. The feminist subject-matter of her novels both influenced, and developed with, her innovations in form and technique.

Finally, Woolf's novels are distinctively 'modern' in the broadest sense, which is also the most difficult to define. If we imagine that the combined ideas of Marx, Darwin and Freud, and many other thinkers of about the same time, are like a vast axe that chopped away the supports on which the Victorian world-view was built, we can think of the shock and the new challenge felt by individuals in their attempt to confront life. It must have been both frightening and stimulating. In a context of atheism, disturbing news from the subconscious, an unjustifiable, crumbling social structure and ruinous war, the 'new' individual had to search for a meaning in life. In other words, the search for a meaning in life had never been so apparently hopeless. Virginia Woolf's novels are distinctively modern as they reflect this new, unsupported awareness of the human condition.

10

A Sample of Critical Views

Hundreds of books and articles have been written by academic critics about Virginia Woolf's novels, and many more are published each year. They are often written in a confusing, over-complicated or pretentious style: academics are just as fond of showing off as anybody else. It is important to remember that, since you have read the novels, your ideas are just as valid as theirs. Always be critical of their ideas: you are not under an obligation to agree with them. Your mind can be stimulated by discussing the text with your teachers and lecturers, or in a class. Treat the critics in the same way: it is stimulating to debate the text by reading their books and articles, challenging your ideas and theirs. This is the spirit in which you should read 'the critics'.

With Virginia Woolf you should be alert to the added problem that much of the published criticism includes analysis of Virginia Woolf, the historical person, rather than analysis of the texts; and it is useful to keep this in mind to avoid pursuing unjustifiable or non-literary conclusions in your own studies.

In this chapter we sample three different critical views of Virginia Woolf's work as a novelist. We assess and discuss these views in relation to each other and in the light of what we have found in our own study of the texts.

* * *

The first critic we look at is Erich Auerbach. His great work,

Mimesis: The Representation of Reality in Western Literature, appeared in 1946, five years after Woolf's death. His final chapter takes an extract from *To The Lighthouse* as the basis for an analysis of how reality is represented in the modern novel. This recognition of her work was a significant milestone in the development of Woolf's critical reputation, and Auerbach's analysis tends to stand at the front of anthologies of Woolf criticism, to this day.

The passage Auerbach takes is Chapter 5 of Part I, 'The Window', from *To the Lighthouse* (pp. 24–8, from '"And even if it isn't fine tomorrow," said Mrs Ramsay' to '"Let's find another picture to cut out," she said'). Auerbach comments – as we found in Chapter 1 of this book – that the situation the characters are in can be deduced from the text without difficulty, even though it is not presented in a continuous form. He then points out that this passage has a very slight narrative framework: what he calls the 'exterior occurrence' of Mrs Ramsay measuring the stocking she is knitting for the Lighthouse-keeper's boy, against the leg of her son James. Auerbach begins his argument by noticing that this insignificant 'exterior' event is interwoven with other elements, so the extract takes longer to read than the event would have taken to happen. Most of these other elements are:

> inner processes, that is, movements within the inner consciousness of individual personages, and not necessarily of personages involved in the exterior occurrence but also of others who are not even present at the time: 'people', or 'Mr Bankes'.[1]

Not only are these inner consciousnesses of several people brought into the passage: there are other exterior details imported from other times and places, as well. Auerbach proceeds to write a detailed commentary, following the twists and turns of Virginia Woolf's subject-matter through the extract. It emerges from this commentary that

---

[1] Erich Auerbach, *Mimesis: The Representation of Reality in Western Literature*, first published Berne, 1946; trans. Willard Trask, Princeton University Press, 1953, reissued in Anchor Books, New York, 1957, p. 467. During the remainder of the summary of Auerbach's argument, page numbers of quotations from this edition appear in the text.

the passage begins and ends in the 'exterior occurrence' or framework. In between this beginning and ending there are two major
excursions or parentheses, divided by a brief return to the framework
when Mrs Ramsay speaks sharply to James, saying 'Stand still', measures the stocking and finds that it is still too short. The second
parenthesis begins with the paragraph which starts and ends with
'Never did anybody look so sad' (*To the Lighthouse*, p. 26). Who is
the speaker in this paragraph? 'Who is expressing these doubtful,
obscure suppositions? – about the tear which – perhaps – forms and
falls in the dark, about the water swaying this way and that,
receiving it, and then returning to rest?' (p. 469). It cannot be either
Mrs Ramsay or James, and there is nobody else there, so it may,
perhaps, be the author herself. However, she does not speak in the
manner we expect of an author, one who has objective knowledge of
the characters. Instead, she sounds vague and wonders about Mrs
Ramsay.

Auerbach suggests that Virginia Woolf is acting the part of one
who has only an impression of Mrs Ramsay. The subjective statement 'Never did anybody look so sad' 'verges upon a realm beyond
reality', so that Auerbach imagines the speakers to be not human at
all but 'spirits between heaven and earth, nameless spirits capable of
penetrating the depths of the human soul, capable too of knowing
something about it, but not of attaining clarity as to what is in
process there' (p. 469). A detailed commentary explaining the
second long excursion follows. The exterior occurrence of the
stocking reappears 'suddenly, and with as little transition as if it had
never been left'; but the change from excursion to exterior reality is
only an 'exterior change' because:

> the theme (Mrs Ramsay, her beauty, the enigma of her character . . .)
> carries over directly from the last phase of the interruption (that is, Mr
> Bankes's fruitless reflections) into the situation in which we now find
> Mrs Ramsay: 'with her head outlined absurdly by the gilt frame', etc.
> (p. 471)

Analysing this passage has highlighted a number of 'distinguishing
stylistic characteristics' which Auerbach will discuss.

First, there is no objective narrator: the author has withdrawn from that position and there is no viewpoint outside the novel, except for the wondering and indefinite observation of characters which suggests that the author looks at them 'with doubting and questioning eyes' (p. 472), in the same way as another character, involved in the novel, might observe them. Auerbach has found a number of the techniques by which authors express the contents of their characters' consciousness in his study of earlier literature; but Virginia Woolf 'achieves the intended effect by representing herself to be someone who doubts, wonders, hesitates, as though the truth about her characters were not better known to her than it is to them or to the reader'. This attitude to the reality she represents 'differs entirely from that of authors who interpret the actions, situations, and characters of their personages with objective assurance, as was the general practice in earlier times' (p. 472). The description of this technique is refined: not only does the author withdraw from objectivity, but also there are a number of viewpoints, or a 'multiplicity' of different consciousnesses, and the viewpoint frequently changes from one to another. These viewpoints include Mrs Ramsay, 'people', Mr Bankes, James, the Swiss maid, and the nameless consciousness – whether author or another – who speculates over a tear:

> The multiplicity of persons suggests that we are here after all confronted with an endeavour to investigate an objective reality, that is, specifically, the 'real' Mrs Ramsay. She is, to be sure, an enigma and such she basically remains, but she is as it were encircled by the content of all the various consciousnesses directed upon her (including her own).
>
> (p. 473)

There is a difference between this 'multipersonal representation of consciousness' and the 'unipersonal subjectivism' that traditionally admits only one person's way of looking at reality. Moving on, Auerbach considers Woolf's treatment of time, which is 'closely and necessarily connected' with the 'multipersonal' technique he has described. It is commonplace to remark that there is something odd about the treatment of time in modern literature. There are two rela-

tions between the 'exterior occurrence' and the time represented in
the excursions. First, the time it takes to read the passage attentively
is much longer than the time it would have taken for Mrs Ramsay to
measure the stocking, so it takes longer to read than it did to
happen. Secondly, there are the times we travel to in memory,
during the excursions. Additionally, there are two long excursions
'whose relations in time to the occurrence which frames them seem
to be entirely different'. The first 'excursus' technically takes place
within Mrs Ramsay's mind in between her two orders to her son to
stand still, so it belongs in time within the exterior occurrence:

> it is only the representation of it which takes a greater number of
> seconds and even minutes than the measuring – the reason being that
> the road taken by consciousness is sometimes traversed far more
> quickly than language is able to render it.
>
> (p. 474)

Mrs Ramsay's mind is easily intelligible, unlike those, for example,
of characters in James Joyce's novels: the ideas that pass through her
mind are normal, ordinary, everyday thoughts. However, Woolf's
technique does create a sharp contrast between 'the brief span of
time occupied by the exterior event and the dreamlike wealth of a
process of consciousness which traverses a whole subjective universe':

> These are the characteristic and distinctively new features of the tech-
> nique: a chance occasion releasing processes of consciousness; a
> natural and even, if you will, a naturalistic rendering of those
> processes in their peculiar freedom, which is neither restrained by a
> purpose nor directed by a specific subject of thought; elaboration of
> the contrast between 'exterior' and 'interior' time.
>
> (p. 475)

The author cannot help selecting and stylising the raw material of
the real world, but in this technique Woolf does not do so in order
to achieve any continuous, explained sequence of events with
motives and rationalisation. The exterior events have lost their position of importance: they are only slight, chance occasions which
release the much more significant inner process.

In the second excursus of the extract, other times and places are brought into play, such as a telephone conversation between Mrs Ramsay and Mr Bankes which may have taken place some years before; and the room in a city where Mr Bankes was when the telephone conversation took place. Auerbach compares this with a digression which told the story of the origin of Odysseus's scar, in Homer's *The Odyssey*, which he analysed in the first chapter of his work (see *Mimesis*, pp. 1–20). However, there is still a difference, because in the case of Odysseus's scar, the digression is linked as an exterior cause of an exterior fact, and gives a clear narrative of the earlier time which seems to take the place of the interrupted narrative completely. In the case of Mrs Ramsay, by contrast, her 'sad' facial expression is the point of departure which begins the excursus, and this same point of departure actually gives rise to three separate scenes from the past. These three all differ in time and place, and in the definiteness with which they are treated. The first is placed 'vaguely', the second 'more definitely', and the third quite clearly. These three separate scenes are linked because, as Auerbach argues that Mr Bankes visualises Mrs Ramsay's face during their telephone conversation, 'not for an instant does the theme (the solution of the enigma Mrs Ramsay), and even the moment when the problem is formulated (the expression of her face while she measures the length of the stocking), vanish from the reader's memory' (p. 476). The three scenes have no other connection in time or in place, but their connection to the central theme of the enigma of Mrs Ramsay makes them seem 'nothing but attempts to interpret' that theme. As a result, there is continuity of theme, rather than of exterior action, despite the excursus. Auerbach therefore reasons that the two excursuses are not essentially as different from each other as they appeared to be at first. It does not matter that they make use of different kinds of time, because they are both part of one continuous investigation into the single theme of the extract.

This again reminds us of the viewpoint of some person who sees Mrs Ramsay and the exterior occurrence, and meditates on the mystery of her beauty and her character. This meditation might contain memories of 'what other people say and think about her'. Auerbach explains that Virginia Woolf thus focuses attention away from a superficial exterior reality, and 'attempts to fathom a more genuine, a deeper, and indeed a more real reality': 'The important point is that an insignificant exterior occurrence releases ideas and chains of ideas which cut loose from the present of the exterior occurrence and range freely through the depths of time' (both p. 477). Auerbach then includes a discussion of Proust's technique in comparison to Woolf, and enters a more general development of ideas about the direction of different forms of art: the novel and film, in particular, because film's ability to move through time and space with great freedom and speed has made novelists more aware than ever of the limitations imposed by their instrument: language. He then sums up what he calls the 'distinctive characteristics of the realistic novel of the era between the two great wars', which he has found in the passage from *To the Lighthouse*, as 'multipersonal representation of consciousness, time strata, disintegration of the continuity of exterior events, shifting of the narrative viewpoint'. He suggests that these characteristics originate in the history of the time, because they all belong to one distinctive effort: 'a striving for certain objectives, of certain tendencies and needs on the part of both authors and public' (pp. 482–3).

Finally, Auerbach advances a theory to account for why authors and public should have developed these particular needs and objectives during the period between the wars. He describes a wide range of developments in natural science, social and philosophical thought, knowledge of the world, and particularly in communications and the dissemination of information. His main point appears to be that it was at this time, at the start of the twentieth century, that mankind became conscious of an information explosion. It was now impossible for any one person to know very much about the world. Even at the beginning of the twentieth century, there was still enough 'clearly formulable and recognized community of thought and feeling' to provide reliable criteria for a writer who sought to represent reality: 'At least, within the range of contemporary movements, he could discern certain specific trends; he could delimit opposing attitudes and ways of life with a certain degree of clarity (pp. 486–7). As the twentieth century developed, however, the writer realised that he could no longer do this, because knowledge was suddenly too varied and complex for one person to grasp. This would seem to suggest that the modern novel – and Woolf in particular – simply reflects confusion and helplessness in the face of life, but there was something else as well. Yes, life became too complex to be known, so that authors would 'hesitate to impose on life, which is their subject, an order which it does not possess in itself' (p. 485). On the other hand, it was the complexity of exterior life that became overwhelming and impossible to represent, and these authors have therefore turned their attention to representing an inner reality:

> the wealth of reality and depth of life in every moment to which we surrender ourselves without prejudice. To be sure, what happens in that moment . . . concerns in a very personal way the individuals who live in it, but it also (and for that very reason) concerns the elementary things which men in general have in common . . . the more it is exploited, the more the elementary things which our lives have in common come to light.
>
> (p. 488)

Auerbach ends his argument with this theory, then: that in the proliferation of complexity and faced with the suddenly incomprehensible world of rapid communications and multiplying societies, the modern writer such as Virginia Woolf found a traditional representation of exterior reality impossible to achieve. She therefore developed techniques to marginalise the elements of exterior reality in her novel, and to concentrate on representing an inner reality that is 'more real', because it is both extremely personal, and is made up of life-experience itself, which is universally shared by all human beings.

We can notice certain points about Auerbach's argument, before we move on to sample another critic. First, Auerbach's analysis rests on his perception that Virginia Woolf's narrative stresses 'inner' elements of character at the expense of 'exterior' – events, speech and actions. This is very similar to the point we noticed in our first chapter, when we concluded that 'The features we have noticed point to a consistent interest: Virginia Woolf's effort to create and express mental experience at a pre-rational level.' However, Auerbach takes a longer extract than any of ours, and so he notices that the exterior event is briefly treated, while longer passages are devoted to inner explorations, and narrative journeys through memories, and other consciousnesses. Remember that in our extracts, we often found this same relationship but between sentences rather than between whole blocks of the text: short sentences are used for exterior narrative, and much longer ones for the processes of thought within the characters.

Second, Auerbach's analysis of Woolf's use of time is illuminating, and can be added to our suggestion that there is an effect of richness and intensity gained from such detailed, expanding exploration of short moments. Third, we can feel that we have gone much further than Auerbach did in analysing the impersonal, hesitant voice he identifies as the author's voice, from one paragraph of his extract. Our work on imagery and nature (see Part 1, Chapters 5 and 6) has discovered consistent significance among the apparently 'shadowy' metaphors Virginia Woolf uses when describing the internal landscape of the mind: there is a more positive, structuring intelligence at work in these interludes than Auerbach has allowed for.

Finally, notice that this critic explains the techniques he sees as peculiar to Woolf and modern novelists, in terms of a generalised development through the history of Western civilisation. This development of ideas, coming from such a commanding and widely learned authority as Auerbach, should reinforce the suggestions we have made at certain times in our own analysis: that Woolf describes characters who are confronting a 'chaos', a world that they are unable to rationally explain. In Chapter 7 we looked at the theme of art and commentated on Lily Briscoe's struggle to find a new way in which she can understand this baffling world.

In this case, then, reading the critic is a reassuring supplement to our own work. Notice that we have been able to reach similar perceptions, and in some cases more thorough and advanced understanding, through our own unaided approach to these texts. Additionally, reading Auerbach adds to our appreciation of Woolf's writing, since his mind naturally highlights a slightly different aspect of the novels, from his slightly different angle, which supplements and enriches our own.

*   *   *

We now turn to our second critic. Elizabeth Abel has written widely on the subject of Virginia Woolf. She is a modern critic who makes full use of both Freudian and feminist viewpoints. Our sample comes from her article 'Narrative Structure and Female Development: the Case of *Mrs Dalloway*', which first appeared in *The Voyage In: Fictions of Female Development* (1983), edited by Elizabeth Abel, Marianne Hirsch and Elizabeth Langland.

Elizabeth Abel begins her article by observing that, although Virginia Woolf's novel has an experimental narrative structure, the author inevitably invokes conventional structures even if only to alter them. This enables an 'iconoclastic plot to weave its course covertly through the narrative grid'.[2] This is the story of 'female development' in Mrs Dalloway, which is 'clandestine' and 'disguised' by being dispersed to different parts of the novel and disjointed so that it resists attempts to put it together as a clear continuous narrative. This is an 'intrinsically disjointed' story because it is about a woman's development, so the book's structure reflects 'the encounter of gender with narrative form' (all p. 78). She quotes Woolf to the same effect as we do in Chapter 9 above, pointing out that traditional fictional forms have been determined by male values, so a woman novelist must, to preserve feminine values, be in conflict with traditional narrative structure and methods. Woolf disguised the feminine story for tactical reasons, as she wrote for a literary world still dominated by men: 'If the early nineteenth-century woman novelist betrayed her discomfort with male evaluation by overt protestation or compliance, the early twentieth-century woman novelist, more aware of this dilemma, may encode as a subtext the stories she wishes yet fears to tell' (p. 79). One of the tasks of feminist criticism has been to excavate buried plots in women's texts because feminism radically changes the reader's per-

---

[2] Elizabeth Abel, 'Narrative Structure(s) and Female Development: the Case of *Mrs Dalloway*', in *Virginia Woolf*, ed. Rachel Bowlby, Longman, London and New York, 1992, pp. 77–101, p. 78. During the remainder of the summary of Abel's argument, page numbers of quotations from this edition appear in the text.

ception, allowing the orthodox plot to fade and previously hidden stories to appear. In particular, these have been plots concerned with the mother–daughter relationship, or the pre-Oedipal stage of female development. 'In *Mrs Dalloway*, written two years before *To the Lighthouse*, Woolf structures her heroine's development, the recessive narrative of her novel, as a story of pre-Oedipal attachment and loss' (p. 80).

The story of Clarissa's female development is hidden behind a dominant romantic plot, which is a revision of a courtship model borrowed from Jane Austen. Clarissa has to choose between two men, but the courtship period is condensed into a few memories of what was essentially a single scene, and marriage itself – which is the closure of an Austenian plot – is the opening of the main plot of Clarissa's party thirty years later, and her persisting uncertainty about whether she married the right man: 'The elongated courtship plot, the imperfectly resolved emotional triangle, becomes a screen for the developmental story that unfolds in fragments of memory, unexplained interstices between events, and narrative asides and interludes' (p. 81). There is a remarkable difference in emphasis and subject-matter between Clarissa's and Peter's memories of the crucial time at Bourton in the past, when Clarissa made her fateful choice to marry Richard:

> Although Clarissa vacillates emotionally between the allure of Peter and that of Richard, she remembers Peter's courtship only glancingly; the burden of that plot is carried by Peter, through whose memories Woolf relates the slow and tortured end of the relation with Clarissa. Clarissa's memories, by contrast, focus more exclusively on the general ambience of Bourton, her childhood home, and her love for Sally Seton. Significantly absent from these memories is Richard Dalloway, whose courtship of Clarissa is presented exclusively through Peter's painful recollections.
>
> (pp. 81–2)

The connection between past and present is made up of gaps, silences and juxtaposition. Clarissa's present is in a male-dominated London where she does not have any close female bonds (for example, she is not close to her daughter, and not invited by Lady

Bruton); this is starkly contrasted with her memories of Bourton. The connecting elements of narrative – the wedding, the move to London, childbirth, all the other events of the intervening thirty years – are rigorously omitted. The ultimate effect of this structure is to form the developmental plot which lies beneath the more familiar romantic one, into 'two contrasting moments and the silence adjoining and dividing them' (p. 82).

The earliest scene is that of Sally's arrival at Bourton. Prior to her arrival there is an atmosphere of female loss and deferred childhood desire, with mentions of a dead mother and sister, a distant father and a strict maiden aunt. Sally's arrival brings a 'vibrant female energy' and 'replaces Clarissa's dead mother and sister . . . inspiring a love equal to Othello's in intensity and equivalent in absoluteness to a daughter's earliest bond with her mother, a bond too early ruptured for Clarissa' (pp. 82–3). Abel quotes the moment when Clarissa and Sally kiss, including the metaphor of 'a diamond, something infinitely precious, wrapped up' (see *Mrs Dalloway*, p. 30) that Sally gives to her as a present, and comments:

> This kind of passionate attachment between women, orthodox psychoanalysts and feminists uncharacteristically agree, recaptures some aspect of the fractured mother–daughter bond. Within the sequence established by the novel, this adolescent love assumes the power of the early female bond excluded from the narrative.
>
> (p. 83)

The bond described predates the female experience of the Oedipus complex, the traumatic turn from mother to father. French psychoanalytic theory has suggested that the Oedipus complex has more to do with socialisation than with instinct: it is a necessary change in order that adults are produced with proper sexual orientation for perpetuating the species. Both women and men have to renounce something when they undergo this change, but boys are better compensated because their reward is a woman like their mother, and they gain paternal power over their own family. Girls, by contrast, have to lose the original female bond completely and turn to the other sex. Their reward is not power, but a renewed submission to an imitation of the paternal authority. This means that women have to make a double renunciation and a radical change of sexual orientation during their development, and no comparable sacrifice is demanded of men.

In *Mrs Dalloway*, Clarissa and Sally think of marriage as 'a catastrophe' (*Mrs Dalloway*, p. 29), and Woolf increases the shock of the rupturing of this female bond by juxtaposing the kiss – the purest moment of Clarissa's and Sally's relationship – and Peter's interruption: 'the moment of exclusive female connection is shattered by masculine intervention . . . Clarissa's response to this intrusion images an absolute and arbitrary termination: "It was like running one's face against a granite wall in the darkness! It was shocking; it was horrible!"' In revenge, Clarissa refuses to marry Peter, and chooses instead 'the less demanding Richard Dalloway in order to guard a portion of her psyche for the memory of Sally' (p. 84).

Woolf's reference to the death of Clarissa's sister is carefully off-hand, and recalled by Peter rather than by Clarissa herself. It includes a contradictorily shocking but brief accusation: it was all her father's fault. In addition, the dead sister's name, Sylvia, reminds us of 'Sylvan', meaning 'to do with woodland and trees'. This suggests something pastoral and implies a larger female story of natural existence. On this basis Abel reasons that Sylvia's death and Clarissa's traumatic experience of rupture from her female bond with Sally are implicitly parallel events; and that the deliberate brevity of Woolf's mention of Sylvia emphasises the silences and gaps in which the rest of the female developmental story exists. It suggests 'a story intentionally withheld, forcibly deprived of its legitimate proportions, deliberately excised from the narrative yet provocatively implied in it, written both into and out of the text'. In this way, 'Woolf creates an inconspicuous subtext perceptible only to an altered vision' (both p. 85).

Freud only revised his theory of female development in an essay published in 1925, the same year which saw publication of *Mrs Dalloway*. Therefore, the correspondence between the hidden developmental plot of the novel, and Freud's later theory, is an extraordinary instance of literary intuition working simultaneously with the theory of psychoanalysis. Freud's new theory was that female identity is achieved after a series of costly repressions that the male child does not have to undergo. The girl's progress is much harder. The boy, for example, has to repress his sexual desire for his mother; but he does not undergo a change in sexual orientation, since the mother will eventually be replaced by other women. So the interruption to the boy's progress is an 'arrest' rather than a 'dislocation'. In contrast, the girl must completely change her direction. She begins, like the boy, bonded with her mother in the pre-Oedipal stage; but she then has to replace this with a heterosexual attraction to her father. Then she has to repress this in turn, in favour of an attraction to some other man. Freud points out the monumental dislocation of this shift. He calls it a 'change in her own sex' because in the pre-Oedipal stage 'the little girl is a little man'.

Freud outlines three developmental paths women follow. The girl who follows the first path realises that she cannot compete with her brother for her mother because she lacks a penis. She renounces her sexual orientation towards her mother, and becomes passively oriented towards the superior father. Freud suggests that the result of this path is long-term sexual inhibition and neurosis. The second path is followed by girls who fight against this first renunciation and develop a 'masculinity' complex which often results in homosexuality later in life. The third route leads to normality, but Freud does not describe it as a distinctly different route. It seems, rather, a less damaging version of the first route, from which a more fortunate girl may manage to emerge. However, even if normality has been achieved, Freud thought that a woman of thirty was psychically rigid and used-up, while a man of the same age was still psychically active and flexible. The woman seems 'as though, indeed, the difficult development to femininity had exhausted the possibilities of the person concerned'.[3]

Woolf, like Freud, accentuates the traumatic dislocation stage of female development, by juxtaposing the moments of fulfilment with Sally and violent intrusion by Peter in as sharp a contrast as possible,

---

[3] Sigmund Freud, 'Femininity', quoted by Elizabeth Abel from *Women and Analysis*, ed. Jean Strouse, Grossman Publishers, New York, 1974, p. 92.

in *Mrs Dalloway*. She also portrays the sexual and emotional 'calcification' Freud describes in the older woman. Clarissa has always responded coldly to men, and she sees this as a failure, letting Richard down; while her idea that her virginity has remained despite motherhood is symbolised by the narrower and narrower attic bed, where she reads about Baron Marbot and the retreat from Moscow, 'a victory achieved by icy withdrawal' (p. 88). The narrow bed is implicitly linked with a grave, so her sexuality is associated with death. In contrast, and in the same paragraph (see *Mrs Dalloway*, pp. 26–7), Woolf writes an extraordinarily erotic description of her passionate responses to women.

Abel takes the image of 'a match burning in a crocus', together with other elements of this erotic passage which bring together 'male and female, active and passive, sacred and profane' as suggesting an experience of 'completeness' which is simultaneously masculine and feminine, in Clarissa's relations with women. This brings 'fusion' rather than the either/or distinctions Freud's theory insists upon, and bypasses the Freudian claim that some developmental paths or outcomes are 'immature' or 'abnormal'. In short, 'she valorizes a spontaneous homosexual love over the inhibitions of imposed heterosexuality':

> The opposition between Clarissa's relationship with men and women modulates to the split between her present and her past, her orientation and emotional capacities on both sides of the Oedipal divide. Woolf, like Freud, reveals the cost of female development, but she inscribes a far more graphic image of the loss entailed, questions its necessity, and indicates the price of equating female development with acculturation through the rites of passage established by the Oedipus complex.
>
> (p. 89)

There are carefully orchestrated echoes of Clarissa's developmental story, in that of Rezia Warren Smith, who passed from a feminine and pastoral world of sisters and mother in Italy, to the arid masculine ugliness of London. Several verbal echoes and common images link the two women's stories. However, when Virginia Woolf decided to make Septimus the sacrificial hero, preserving Clarissa from death instead, she 'reverses narrative tradition' (p. 91) in which women are sacrificed in place of men.

There are many close echoes between the language and structure of two 'meditative interludes': Clarissa's reminiscence about Sally Seton, and her meditation on the death of Septimus. Abel suggests that this latter passage completes the hidden story of Clarissa's female development:

> By interpreting Septimus's suicide in her private language of passion and integrity, Clarissa uses the shock of death to probe her unresolved relation to her past. The suicide triggers Clarissa's recurrent preoccupation with this past, providing a perspective that enables her belatedly both to admit and to renounce its hold. On the day in June that encloses the action of *Mrs Dalloway*, Clarissa completes the developmental turn initiated thirty years before.
>
> (p. 91)

There are many linguistic and structural similarities between the two passages. For example, Clarissa withdraws from the party (*Mrs Dalloway*, p. 162), and the phrase 'as if she had left a party' (p. 25) appears as she goes upstairs at the start of the earlier passage. Also, there are several verbal echoes that are too close to be accidental: 'closeness drew apart; rapture faded, one was alone' (p. 163) and 'But the close withdrew; the hard softened. It was over – the moment' (p. 27) is one example.

There is a sudden juxtaposition of present and past moments in the later passage, when Clarissa suddenly interposes 'And once she had walked on the terrace at Bourton' into a description of her forced and artificial present life; and Abel argues that it was the thought of Richard (from the preceding paragraph) that brings Clarissa a sudden joy: 'she had never been so happy' (see *Mrs Dalloway*, p. 164). She continues:

> We can only speculate that Septimus's sacrificial gift includes a demonstration of Clarissa's alternatives: to preserve the intensity of passion through death, or to accept the changing offerings of life. By recalling to Clarissa the power of her past *and* the only method of eternalizing it, he enables her fully to acknowledge and renounce its

hold, to embrace the imperfect pleasures of adulthood more completely.

(pp. 92–3)

Finally, Elizabeth Abel comments on the significance of the old woman in the house opposite, who is going to bed as Clarissa looks out through the window. This points to 'a positive commitment to development – not to any particular course, but to the process of change itself' (p. 93) in Clarissa. Following this hopeful interpretation of the final scene in the plot of female development in *Mrs Dalloway*, the remainder of Abel's article discusses the analogy between these theories of female development, and developments between Mycenean and Athenian cultures, which is mentioned by Freud and is a theme of the *Oresteia* which Woolf read while writing *Mrs Dalloway*. She briefly comments that there may be a relation between developing awareness of gender and cultural evolution; and elaborates this with a survey of the contrast within the novel, between a pre-war 'feminine' world (Bourton) and the masculine tenor of post-war society in the novel's present. Elizabeth Dalloway stands at the end of the novel, next to her father, basking in the glow of his admiration of her beauty, as the unwritten and unexplored story of future female development.

Elizabeth Abel's article is a fascinating and illuminating study. It is extraordinary that so much confluence occurred between Woolf's intuition and Freud's developing theory of femininity, at the same time – but this should not deflect our attention from the fact that Abel has highlighted this 'female developmental story' in the text itself, not merely by importing a theory from outside. Again, as with Auerbach, several elements of her insight are points that we have noticed in the analytical chapters of this book. For example, we already commented on the traumatic violence of Peter's interruption (*Mrs Dalloway*, p. 30) and the primacy of Sally's kiss as the most blissful and influential moment in Clarissa's memory. Also, we discussed the relative sexual threats of Peter and Richard as crucial in determining Clarissa's choice.

Abel is particularly adept in describing the 'subversive' narrative structure Virginia Woolf adopts to 'encode' her story of female development; and in illuminating the effects achieved by means of revision of conventional plot-structures, and the use of silences, gaps, or omissions. On the other hand, I disagree with some of her interpretation of the final interlude, because I do not think the text is as optimistic as she does, and I see the completion of Clarissa's developmental story as ironic.

The fact that I state my disagreement is positive: Abel's analysis has stimulated me to return to the text, rereading the vital interlude for myself in the light of her interpretation; and her views have helped to crystallise and further define my own.

*   *   *

The third critic we sample in this chapter is Gillian Beer, whose article 'The Island and the Aeroplane: The Case of Virginia Woolf' appeared in 1990. Ms Beer discusses an English island tradition, the 'cultural discourse' that has evolved around the use of the island as a cultural sign, and the alterations wrought in that English perception by the coming of the aeroplane: 'England's is, so writers over the centuries have assured us, an island story. What happened to that story with the coming of the aeroplane?'[4] Much of Ms Beer's essay is devoted to a wide-ranging discussion of various works and analysis of quotations drawn from a variety of sources in English literary and cultural history. The two parts of her argument that concern us are her discussion of the 'island' motif in relation to *To the Lighthouse*, and her analysis of the aeroplane from *Mrs Dalloway*, which leads into a brief comment on *The Waves*.

Beer begins by pointing out that the house, and the family, can also be thought of as contracted 'islands' in the metaphoric structure of *To the Lighthouse*; and that 'the final separation of the individual each from each is figured' (pp. 140–1) when Mr Ramsay obsession-ally recalls 'We perish each alone':

---

[4] First published in *Nation and Narration*, ed. Homi K. Bhabha, Routledge, London, 1990. The extracts in this chapter are drawn from *Virginia Woolf*, ed. Rachel Bowlby, Longman, London and New York, 1992, pp. 132–61, p. 132. During the remainder of the summary of Beer's argument, page numbers of quotations from this edition appear in the text.

Throughout the book, sometimes louder, sometimes muted, the sound of the waves is referred to. The sea is as much the island as is the land. The fisherman's wife, in the story Mrs Ramsay reads to James, longs for possession and for dominance, for control: that last wish is shared with Mrs Ramsay, and perhaps the other wishes too. 'That loneliness which was . . . the truth about things' permeates the book. The lighthouse itself is the final island, the last signifying object, amidst the timeless breaking of the sea . . . At the end of the book the First World War is over; the family is fragmented: the mother is dead, a son, a daughter; the fishes in the bottom of the boat are dead.

(p. 141)

Beer then quotes Cam's retrospective musing about the island, which looks much smaller from the perspective of the boat, now out at sea; yet which contained the complexity of the house and garden and 'all those innumerable things' (*To the Lighthouse*, p. 194). Cam achieves distance and retrospect at the end of the novel:

The long backward survey to the politics of Edwardian family life, to England before the First World War, which began to unravel through the image of the abandoned house in 'Time passes' here reaches conclusion: 'It is finished'. Lily's words – and those of the Cross – means also what they say. Things have come to an end. The period of empire is drawing to its close. The book ends; the picture is done; the parents' England is gone.

(p. 141)

Therefore, the final section of *To the Lighthouse* is a last review of a past culture that no longer exists and that Woolf does not wish to resurrect, which is associated with the image of an island:

In *To the Lighthouse* Woolf frets away the notion of stability in the island concept. The everyday does not last forever. The island is waves as well as earth: everything is in flux, land as much as sea, individual as well as whole culture. The last book of *To the Lighthouse* looks back at the conditions of before 1914. Implicit is the understanding that this will be the last such revisiting for the personages within the book.

(p. 142)

Turning to the aeroplane in *Mrs Dalloway*, Beer points out a contrast with the closed car in which royalty travelled. The car is a focus for nationalism, and the several characters who either get out of its way, or speculate admiringly about who is inside, provide sharp satirical comment on the structure of society and social class. The aeroplane is contrasted because everybody looks 'up', and the emphasis on 'up' suggests equality and freedom in contrast to the car's evocation of fixed social class and hierarchy. Beer closely analyses the mood of the passage describing the aeroplane:

> It becomes an image of equalizing as opposed to hierarchy, of freedom and play, racing and swooping 'swiftly, freely, like a skater'. It includes death, 'dropping dead down', the baby 'lying stiff and white in her arms', but it does not impose it . . . Each person reads the plane's message differently. To Septimus 'the smoke words' offer 'inexhaustible charity and laughing goodness'. The communality is not in single meaning but in the free access to meaning. The ecstatic joke is about insufficiency of import: 'they were advertising toffee, a nurse-maid told Rezia'. The message does not matter; the communal act of sky-gazing does.
>
> (p. 144)

As the aeroplane flies, the narrative viewpoint both soars over the 'little island of grey churches' that is London and off over the patch-work of countryside that the watchers cannot see but only imagine by means of contemplating the aeroplane; and dives with sudden magnification down to 'where adventurous thrushes' tap snails on stones to knock their shells away. The aeroplane not only has an 'egalitarian' height that 'dissolves bonds and flattens hierarchies'; it also represents a human aspiration towards something beyond ordinary life that can be achieved by means of 'man's soul' or 'thought', as the momentary character Mr Bentley meditates when he sees it pass (see *Mrs Dalloway*, p. 23). In conclusion of this part of her analysis, Beer elaborates this idea:

> So the aeroplane becomes an image of 'free will' and ecstasy, silent, erotic and absurd . . . Virginia Woolf's disaffection from the heavily bonded forms of English society often expresses itself paradoxically

thus as affection and play – and in this novel, as in *Orlando*, the aeroplane figures as the free spirit of the modern age returning the eye to
the purity of a sky which has 'escaped registration'.

(p. 145)

In the remainder of the article, Beer briefly discusses *The Waves*, suggesting that the image of waves that cover everything, the sea and
the land, and that constantly give motion to life, people and things,
is a progression from the opposition of land and sea in the island-
image: 'this book engages with an imaginative scientific world in
which substance is unreal, motion universal' (p. 149). Virginia
Woolf has achieved her effect by pushing to the edge of the novel or
out of it all that is normally central to a work of fiction: 'private love
relationships, the business of government, family life, city finances,
the empire. Each of these topics is, however, marked into the narrative so that we also *observe* how slight a regard she here has for them'
(p. 149). She has done this by taking a fresh look at the world in the
light of some popular scientific theories of the time, including wave
theory, as put forward by the two scientists Eddington and Jeans.
Eddington pointed out the effect of science's new understanding of
particles, in 1927, saying that the most striking thing about new
scientific knowledge was this breaking-down of what we have
traditionally thought to be a solid world into particles. Beer
quotes from Eddington's *The Nature of the Physical World* (1928),
where he writes that the shock of new understanding lies in 'the dissolution of all that we regard as most solid into tiny specks floating
in a void'.

Following this short discussion, Beer enters a longer consideration
of Woolf's final novel, *Between the Acts*, then draws together her conclusions about island and aeroplane images in Virginia Woolf, and
their place in both signifying technological change, and in the con-
tinuum of a wider 'cultural discourse'.

This kind of criticism allows itself enormous freedom, and is vulnerable to many objections: the sweeping and cavalier manner in
which whole cultures through several centuries are reduced to a few,
apparently randomly selected quotations, is in contrast to the academic caution many critics display. We can easily argue against such a

critic, simply by finding different quotations from other writers (or the same writers!).

On the other hand, Ms Beer has made free and confident use of her reading through contemporaneous and earlier literature, and other writings, allowing herself to propose movements, connections and changes. Her suggestions throw a light upon the backdrop against which we see the novels of Virginia Woolf; and her work on the texts themselves deserves attentive reading. Certainly, the idea of an island is a significant symbol in *To the Lighthouse*. Beer's emphasis on the relation between Virginia Woolf's writing and the shocks of developing scientific awareness, and developing technological capability, is very much in the same direction of thought as the theory with which Auerbach concludes his analysis of the brown stocking. The more psychoanalytically viewed examination of dislocation or disjunction in experience that is the focus of Elizabeth Abel's article, is ultimately a related observation.

The three critics we have sampled in this chapter, then, have this in common: they all write of Virginia Woolf as responding to a new and baffling world. They seem to agree that the radical innovations in her writing: her 'tunnelling' technique and her ironic use of narrative structures, are part of an attempt to respond to a new perception of human experience, in a new way. Many of the specific insights contained in the critics' analyses are similar to those we have already reached; but in each case the critic has added an 'angle' – a particular preoccupation which enriches our own understanding. The critics have also put forward some interpretations that provoke us to disagree, so we return to the text to argue our case against theirs.

The broad agreement between critics may seem surprising, since we have sampled one traditional critic, one psychoanalytic feminist, and one whose focus is on cultural history. In each case, however, some light at least has been thrown upon the novels themselves, which are the crucial focus of our attention.

Further Reading

Your first job is to study the text. There is no substitute for the work of detailed analysis: that is how you gain the close familiarity with the text, and the fully developed understanding of its content, which make the essays you write both personal and convincing. For this reason I recommend that you take it as a rule not to read any other books around or about the text you are studying, until you have finished studying it for yourself.

Once you are familiar with the text, you may wish to read around and about it. This brief chapter is only intended to set you off: there are hundreds of relevant books and we can only mention a few. However, most good editions, and critical works, have suggestions for further reading, or a bibliography of their own. Once you have begun to read beyond your text, you can use these and a good library to follow up your particular interests. This chapter is divided into *Reading Around the Text*, which lists some other works by Virginia Woolf, and some by other contemporary writers; *Biography*; and *Criticism*, which will introduce you to the varieties of opinion among professional critics.

Reading Around the Text

If you have any one of the three novels studied in this book as a set text, your first job is to read the other two, if you have not already done so. Then look at Woolf's other novels, beginning with *Orlando* and *Between the Acts*. *Jacob's Room* would be the next one to try, leaving the other three (*The Voyage Out, Night and Day* and *The Years*) until last. All of Woolf's novels are available in the Vintage Books edition (London, 1992). You could also try some of her short stories. *Virginia Woolf: The Complete Shorter Fiction*, edited by Susan Dick (Triad Grafton Books, London, 1987), has all her published stories. Begin by reading *The Mark on the Wall*, which, together with a story by Leonard Woolf, was the first publication of the Hogarth Press.

If you wish to pursue an interest in Virginia Woolf's ideas and theories, read the two most important full-length works, *A Room of One's Own* and *Three Guineas* (both are available in Penguin). Following these you should read among her many essays. There are collections in Penguin Books published under the title *A Woman's Essays*, or the Hogarth Press publishes *The Essays of Virginia Woolf* edited by Andrew McNeillie. There are several volumes, and you could begin by reading *Mr Bennett and Mrs Brown*, which we discussed in Chapter 9. However, I suggest that you pick titles that intrigue you among her essays, or follow leads to interesting essays, from biographies or critical works which refer to them or quote them.

Among Woolf's contemporaries, it is worth reading the novels of her time for the purposes of comparison. She was concerned to assess the notorious James Joyce, and reading *A Portrait of the Artist as a Young Man* will introduce you to this most 'stream-of-consciousness' of writers, although *Ulysses* is the famously controversial novel. D. H. Lawrence's *The Rainbow* or *Women in Love* are both fine novels, and his highly personal method of expressing the half-unconscious emotions of his characters makes an interesting contemporary comparison with Woolf. Finally, E. M. Forster's *Howard's End* is a thoroughly modern novel in theme, written by one of Woolf's friends. I would also suggest reading *The Waste Land* and *Four Quartets*, which are poems by T. S. Eliot. He was another contemporary and friend, and his work revolutionised poetry, attacking and reshaping traditional forms, in much the same way as Virginia Woolf's work reinvents the novel.

Biography

The first recommendation if you become fascinated by Virginia Woolf herself, and her life, is to read her own accounts. Begin by looking into the autobiographical sketches she called *Moments of Being: Unpublished Autobiographical Writings*, which were collected and published after her death. In these, Woolf reflects on her life and seeks explanations for her character. However, the primary autobiographical document is *The Diary of Virginia Woolf*, edited by Anne Olivier Bell (five volumes, Hogarth Press, London, 1977–84).

I shall only mention three biographical titles of the many available. Her nephew Quentin Bell wrote the definitive biography of Virginia Woolf. This was published by the Hogarth Press in 1972, and has come out in a two-volume paperback edition since (Triad/Paladin, London, 1976). You could also read Leonard Woolf, *An Autobiography* (Oxford University Press, Oxford, 1980). The second volume contains his memories of the years 1911–69, which span the whole of his and Virginia's married life. Finally, for a clearly written and well-argued assessment of her life together with her literary works, read *Virginia Woolf: A Literary Life*, by John Mepham (Macmillan, London, 1991).

Criticism

The critical works sampled in Chapter 10 are: *Mimesis: The Representation of Reality in Western Literature*, by Erich Auerbach, translated by Willard Trask (Princeton University Press, Princeton, NJ, 1953); Elizabeth Abel's 'Narrative Structure(s) and Female Development: the Case of *Mrs Dalloway*', in *Virginia Woolf*, ed. Rachel Bowlby (Longman, London and New York, 1992), pp. 77-101; and 'The Island and the Aeroplane: The Case of Virginia Woolf', by Gillian Beer, from *Nation and Narration*, ed. Homi K. Bhabha (Routledge, London, 1990), pp. 255–90.

Anthologies of critical essays and articles are a good way to sample the critics. You can then go on to read the full-length books written by those critics whose articles you have found stimulating. *Virginia*

Woolf, edited by Rachel Bowlby (1992), includes the editor's introduction and brief comments on each of the selected articles. *Virginia Woolf* in the Modern Critical Views series, edited by Harold Bloom (Chelsea House Publishers, New York and Philadelphia, PA, 1986) and *Virginia Woolf: A Collection of Critical Essays,* edited by Margaret Homans (Prentice Hall, Englewood Cliffs, NJ, 1993) are two further anthologies containing a range of critical opinion.

The following full-length critical works may also be of interest and should be stimulating whether you agree or disagree with the writer's analysis. Rachel Bowlby's *Virginia Woolf: Feminist Destinations* (Basil Blackwell, Oxford, 1988), *The Interrupted Moment: A View of Virginia Woolf's Novels,* by Lucio P. Ruotolo (Stanford University Press, Stanford, CA, 1986), and Jane Marcus's *Virginia Woolf and the Languages of Patriarchy* (Indiana University Press, Bloomington, IN, 1987) will all enrich your own analysis with challenging ideas. For a concise survey of the form of Woolf's novels, look at *Virginia Woolf,* by Susan Dick (Arnold, London, 1989).

When you are in a library, use the catalogue system resourcefully to locate further interesting critical work on Virginia Woolf. There are numerous books which appear to be on different subjects – Modernism, Feminist Writing, Twentieth-Century Narrative Experiment, Psychoanalysis in Literature, and so on. A large number of these contain chapters or essays about Virginia Woolf which may bring an illuminating angle to bear upon her writing.

Index

222